A Journey Along the World's

GREAT TREKS

by

Jeff Salvage and Kirk Markus

edited by Diane Graham-Henry

Walking Promotions
79 North Lakeside Drive W
Medford, NJ 08055
www.greattreks.com

Copyright 2011
ISBN: 978-0-9827107-1-5
First Edition

Printed in China

Dedications

To Jennifer, my beloved wife. For years I walked the trails taking in their beauty
and adventure, but something was missing. Actually, it was someone. Now my
trips and life are fulfilled as we trek together for all that life has to offer.

- Jeff Salvage

To my indomitable grandfather Francis W. Markus [1903 – 2001],
a genuine 20th century man. His travels and passion for America's
National Parks inspired my own travels and initiated a desire to
get out in those mountains and see what's on the other side.

- Kirk Markus

Acknowledgements

Thanks to our tireless editor Diane Graham-Henry whose countless hours word smithing our text can't be thanked enough. Her patience with our grammatical faux pas was greatly appreciated. In addition, thanks go to those that proofed the early versions of the text Erin Talcott, Kristy Peterson and Jennifer Salvage.

Thanks to travel, trekking partners and friends: Keri Cohn, Heather Cohn, Nancy Benjamin, Matthew Dormond, Chuck Meyer, Ben Rockstroh, Jennifer Salvage, Ruben Cashler, Ralph Markus, Mark Rogers, Phil Gray, David Steingard, Dean Ottati, Annette Monreal, Dave Sockel and Randy Ackerman. Good trails can be hard to find but good friends are even harder.

Many thanks to our friend and guide Padam. Over numerous trips to Nepal, including countless days on the trail and around Kathmandu, he has our treks and visits much more enjoyable and educational.

After many unfruitful attempts at producing quality maps for the trails, the maps in this text were derived from NASA's Blue Marble project using LANDSAT7 data purchased and polished by Scapeware 3D (www.scapeware3D.com). The trails were added manually to these satellite images. The very difficult to obtain coordinates for the Kachin Tribal Village Trek were provided by Henk de Jong. Check out his website at http://www.hsdejong.nl/myanmar/. All of the photos in this book were taken by Jeff Salvage and Kirk Markus except for two images in Chapter 11. They were bravely photographed under horrendous conditions by Karl Scheibe.

Finally, thanks to all the guides and porters in all the countries we visited. We would bear a much heavier load without them.

-Jeff Salvage and Kirk Markus

Thanks to my parents Ralph Markus and Grace Jameson for all their love and support over the past 46 years. Special thanks to my mom, Grace, for demonstrating a keen passion for life and teaching me many of the joys and techniques of writing. I recently discovered on our first high altitude hike together at 11,000 feet in Colorado that she does pretty darn well on the trail.

Also thanks to Kristy Peterson, my partner and trail-mate, who enhances all aspects of my trekking and home life experiences.

Of course, thanks to my friend and co-author Jeff Salvage. I am a better trekker and photographer with Jeff on the trail. His often stinky feet not withstanding, it's always an entertaining and quirky (think Monty Python quirky) adventure with Jeff. Alas, without his perseverance it is likely my participation in this project would not have happened.

-Kirk Markus

While Kirk Markus credits me with his participation in this book, without Kirk I never would have had the courage to venture so far from my comfort zone.

- Jeff Salvage

Table of Contents

Preface

Great Treks is the culmination of a seven-year quest to walk the world's ten best treks. We've stood in awe at the foot of the world's largest mountain; traversed home-strung rickety rattan bridges above white water rapids in the mountains of Burma; endured four seasons in a single day on the trails in Patagonia; and much more. The list of the "top ten" treks is subjective by nature since different people value varied aspects of a trek. In general, we followed the consensus of treks that topped most outdoor/hiking publications and trekking enthusiast's lists.

Hiking through diverse ecosystems, sometimes several on a single trek, and completing the world's greatest treks fosters a new appreciation for the grandeur of our planet. A former international race walking competitor, my racing days ended early due to knee injuries. I threw myself into a more formal career, but a sedentary life was not for me. By happenstance, I followed a friend to Nepal for a trek to the foot of Mount Everest. With little camping or hiking experience, the trip to Nepal dramatically changed my life. It's where I met *Great Treks* co-author Kirk Markus, a far more experienced traveler and trekker than myself. Our journeys filled the void, left from a lack of competition, with the quest to walk along the preeminent treks in the world.

We've written *Great Treks* to inspire you to get off the couch and explore the vast and diverse world. Maybe after reading this book, you'll go out for an afternoon hike. Perhaps the hike will lead you to walk one of the treks described here. And maybe, just maybe, you'll be inspired to complete all ten of the Great Treks!

- Jeff Salvage and Kirk Markus

Chapter One
Stepping Out of Your Comfort Zone

Most people walk every day. You may walk for health, you might walk for charity and maybe you have even walked to race, but have you trekked? Merriam Webster states to trek is "to make one's way arduously." This could happen on the steep streets of San Francisco, dodging taxis in New York, or even battling a strong winter head-wind on the flat streets of Chicago. However, for us the term takes on the greater colloquial meaning of a multi-day walk through spectacular mountains and scenery. How arduous a trek may be is determined by factors like how far, how high and how treacherous the path is that lies before you.

Imagine forging your way through fog-laden forests in the high Andes, camping along 600 year-old Incan trails, climbing 13,000-foot passes and braving rain storms as your trail turns to slippery mud. After four difficult days, you wake up in the darkness of the early morning and walk two miles to an overlook to await the sunrise. Within minutes the clouds lift and rays of golden light begin to uncover one of the most majestic ruins on the planet. Machu Picchu's stone secrets are slowly revealed in the breaking dawn.

It is moments like this that make a trek worthwhile and set it apart from a typical walk. We describe trekking as a non-technical hike lasting a few days to a few weeks and for some, even a month or more. The key is that it is non-technical. Many people falsely assume when I say I trekked on Mt. Everest that I reached the summit of the beast. Hell no, people die there! Trekking with the proper precautions is adventurous, but relatively safe.

In the United States one of the most famous treks is the Appalachian Trail, which spans from Georgia to Maine crossing fourteen states. It takes approximately six months to hike in its entity. Hard core thru-hikers complete the entire trail from end to end without pause. This requires a great deal of planning and coordination, as well as substantial physical and mental fortitude. If you don't have six months to devote to a hike, you can complete smaller sections of the trail at your leisure over several years. There are so many wonderful treks which require as few as three days or up to a several weeks of time.

While we will go into great detail about each of the ten greatest treks, there is a fair amount of general information that is helpful to review before delving into individual treks.

Guided vs. Independent Treks

In the "old days" before guided treks, independent travelers ventured forth into the mountains going from village to village staying in the same little houses where locals stopped for a night's rest on their own journeys to and from their homes in the mountains.

Ultimately, as more travelers reached these remote areas, "official" guest houses were built and small restaurants opened— allowing one to pack a sleeping bag and head off. This was all before the birth of the guided trek. Today, in many places it is still an easy economical option to hike independently.

On the other hand, if time is in short supply you can pay a premium to an international guide service. The upside of a guided trek is they complete all the planning and set up. You just have to show up ready to start. The downside of travelling with a guide is the decreased local interaction in the guest houses. Regardless, of your desire, it is not always a choice, as some sensitive areas require supervision.

There is also a third way to trek. You can easily hire a guide in the closest major access town. In popular trekking regions there are usually many local companies and with a few days time you can find a reliable, reasonably priced guide and set off. In fact many of the international guide companies subcontract to such firms. You can even have your guide hire porters so all you need to carry is a daypack.

Bearing the Load: Porters

There is often a lot of debate about the ethics involved in using porters to share the burden of carrying your gear. The countries we trek are often very poor and working as a porter can earn a fairly decent wage. A friend of ours from Nepal, Padam, started out as a poor porter in the Everest region and earned enough to buy a small house in Kathmandu. You'll get to know him when you read the treks in Nepal in Chapters Two and Seven.

Porters often carry the supplies and equipment for the trek. If you splurge they may also carry your personal belongings. Typically, a porter can carry the belongings of one or two people, not more. When porters carry everything, it's like traveling with a small army; it is not unusual for 10-20 porters to support 5-10 trekkers.

It's important to be aware of how your porters are treated. Different countries have different regulations. In Peru porters are strictly limited to the amount of weight they are allowed to carry and are inspected multiple times on the trail. In contrast, in Nepal it is common practice to overweigh porters whose difficult load is compounded by their improper clothing for the high mountainous conditions. Even the guides from agencies rarely show genuine concern; they tell you what you want to hear.

During our trek in Nepal we ended up buying gloves and hats for our porters. As we reached the summit of Kilimanjaro, we offered a spare set of gloves to our assistant guide, but he turned them down claiming they made him uncomfortable. Sometimes it is difficult to know what to do.

Lodging: Where to Get a Little Shut-Eye

Some trekking regions are inhabited and afford the option to stay in local villages. Other areas are so remote that tenting is the only option. This is especially true in the far reaching wilderness. Sometimes your budget dictates where to stay. Other times tenting allows guided companies to maintain a consistent experience. The quality of a tent varies, not surprisingly usually with the price. Typically two people sleep in a tent and you can either bring your own sleeping bag and pad or have them provided for you by a trekking company. We recommend you bring these yourself, as you can be sure about the quality and cleanliness. Once embarked, you are pretty much stuck with what you have, so it's best to be prepared.

Lodge-based trekking differs greatly from trek to trek and from group to group. Lodges can be very fancy, like the Everest View Hotel or as simple as a local villager's house. Depending on the country and altitude, warmth at night varies widely. While trekking in Burma, they burn firewood at the center of the hut, at least providing reasonable warmth until the fire dies. However, in Nepal, where there is no firewood at high elevations, yak dung is used to keep the main room warm for a few hours. Sadly, once the poop runs out, it turns bitterly cold. Imagine being upset that there is no more yak dung!

What to Bring: Gear, Food and Clothing

Each trek usually brings with it a unique character in terms of climate and culture. Part of the joy of any travel experience is sampling the many local dietary delights that your journey offers. No matter where you go, however, you should always be prepared and bring the right gear.

First and foremost, a good pair of broken in, waterproof, trail-tested hiking boots is highly recommended. A high quality sleeping bag, reliable rain gear and thermal wicking layers are important for virtually any trek. As for other equipment, we are often a little gadget heavy (our nerdy side.) So, devices like an altimeter, a compass or even GPS are useful tools and sometimes fun to have on a trek to monitor your progress and location. Good maps are essential if you are on your own, but not necessary if you take a guided trip. An extensive list of equipment is included in Appendix A.

The culinary experience might vary depending on whether you go with a guided company that attempts to cook western style food versus local fare. However, usually the style of food is similar along the entire trek. Even meals seemingly great on the first day, become monotonous after two weeks of it. Therefore, it's a good idea to bring some treats, but think before you buy. Whatever you bring must be carried and it has to keep well. Energy bars (non chocolate covered, because chocolate melts), nuts and dried fruits are all obvious choices. A great addition on any trek is tea or a powdered electrolyte drink, which helps give your water a little flavor. We can't emphasize enough how important it is to keep hydrated. It is the key to performance, comfort and safety.

Get off the Couch

So why not make your next walk a trek? Take your passion to the next level or maybe even another country. Wake up to the challenge of Mt. Everest Base Camp or a sunrise from the summit of Mt. Kilimanjaro. Step out of your comfort zone. We hope that this book inspires and educates you to get on the trail. See you there!

Chapter Two
Everest Base Camp
Nepal

Mysterious and exotic, Nepal holds prime position in the imagination of every mountain lover and trekker in the world. It is home to the bulk of the Himalaya and of course Mt. Everest, planet Earth's highest peak. In fact, of the world's fourteen highest peaks, eight are in Nepal. It is also the birthplace of Buddha and home of the famed porters and mountain climbing Sherpas. The mixture of mountains and ancient culture make Nepal a magical land of superlatives and an absolute delight for walkers and trekkers. Himalaya means "abode of the snows," and the main purpose of any respectable pilgrimage to Nepal is to reach out and touch a piece of these wild and jagged mountains, to feel their power and of course, to walk among the high peaks and deep valleys. It is the embodiment of a trek. It is no surprise Nepal is one of best places in the world to do just that. Considering 80% of the villages of Nepal are not connected by roads, walking is the means by which everybody and every-thing is transported, usually by porters. Trekking is second nature there and a habitual way of life.

It's hard to imagine any other trek that offers as much classic Himalayan scenery step after step, day after day, than the trek to the foot of Mt. Everest. In addition to the fantastic vistas, there are rewarding visits to the friendly villages along the trails. While most of the culture is Sherpa, who are akin to Tibetan Buddhists, you will also find some migrant Hindu Nepalese who work in the shops and guest houses. This gives you a taste of the two predominant cultures in Nepal. Synchronize your visit with the market days and you will probably see traders who have ventured from Tibet to the markets in Namche and even farther south. Their distinctive red braided head garb makes them easy to spot.

There are two primary destinations for the average trekker. Everest Base Camp at 5,300m / 17,500' is the stepping off point for most mountaineering expeditions to summit the peak and is the destination most people imagine when trekking to Everest. The other destination is probably more impressive from a trekker's standpoint. It is a small chunk of rock nestled at the foot of Pumori Mountain overlooking Everest Base Camp. This modest piece of earth is called Kala Pattar (Black Rock) and its peak sits at 5,550m / 18,200' commanding stunning views of Mt. Everest, the surrounding massif, Everest Base Camp, the

Khumbu Glacier and finally, the famous, deadly Khumbu Ice Fall. All are part of one of the most breathtaking 360 degree panoramas available in the world! Amazingly, this is all accessible without using a rope and ice axe.

Fundamentals

Days Trekking: 12	**Approximate Elevation Change:** 2,650m / 8,800' one way
Distance: 92 km / 57 miles, roundtrip	**Price Range Independent:** $300 - $700
Maximum Elevation: 5,500m / 18,200' Kala Pattar - 5,300m / 17,500' Everest Base Camp	**Price Range Outfitter:** $1,200 - $3,500
Starting Elevation: 2,850m / 9,400'	**Challenge Level:** Difficult

When to Go

The prime trekking seasons in Nepal are fall and spring. Fall in Nepal is October to early December and the spring season runs from mid February to mid April. Fall offers clearer skies and more crowds on the trails. Spring presents a greater possibility for dusty or hazier skies, but it gives you a chance to see the spectacular Rhododendron trees in full bloom.

Guided vs. Independent Treks

Nepal provides a full array of choices when it comes to trekking independently or with a guide service. For those with little experience, an internationally guided trip removes a lot of the complexities of following the trail and selecting lodging. For those a little more adventurous and wishing to save on expenses, it is fairly easy to hire a local guide in Kathmandu. You can even make the arrangements over the Internet, just make sure you check out the company carefully as their quality can vary widely. Finally, for the truly bold, you can hike independently without a guide. While you might be tempted to opt for this latter option, we recommend splurging for a guide and/or porter as it helps support the local economy and we've always found it to be a rewarding experience. One of our guides, Dhruba, now has his own guiding company, World Vision Tours. You can visit his website at *www.worldvisiontours.com*,

Access / Local Information

Kathmandu is the gateway for most Himalayan treks. It is an easy flight from Bangkok, a little longer from Hong Kong, and a puddle jump from New Delhi, India. You can also cross into Nepal by land from India. Kathmandu is a traveler's paradise. Everything you need is available there; hotels in any price range, culinary feasts of any world-wide cuisine, cheap and relatively fast Internet access and a wealth of western bookstores are found in the honky-tonk backpacker ghetto of Thamel. You can find any trekking gear, souvenirs and supplies you require.

To begin your journey you can fly from Kathmandu to Lukla. Flights can be arranged in Kathmandu. The overland approach for those who have more time is to take a bus from Kathmandu to Jiri and trek 11 days to Lukla, including five 13,000' passes. It is a beautiful way to get there and you will be in tip-top shape for the final ascent to high altitude.

Difficulty

The Everest Base Camp Trek requires no technical knowledge, but it's no easy walk in the park. The altitude, cold and terrain can wear on the unprepared. This is definitely a difficult trek, but one that can be completed by most fit individuals with an iron will.

Orientation

The Himalayan range crests across northern Nepal sharing the border with Tibet. The Solu Khumbu region is home to Mt. Everest and is 200 kilometers east of the Nepal capital, Kathmandu. Lukla is at the meeting point of the Himalayan foothills and the Himalayan range. The trail winds north toward the Base Camp with Everest saddling the border of Nepal and Tibet.

Alternative/Additional Treks

A great alternative to the Everest Base Camp Trek is to hike to Gokyo Ri. Starting in Lukla and passing through Namche, it offers much of the grandeur of the Everest Base Camp Trek, but without the crowds. If weather permits, you can combine the two treks, but this is usually quite difficult.

On the Trail with Jeff

The trek to Everest Base Camp carried with it a mystique like no other I've experienced. The multitude of stories surrounding the successes and failures of many people's journey to the peak built an aura about this trip that had me a tad bit apprehensive. Even though I was going no farther than Base Camp, I didn't know what to expect. As my first real trek, it was an odd choice, but when one of my athletes, Keri, invited me along, how could I refuse? While I had a reasonable amount of world travel under my belt and thousands and thousands of miles of race walking, I had virtually no hiking, trekking, or camping experience.

As a coach and walking expert, I prepared diligently. Physically, I worried how my knees would handle the assault up the mountain. I felt well prepared, walking daily and including strength training and step workouts, lots of step workouts. Before the trip I had built up to about 100 flights of steps a day. Importantly, I walked up and down each flight so my body was prepared for whatever the trail would throw at me. Despite my preparation, my anxiety was high. Sadly, my companions on this trip only added to my angst. Immediately before the trek, Keri was participating in a medical rotation in India, where she found it difficult to train. She was tough. Years earlier her competitive race walking career ended with a car accident that broke her back but not her spirit. While I had faith she could persevere, her sister Heather wasn't training enough either. It concerned me so much I politely emailed our guide and inquired what it would cost to hire two guides. Not understanding why, he quickly talked me out of the additional expense, so I simply hoped for the best. Heather and I left the States and headed to India where we picked up Keri, before flying to Kathmandu, Nepal, to meet our guide Dhruba and our two porters Ganesh and Kristna.

Our trek started with a short flight from Kathmandu to the small village of Lukla. There was a jostle for seats on the left side of the plane for those in the know, as these are the best seats for a view of the mountains. Eager anticipation was in the air while

waiting to receive clearance for take-off. Once airborne the tiny prop plane was engulfed in the majesty of the Himalayas. Imagine flying at over 3000m / 10,000' and having mountains towering above you! The flight was short and soon we were approaching the short strip of land they called a runway. Everyone was anxious as the landing strip was tiny and surrounded by peaks and valleys. The runway was sloped to assist landings and takeoffs; however, there was still little margin for error. We wondered if the sandbags surrounding the runway were part of military security for the ongoing civil war in Nepal or if they provided a barrier in case the plane didn't not stop in time.

While the town of Lukla doesn't have much charm, it is an effective launching point and a good place to hire porters if you don't already have them. Just standing around at over 2,850m / 9,000', the thin air taxed our lungs. Walking around the town breathing was further strained, but after a long morning the quest for breakfast distracted us from respiratory issues. Surprisingly, there were many choices from a traditional western fare to Tibetan bread called chapati and a dish similar to Cream of Wheat called champas.

After our meal we set forth upon the business we came here for, to walk. We actually descended 200m / 656' on our trek to Phakding, the first night's destination, rolling along a two-hour trek on a "Nepali Flat" series of ups and downs. The trail was incredible, passing aqua blue rivers reminiscent of the Caribbean with towering mountains littering the backdrop.

Lunch was our first taste of the traditional meal of dal bhat - the Nepalese national dish. It is basically a thick lentil soup poured over a Mt. Everest sized pile of rice. To add a little spice, it was augmented by curry and a vegetable or mystery meat if you dare. The Nepalese eat it in copious quantities for breakfast, lunch and dinner, every day without complaint. While advertised as not too appetizing, our first taste of dal bhat was surprisingly delectable. In addition, we had momas (a perogi

like potato dish), curried vegetables, and fried noodles. It all tasted great, but we didn't fully appreciate it because we didn't know as we progressed higher up the mountain the choices became as thin as the air. The trail was lined with countless prayer wheels and carved prayer stones. While these mantras were probably meant only to pacify general fears, we worried why there was so much need for prayer. Thankfully, we were going no farther than Base Camp.

When we reached the first night's guest house it exceeded expectations. It even had electricity, albeit the lights all dimmed when anything was plugged in to charge. This is where Kirk and I met the first time. While sipping a cup of tea, Kirk was intrigued by the invasion of electronic gadgetry I brought to such a remote area. I had a small laptop, one of the first digital SLR cameras and lots of accessories.

"Why do you have such a big lens?" Kirk's fiancé Nancy inquired. Being a smart ass, I replied, "because I take pictures of race walkers." Expecting a strange look, I was startled by Nancy's one word reply, "Really!"

Sensing her enthusiasm, I was unsure why she would be so intrigued. She explained how she knew all these "great" race walkers. Now, while I don't hear too many people boasting that they know race walkers, usually the names I hear are not truly amongst the elite of America, but some quick local walkers. Nancy proved my assumption dead wrong listing name after name of America's fastest "pedestrians." Most of these people were my friends and she even dated my college coach. She knew them from her days working at the Olympic Training Center in Colorado Springs. Who would guess that race walking would bring people together in such a remote corner of the world? An instant bond was formed, leading to a new friendship and many more treks together. Although our groups would travel separately at this point, our paths would crisscross many times over the next several days, ultimately joining forces for our summit bid on Kala Pattar.

The Worst was Yet to Come

As cold as it was in our sleeping bags that night in our Spartan room, the true bite of the cold hit exceptionally hard the next morning while filtering the icy water for our day's travel. Fortunately, as the sun rose its glow warmed us considerably. The beginning of the day's trek wasn't challenging at all. While physiologically one cannot significantly adapt overnight, breath-

ing did feel a lot easier walking along the relatively flat terrain, at least at the beginning of the day's hike. Perhaps the distraction from our labored breathing was more due to being engulfed in the soaring mountains as opposed to an easy trail.

Not too far into the day we officially entered Sagarmatha National Park. Seeing the park visitation chart we were amazed to discover that in February the average was barely 500 trekkers entering the park. By March this increased to over 2,000 and by the peak month of October there were over 6,000 people hitting the trail. Indeed, the pleasant emptiness of the trail we were experiencing was not the standard. Breaking for lunch, we relaxed with the sights of Nepalese children and cute puppies playing just outside the village. This relaxation was short lived because once we resumed hiking we had a rude awaking. The jump from 2,620m / 8,594' to almost 3,445m / 11,300' all occurred in the latter part of the day's hike. This was the single biggest altitude gain in a day.

As we began the lung-sucking climb to reach the village of Namche Bazaar, the center of commerce and tourism for the region, my group's pace slowed to a crawl. With Heather's heart rate climbing over 170, I knew we were in trouble. While a trained athlete can sustain this for some time, we needed to hike for hours and Heather was definitely not a trained athlete. We advanced one step at a time, trying to catch our breath as we continued upward. The thought of the next day's rest for acclimatization helped soothe the pain as we marched higher and higher.

The cluttered sight of small shops, houses and lodges clinging to the steep mountainside was a blessing to our weary eyes. Namche Bazaar had a good variety of facilities. Internet was available as well as several little European-style bakeries serving tempting sweets. In fact, there was so much trekking gear and western-style goods that it was hard to believe Namche Bazaar is not connected via paved roads with trucks bringing supplies on a daily basis. It is truly a place where the medieval world meets the modern. However tempting it may be it's not worth buying any souvenirs until your return to Namche Bazaar. Most items are readily available when you come back to either Namche Bazaar or the comfort of Kathmandu. Hopefully you've planned ahead and do not have to purchase anything. Often the trekking equipment sold in Namche Bazaar are knock-offs and poorly built. What looks reasonably constructed may not hold up to the rigors of the remainder of your climb. We sought basic lodging with our only expectations being a power source and a rejuvenating hot shower, as we assumed this would be the last chance for such amenities. Fortunately these are not rarities in Namche Bazaar.

Sleeping at altitude can always be a challenge. My first night in Namche Bazaar was tough, waking many times; but no one ever said this would be easy. Keri and Heather stayed in a separate room while I stayed by myself. The solitude was not ideal. With my respiration still challenged by the thin air, my mind started to dwell on what had I gotten myself into and how much more difficult it might become.

Due to the large increase in altitude in just over 24 hours, a day of rest and acclimatization was on tap for the next day. We planned a circular route through the surrounding countryside which would take us to approximately 3,840m / 12,600'. Our simple trip did not start well and forebode things to come. Keri developed problems with her relatively untested hiking boots. This led to our porter Ganesh and I running back to the room to get her sneakers. Figuring the day wouldn't be that difficult of a hike, it seemed like a reasonable decision at the time. Unfortunately, we were wrong. The muddy, cold trail engulfed her sneakers leading to further discomfort instead of a pleasant recovery day.

Still our group plodded along past the tiny airport and up to the Everest View Hotel where we stopped for a bit of hot chocolate and our first clear view of Mt. Everest. Seeing our goal in sight curbed the doubts and our pains shed away. However, the vision of Everest was not the giant granite monolith one sees in photographs, but a tiny speck small and far in the distance. It was dwarfed by the closer mountains in the foreground, showing just how far we still had to go. We headed back with a circuitous route that passed through a few villages. The porters were having a blast and got in a friendly snowball fight. However, once the fog rolled in, it got chilly fast. Keri's complaining I was paying too much attention to her sister and that I was walking too fast only added to the icy feeling. My patience was challenged as I didn't even like Heather and was "paying her attention" because I was trying to be nice for Keri's sake. It was going to be a long trip.

Fortunately, we got back and the acclimatization worked, I was feeling much better. The next day was Sunday, market day in Namche. While Kirk and his group were smart enough to plan ahead, we simply lucked out getting to witness the gritty, little market on a steep hillside at the edge of town. Wild-eyed traders came from surrounding villages and even as far as Tibet to buy and sell.

Mountains Don't Care

For the most part we went up (ukalo in Nepalese). Ukalo, ukalo, ukalo – it hummed in our bodies and rung out in our heads. It was tough, especially after we gained 175m / 574' only to go back down and then right back up again. Our hard-earned

altitude was constantly wasted. Kirk's favorite mantra was brought forth: "elevation gain is a terrible thing to waste." However, the mountains don't care, it's just business as usual on the roof of the world. From Namche it was on to the Tengboche Monastery and the surrounding guest houses that serve trekkers and pilgrims. Climbers of Mt. Everest historically come to Tengboche for blessings by the monks in advance of their dangerous summit bids of Mt. Everest. They receive a white scarf, a blessing for a safe journey and offer a prayer to the mountain gods. Hopefully, we wouldn't need such blessings.

Although the initial climb straight up out of the valley from Namche Bazaar was challenging, the good night's sleep helped. From this point the trail eased and we enjoyed bright, sunny blue skies and a relatively flat trail. Along the way were roaring rivers and flimsy bridges littered with prayer flags. As I hesitantly peered down from a bridge as it bounced and swayed unpredictably in the wind, I was reminded why I am a trekker and not a mountaineer. It was a *looong* way down. The sun made hiking comfortable and I thought this is what one hopes for when one treks. The nicer weather led to a jovial atmosphere, at least from my perspective. Our guide Dhruba thought it funny to place rocks in Heather's pack. She, of course, didn't share his perspective. Perhaps too much joviality is a bad thing, then again perhaps not. It was at this point I decided to pile it on. My plan was simple. I'd carried a ceramic ocarina and intended to let Heather discover it on the trail. When she did, I would pick it up and declare it to be an ancient Sherpa's Yeti whistle and start playing it. Having practiced *Blowing in the Wind* by Bob Dylan, I figured it would be good for a much needed group laugh. My plan didn't hatch as I hoped. After I left it on the trail multiple times, with Heather walking by it each time, I enlisted Ganesh to retrieve the Yeti whistle and redeploy our trap. Eventually I gave up and dropped it by her feet. Picking it up, I declared, "Look a Yeti whistle! I hear that these things are really rare and used by the ancient Sherpas." Heather laughed, "They're not so rare, I saw them on the trail for the past few days." While not having the effect I originally desired, we all laughed at Heather, I mean with Heather.

The end of the day's trek once again found us climbing upward. The steep ascent of 500m / 1,640' sapped the cheerful atmosphere from my crew and it didn't return upon reaching Tengboche. The local lodge was quite different from the previous accommodations; with long, body-chilling shadows growing across the village. It was damp, musty and the outhouse reeked worse than a stable.

In contrast, the nearby Tengboche monastery was truly in a stunning setting. As we marched toward it we met back up with Kirk and Nancy. We stopped at the center of the 360-degree panorama while Kirk studied the topographic map and pointed

out the names of the surrounding peaks. Padam, his guide, knew them by heart from his many trips to the region: Ama Dablam, Lhotse, Tamsherku, Kasem Kanguru and a glimpse of Everest over the top of the Nuptse Ridge. Embarrassingly the names of these peaks were foreign to me, but they had engaged Kirk's dreams from many years of studying maps and reading books of this famous region. For him it was great to be there and see them with his own eyes, but I felt a little ignorant not recognizing anything but our destination of Mt. Everest.

We had an added treat during our visit to Tengboche because we arrived just in time for Festival Lo Shar, the Sherpa New Year. The monks, in full red and yellow regalia, were an ocular feast. Centered around a bonfire, they chanted and tossed spears. I chuckled as I watched the young monks take "cheating" glances from their book of chants. I had flashbacks to Hebrew school where I struggled reading prayers I could pronounce but not comprehend.

After the ceremony we had dinner, which was surprisingly good. It was so tasty Keri decided to challenge the food gods. Although we were explicitly told not to drink the unpasteurized buttermilk tea, she proclaimed how great her immune system was and slurped it down. While I like to try all the local delicacies and her bravado against illness was a page out of my proverbial book, I was too paranoid to take chances on the way up. As an added perk, I got to recharge my batteries, although now the guest houses charged for electricity. It's amazing how power becomes such a huge issue just a few days along a trail. Once back at the room with time to think, I took inventory of my many aches and pains. While the altitude wasn't bothering me at all, the pounding of the many ups and downs was showing in my knees, hamstrings and on my sun burnt face (even with SPF 30). I considered myself lucky that I hadn't pressed ahead earlier, but instead had walked at the pace of my group. Their conservative pace probably saved me a good bit of suffering. While I kept my aches and pains to myself, Heather was more than willing to share her discomfort. "It's so cold. My face hurts. Keri doesn't care about me." "Really," I thought? It's one thing to have to battle the mountain, but Heather decided she wouldn't wear sunscreen that day and turned cherry red because of it. Now, on top of this, I had to hear more sibling rivalry?

The next day the foggy, damp atmosphere disappeared quickly as the sun rose over the valley, transforming Tengboche into a winter wonderland. Even the monks were feeling playful as they tested some make-shift skis. However, playfulness would not last long. Beyond Tengboche were the desolate lands above the tree line; the home of the glaciers, mountain peaks, ice falls, rock faces and glacial moraines. The amount of snow on the ground increased substantially and the wind picked up, but we were blessed by a bright sunny day lighting the mountains with outstanding views.

A flatlander all my life, I was finally getting my mountain legs under me as we trekked from Tengboche to Dingboche. The climb of nearly 610m / 2,000' along a moderate, graded trail seemed relaxed in contrast to the previous few days' hikes. However, the easier terrain was marred when Keri intestinal tract rebelled, making her progress difficult, thus wearing down our spirits to a new low. On a positive note, we bumped into a doctor who was going to be stationed at the Pheriche Hospital run by the Himalayan Rescue Association and he offered us a tour of the facilities. While we were bypassing Pheriche on the way up, we promised to stop by for a tour on the way down. Fortunately, I was able to take refuge from my group's strife when we reunited with Kirk and Nancy at dinner. Their fresh blood was just what I needed to reenergize as we spent the evening huddled around the yak-dung stove eating dal bhat, sipping hot tea and sharing friendly conversation. Nobody wanted the banter to end as it meant retreating to the cold "bedrooms," crawling into our sleeping bags and waiting, skin shivering, for our body heat to warm the confines of our sleeping bags.

Higher Than Base Camp

With no place we had to be by a particular time, we decided to sleep in and get a good night's recuperative rest. By morning I was raring to go with Kirk and Nancy joining us for a day hike to almost 5,100m / 17,728'. Keri was still feeling under the weather, but she rallied and joined us. Once we climbed a bit over 4,500m / 15,000', Keri reached her limit and Heather claimed she would go down to keep her sister company. Only later in the trip did I find out she was lying and that she was struggling with the altitude. Quickly, everyone bailed except for Kirk and myself. Dhruba reviewed the map with Kirk, before heading back with the troops. Instead, our marginally English-speaking porters escorted us the rest of the way to our mini summit attempt. Kirk's knowledge of maps and the locale was invaluable as it would be on the many treks we walked together. Although I was tired as well, I knew that hiking high and sleeping lower would help us in the long run, so we continued upward.

As we gained elevation, we had the best views on the trip so far. What was amazing was the ability to see down as well as up at a magnitude that was simply unimaginable in the States. In addition to the uncultivated valleys, some were tamed to act as fields for the warmer months. Unfortunately, we were way too early in the season to see any presence of a farm other than the rock walls surrounding barren fields waiting for the spring to melt away the last of the winter's snow.

The ascent proved more challenging than I thought. Each step was a new personal record in altitude for me and I felt it. With about 30m / 100 vertical feet left, I felt I was close to my limit, but trudged on as the views of the valley and surrounding mountains were breathtaking. In each direction it seemed there was another spectacular towering peak well above our height.

Amazingly, we were higher in elevation than Everest Base Camp. Only six days into our trek our bodies had adapted somewhat to the higher altitude, but only a pittance to what mountaineers at Base Camp experience. To reap the complete benefits of high altitude acclimatization we would have had to spend nearly 60 days at this altitude. No wonder we were tired.

Although heading down was far easier on the lungs, the pounding of the descent was considerable. However, when we returned to our lodge a surprise in the form of a hot shower awaited. Water heated by yak dung was poured in a bucket overhead allowing it to release a bit of it at a time to warm up and clean off a few days' grime. For once gravity was our friend.

On a tourist trek like Everest Base Camp there's not much wildlife to see. While a yak isn't exactly wildlife, shortly after our next day's start toward Lobuche (5,050m / 16,700') a pair of yaks gave us some excitement. Two yaks challenged each other to a duel of sorts, head butting each other until one submitted. I charged towards them to get a photograph. It would be the first, but not the last time that a guide told me I was crazy.

The excitement didn't die down as shortly after Keri and Heather broke out into a screaming match. As Heather storming off ahead of us, I was dumfounded. The mountains, especially this high, were no place for this kind of behavior. Dhruba turned to me and sincerely avowed, "I am very sorry." Puzzled, I replied "Why are you sorry?" "Now I know why you asked for the second guide." We both laughed and regrouped Heather and Keri so that we could continue.

Along the way Keri's stomach problems persisted. Unfortunately, that was not the only issue. Reports of rock slides and avalanches on the way to Base Camp, combined with the fact that we were so early in the season that no mountaineering groups were at the camp, led us to skip it. Instead, we headed directly for Kala Pattar with its great view of Everest. The other group, with my new friends Kirk and Nancy, decided to follow the same plan. Up the trail, we were treated to another taste of "wild" life as a group of crows hovered in the wind like kites, their jet black feathers piercing the cobalt blue sky. On the ground, we passed stone chorten monuments to many who have perished on Everest. This included Scott Fischer and Rob Hall from the ill-fated 1996 climbing season, chronicled in the famous John Krakauer book *Into Thin Air*, as well as Babu Chiri Sherpa who holds the record of 10 ascents of Mt. Everest.

As we approached the group of rock huts known as Lobuche, I started walking along the trail with Kirk and Nancy. I'd hit my limit with the girls and felt my new friends were much better company. In addition, I felt there was a growing likelihood that my group would self-destruct. I recanted the tale of the afternoon and my concerns to Kirk as I heard from down below, "We can hear you, ya know!" My terse response was not warmly received, "I know and I don't care at this point!"

That night we hunkered down and prepared for our summit bid on Kala Pattar with our two independent groups nearly merged together. The physical and mental strain of trekking at high altitude took a toll. We were all worn down, nervous and cold. Before bed we discussed our strategy, and expressed concerns about our ability to reach the summit. We went over decisions for start times, clothing choices and debated taking the altitude sickness drug Dimaox as a preventive measure. This was a once-in-a-lifetime opportunity and we all wanted to succeed. Later, when I was alone in the room, my mind debated over and over again if I could make it. While I was the most athletic of the group, I questioned if I was fit enough to reach the top without a problem. During this internal discussion I heard the gut wrenching sound of someone throwing up. It was Keri. Her stomach was revolting, making it readily apparent she wasn't going to be fit for the climb. After she composed herself, we talked and she indicated she wanted to wait another day. While it made sense for Keri and Heather to wait, I decided to join Kirk and Nancy. Believing my group wouldn't succeed, I definitely wanted the opportunity to reach our destination. How could you come this far and not see Everest up close? I hoped my group would be able to complete it a day later, but from my coaching experience I didn't think they would be ready. My decision didn't sit well, but as our guide said he would stay with them, I saw no reason not to go. I also offered to accompany them on their attempt as well. This did little to change the lack of popularity of my decision. While it was difficult to go back to sleep and the rift with my friends was an uncomfortable feeling, I finally dozed off.

Goddess Lady of the Wind

The next day was truly an epic day. We prepared to leave just before sunrise. Overnight virtually everything not kept in our sleeping bags froze solid. This included water bottles, treasured Snickers bars and even our boots. It's hard to start an ambitious day of hiking only to have to put on a pair of boots that are nearly frozen bricks. We had to get up at 5:30 am and leave by 7:00 am to make sure that we had enough time to get back before sunset. The altitude was clearly clouding my brain, because when I saw that you could order chocolate pancakes for breakfast I got excited and ordered up a plate. It's always a crap shoot when ordering western food, something I try not to do, but it sounded oh, so good. I was oh, so wrong. What I received was a horrendous pancake topped with lumpy, dry chocolate pudding. With no time to waste I forced it down and we headed out on the trail.

Just before sunrise we departed, a little nervous and with a smaller team, but still in good spirits overall. The trails wound up and down, over glacial moraines following along the beautiful Khumbu Glacier. Kirk's expression, "elevation gain is painful

to waste," is doubly applicable at that altitude. Making our way to a place called Gorak Shep, or "Graveyard of the Crows," our energy was depleted by cold and lack of oxygen. We hoped it wouldn't become our graveyard as the steep grade sapped our strength and resolve. Our brains and muscles craved oxygen as the air is so thin at 5,194m / 17,047'. In fact, less than half the amount of oxygen is available there as compared to sea level. Our breathing become more labored with every step. In my competitive days I race walked a six-minute mile and a marathon at close to an eight-minute mile pace. This was significantly harder. At least in a race I knew where to find the finish line. In the end it was sheer will; either we wanted to get to the summit badly enough to endure the pain or we didn't. That day was a triumph of will. After several false summits, we all made it to the very top of Kala Pattar. Prayer flags covered every inch of the summit signaled our arrival and feelings of jubilation were shared by all. Having heard that many Sherpa never got the recognition they deserved, often not even a photograph, I made sure to take pictures of our porters. It is such a simple gift to those supporting your goal. As it turned out, my efforts were rewarded as the photograph of Ganesh was one of my first images to be published.

From the summit the view was absolutely spectacular. We got a good look at the windswept peak of Mt. Everest. The closer peak of Nupste looked more dominating, even though it is several thousand feet shorter. The world's tallest peak is named for Sir George Everest [1790 - 1866] who was the Surveyor General of British India in the 1800's. However, the local names are much more dramatic, even though their exact meanings are sometimes debated. Sagarmartha is the Nepalese name, which translates to "Head of the Sky." The Sherpa and Tibetan name is Chomolungma, which means "Mother Goddess of the Universe" or "Goddess Lady of the Wind." Once again Kirk was educating me that in order to fully appreciate the experience it is good to do a bit more research before embarking.

The summit wasn't the end, we still had to return to Lobuche before sunset. Admittedly, it was easier to go down, but it was still a challenge. It was a long day and all of us were tired after many hours of hiking. We arrived back at our guest house exhausted just as twilight came upon us. My friends didn't seem too upset that I went without them and we agreed to try to walk together to the halfway point of Gorak Shep the next day.

Unfortunately, with Keri quite sick, my second journey through the glacial valley was painstakingly slow. I could tell even our modified destination was out of reach at this pace, so I sent Heather ahead with the porters so at least she could get a view from above the valley. I hung back with Keri until she made it to the end of the glacier valley and needed to start the steep climb. Unable to progress up the incline, we turned around and disappointedly headed back.

Departing the next day we headed toward Lukla. The weather on the return trip was decidedly less welcoming than on our ascent. Much of the way the wind was directly in our face and then the clouds rolled in with some brief rain and snow showers. It was the lack of sun that made the difference, letting in the cold, the bone chilling cold! Another major difference was the crowds on the trail. No longer were we walking in solitude, it was now March and prime trekking season. We diverted to Pheriche Hospital to keep our promise and take the tour of its facilities. Impressively the hospital had solar panels, wind turbines, but most importantly the only clean western toilet higher than Namche.

Ultimately, we made it safely back to Lukla and then flew to Kathmandu. We had just a few days left to experience the rich culture and ancient architecture on the narrow medieval-feeling streets. It really is a fascinating place to explore. For such a small country on the map, Nepal has so much to offer providing one of the most impressive trekking destinations with non-stop Himalayan scenery and a culture rich with Hindu and Buddhist traditions. It was sad to depart but it is good to have reasons to return to such beautiful places.

Epilogue

Trekking to Everest Base Camp as my first major trek wasn't the wisest of choices. Had I gone into it with more experience I definitely would have gained much more from the trip. Sadly, as a result of the challenges on the trek, my friendships with Keri and Heather were permanently damaged. If I had more experience trekking and leading a group, I probably would have handled the situation far better. Fortunately, the fever was lit inside of me and I looked for more opportunities to start exploring the far reaches of our world on foot.

EVEREST BASE CAMP TREK

Everest Base Camp

Kala Pattar

Gorak Shep

Mt. Everest

Lobuche

Pheriche   Dingboche

Tengboche

Namche Bazaar

Phakding

Lukla

N

Chapter Three
Kachin Tribal Village Trek
Myanmar/Burma

Mysterious Burma. Yes, you may have heard that it's called Myanmar these days. For many, however, there is something magical and even foreboding about the name Burma. What often comes to mind are deep jungles, brutal wars, Orwellian military dictatorships and, of course, really hard to build roads. The Kachin State is home to all of these qualities, both historically and in current times. This area is one of the least visited of all Himalayan regions and not surprisingly one of the least visited parts of Burma. Closed to foreigners since shortly after WWII, it just opened up to travelers a few years before our trek. Fascinating new tribes and rare new species from all phyla in the animal kingdom were recently "discovered" in this remote area. You can visit several tribal villages and head out from the "last village" to the untamed forests and ultimately scale the heights of the remote Mt. Phon Khan Razi.

Getting off the beaten path in Burma is like no other place. Burma's isolation over the past sixty years creates a real opportunity to travel back in time and is the main reason for our inclusion of this trek. However, by the time you read this, it may already be too late to have an experience equal to our own. Do some homework and research an equally remote trek for a parallel experience.

Fundamentals

Days Trekking: 10	**Approximate Elevation Change:** 3,178m / 8,745'
Distance: 55km / 32miles roundtrip	**Price Range Independent**: N/A
Maximum Elevation: 3,635 meters / 11,923'	**Price Range Outfitter:** $1,500 - 2,500 from Yangon
Starting Elevation: 457 meters / 1,499'	**Challenge Level:** Moderate

When to Go

The best time for trekking in northern Burma is February through May. The weather is pleasant, leaves are on the trees and bird migrations are passing through the country. Note that Burma is one of the world's best places to bird watch as the geography integrates a wide variety species. After May it gets quite hot and the monsoon season rolls up from the Indian Ocean. It lasts through October. November through February is colder, although trekking is still possible.

Guided vs. Independent Treks

Myanmar is under the leadership of a military dictatorship, which requires permits for any treks or explorations that get off the beaten path. There are only a handful of approved companies that lead trips to these far off places. You will need to coordinate in advance to make sure you will be able to obtain permits and guides. The government will likely provide an escort to keep a watchful eye on your behavior. Don't be deterred, ultimately they are looking after your well being as well as their own interests. They want you to have a safe and enjoyable trip so you can return to your country to say how wonderful, safe and friendly it is in Burma.

Difficulty

The trails and trek are not extremely arduous, however, traveling to and around Burma can be. The trail diminishes to a hunters path after the last village on your way to climb Mt. Phon Kahn Razi. The Kachin state is in remote northern Myanmar and you are required to bring virtually everything you need from Yangon or Mandalay, so be prepared. Additionally, unless you fly everywhere, be prepared for long, very long, bus and train journeys.

Orientation

Myanmar sits geographically between India, Bangladesh, China and Thailand and interestingly combines the geographic, cultural, culinary and religious elements of the Indian subcontinent, the Himalayas, tropical South East Asia and tribal Asian hill country. Putao is about as far north as you can go, near the Indian border and the last stop with internal combustion before beginning your trek.

Access / Local Information

Access to Myanmar is primarily through Thailand. Overland crossings are limited and your best options to access the country are by flights from Bangkok to Yangon. To get to the remote Kachin State from Yangon, fly to Mandalay to Myitchina to Putao. From the dusty dirt landing strip in Putao, it is a several hour jeep ride to the trail head. Alternately and more interestingly, you can take the train most of the way from Yangon. If you do, you will get a real sense of the countryside and small town life of Burma.

On the Trail with Jeff

Friends can be crafty influencers. Once again I found myself headed on an adventure not knowing what to expect. A busy work schedule and house rebuilding were justifications for my ignorance, but these were superficial reasons for my lack of research. Visiting the mysterious country of Myanmar, or Burma, as those of us less aligned with the military regime that took over in 1962 like to call it, isn't exactly on most people's bucket list. I was headed to remote areas of Northern Burma at the invite of my now good friends Kirk and Nancy whom I met in Nepal. Very little reliable tourist information was available and a complete dearth of trekking information existed.

While in 2003 the Internet was maturing into the vast resource of knowledge it is today, Burma was and still is in near complete electronic lock down. People couldn't just hop into a Burmese chat room and start asking questions. No portals existed outside of the government. Outgoing email was completely censored. What hid behind this shield? Nancy assured me Burma was great, but Nancy had a positive, cheery outlook about everything. I wasn't sure I could trust her recommendation. Years earlier, on very short notice, I taught at a university in Kuan Tan, Malaysia. Barely knowing more than where each country existed as I planned my trips, I was experiencing a strange déjà vu with this trip. Teaching in Kaun Tan was one of the best experiences of my life and I hoped this would be similar.

Flying from the U.S. to Yangon, the capital of Burma, is a long, slow process. I said goodbye to my bags, checked them all the way through and pondered the odds of seeing them again. There aren't any direct flights from the States to Burma. Since there's little economic benefit, the U.S. has taken a principled stand against the oppressive Burmese military government. Sanctions are in place and travel is discouraged. Some feel travel helps fund the oppressive government, since they take a healthy skim off the top of every transaction. However, I personally think that interacting with other countries, such as Burma, is important on many levels. Oppression works best under isolation. Taking a personal stake in the Burmese plight doesn't happen without interaction. International access is crucial.

After a long flight to Thailand there was an eight-hour layover in Bangkok. Having spent a few weeks in Thailand several years earlier I opted to take advantage of one of the best airports for killing time. Massages are cheap and plentiful, even at two in the morning. The facilities were clean and professional with no worries about being harassed to buy a "happy ending." After working the kinks out of my pretzeled body I reported home from an Internet cafe and ate a tasty meal. With plenty of time to spare, I wanted to get a haircut, but by 3:00 am the barber shops were not open.

The next morning I flew to Yangon. Like a good curious tourist, once we descended from the clouds I peered out the window. The landscape was startlingly different than almost any other landing I have experienced. All you could see was lush, green farmland with the golden spires of scattered pagodas as the only structures rising up from the foliage. Looking out the window it was hard to believe the stories of the government's ubiquitous, oppressive presence. Before we left the U.S., the Burmese government's restrictions already materialized in very subtle ways. We were told we would not be allowed to have a map of our trek and a government official would be shadowing us during our journey.

Propaganda's Fear

Once I landed the fear of the unknown started to race through my mind. What if my luggage wasn't there? Burma didn't exactly have an REI around the corner. What if Kirk and Nancy weren't waiting for me? Sure, I had the name of the tiny hotel where we were staying, but I wasn't confident I could find it. What would happen when I went through customs? The one piece of knowledge I obtained about Burma was that you were often pressured by government officials to convert currency from U.S. dollars into the kyats, the local currency at a ridiculously poor rate. Strong currency like the dollar was a sought after commodity in the fiscally challenged world of Myanmar. Indeed, I brought one hundred single dollar bills as converting large U.S. bills wouldn't be easy. I reaffirmed that if I were bullied, I would convert as little money as possible.

Most of my fears were unfounded. My luggage slid along the conveyor belt after the few tense minutes that always accompany luggage arrival. I passed through customs without a stare. There was no harassment whatsoever. More importantly, the smiling enthusiastic faces of Kirk and Nancy were waiting as they waved me down like a plane on the runway.

I followed Kirk and Nancy on the way to Yangon as if I were a young pup, making sure I kept them close. As we walked, my fears abated. While there were differences, the scene in Yangon had many similarities to Bangkok. There was lots of useless, low quality merchandise for sale. While there was less bargaining than other Southeast Asian countries, there wasn't much of a reason to haggle. I bought a bunch of cotton T-shirts for the hike at a cost of less than two dollars each. This was before I learned the mantra "cotton kills." Now I only wear moisture wicking shirts.

We went to a Burmese version of a cyber cafe. It wasn't real Internet access as all major email carriers were blocked. I sent a message out through their controlled email and asked my friend to forward it to friends and family so they would know their crazy friend was okay.

Nancy picked lodging well. Although power was intermittent elsewhere our modest hotel had a generator and the lights stayed on most of the time. My confidence for a successful trip was rising. A quick, simple dinner of vegetables, rice and a little fruit juice and I was done. I crashed hard shortly after and barely stirred until morning. Travelling with Kirk and Nancy would be a very different experience than my traditional trips. Nancy has an affinity for culture and seeing everything. Having visited Burma many times, she was my resident tour guide. Kirk visited once before, but when we weren't on the trail, Nancy was clearly our lead.

The day started with a hearty breakfast, but no Lucky Charms in Burma. Instead, we had ohno khauk swe, which was a soup-like dish of coconut milk, spices and noodles. Asian food has always been my favorite cuisine and Burma wasn't disappointing. Our first tourist stop was Shwedegon, the Golden Pagoda, an icon of the country. It was incredibly impressive and ornate. Like many third world countries the contrast between the resources vested in temples stands in strong disparity with individual wealth . . . or lack of it.

We stopped for a quick lunch of biryani (heavily spiced rice with chicken) that cost a whopping $.85, including a drink. Clearly this wouldn't be a very expensive trip. We walked around and wandered through the high-class shopping area. As far as I could tell they weren't catering to tourists, but a tiny minority of locals who could afford luxuries. Not looking to buy a high-end washing machine, we headed to a park to relax before returning to the hotel.

Planes, Trains, but no Automobiles

Next it was time to start the long journey to our trek. The combination of getting a better feel for the countryside with the most efficient form of internal combustion transportation led us to skip a series of easy flights to the start our trek and begin a long, but fascinating series of train rides north. The first leg was a first class train to Mandalay. The seats were comfortable enough, but this was no Amtrak experience. The windows were wide open and a series of broken-down fans littered the ceiling overhead. It was a shame we were starting late in the day as the first major portion of the trip would be in the dark. I was eager to see the countryside up close. Thankfully, before we went to sleep, the train conductors closed the windows. I feared rolling over and dropping out of one, as the poorly-maintained rails thrust the car side to side as much as forward. As we readied for sleep, distorted music blared from speakers. I found the switch to kill it, but was a little shy about flipping it. Fortunately, the more experienced Mighty Kirk did the honors. Normally known as the "Geek of Sleep," I stirred constantly. My night turned into a series of 40 naps ranging anywhere from 10 minutes to an hour. This was certainly not the best way to prepare for a long trek.

As the sun rose, I gave up on getting any more sleep and gazed out the window. Farmland stretched out to the horizon, all ox-tilled. We were truly going back in time where people and animals provided the power. A golden haze rose from the morning fields making the picture even more dreamlike. Upon arriving in the less congested city of Mandalay, Nancy had a busy itinerary for us. We checked into our hotel. It wasn't as clean or quaint as the previous one, but it was only eight dollars. We gobbled a quick lunch and headed to the famous pagoda, Maha Muni. It was interesting, but in contrast to Yangon there were many people begging. The highlight of the experience was interacting with a group of students on a class trip. Surprisingly, they weren't shy. "What is your name? Where are you from? What is your job?" were standard questions they read from a printed piece of paper. As each student progressed down their prepared list, they struggled with any questions beyond what was transcribed on their crib sheets.

Next we visited the handicraft center of Mandalay. It was a nonstop whirl-wind tour. Starting with the carving of marble and casting of brass statues, we learned the secret of cheap production, child labor. In reality most were at least teenagers as this work required skill. There was little concern for environmental or health issues. It was so dusty that the trees appeared covered by a recent snowfall. However, it was watching how the gold foil was manufactured for use in the temples that captivated my interest. Young looking kids pounded gold wrapped in leather packets with heavy mallets for what seemed like forever. Instead of counting how many strikes it took to complete a series, they simply used a very advanced water timer. A cup with a hole in the bottom was filled and flipped when it emptied. After a sufficient number of flips they divided the gold and pounded it some more. In contrast, the girls worked in the clean room packing the micro thin foil. This was not as easy as it seemed because, if they touched the fragile foil, it would stick to their skin. So they worked with small lifting and spreading sticks in a tiny room with no breeze.

As the sun lowered in the sky we journeyed to Mandalay Hill where a pagoda crests the peak, a perfect place to view the sunset across the city. Mandalay seemed visited by more tourists than elsewhere, or at least they were more concentrated in the sparse, scenic spots. I even met a group of Israelis who knew Shaul Adani, a great Israeli race walker I competed with 15 years earlier. We also conversed with a group of monk boys who were very friendly. After being harassed for money all day, it was refreshing talking to people who wanted nothing more than friendship. After the sun set we got a quick dinner. The food here was spicy and flavorful at the local treasure, Pakkoku Daw Malay. Be forewarned, however, little chilies foreshadow the spiciness of foods in Burma. A small salad I ordered took me by surprise, setting my gut on fire.

The next day we played tourist again. We arrived at the docks in Mandalay to catch a sightseers' ferry as we weren't allowed to ride the local one. The docks swarmed with kids begging for money. However, once we were headed downstream, it was the river itself that took center stage. It was a wide, muddy affair that merged with the shallow shore. Rice paddies and small shacks lined the river bank that seemed nearly devoid of settlers. Our destination was Mingun, a gargantuan ruin of a partially built pagoda. Over 50m / 164' high, it was called King Bodawpaya's Folly, as he planned it to be the largest temple in Asia. By the time of his death, only the brick base was complete. Landing at Mingun's dock we were greeted by more kids. Unlike the usual group of youthful salesmen, they followed us everywhere. Each one of us had a child alongside. They wanted us to buy their cheaply made fans for the equivalent of a few dollars, which they continually demonstrated by fanning us. We decided to offer them a "present" of a few kyats for their "escort." At first they refused, but when they realized there was no sale coming, they graciously accepted it.

Checking out of our hotel we then headed to the train station for the next leg of our travels, a 25-hour train ride. Although the outside looked modern, the station was just a concrete façade, no more substantial than a Hollywood set. Of course, the train was late, as if a trip wasn't going to be long enough already. I occupied myself by people watching. When you are the only Caucasians this becomes an interesting sport because as many people are looking at you as you are looking at them. While we certainly stood out more than anyone else, there was a clear division of travelers. The upper class locals were adorned in rubies and other gems, while the general public wore a bit of gold with amulets or ruby chips. When our train finally arrived, porters darted out, grabbing our bags and loading them onto the train with lightning speed.

We shared a sleeper car with a man in the military. He was a treat and nothing like we expected having heard the stories of the government's tyranny. I crashed early, hoping to catch up on sleep. However, my sleeping skills failed me again as the side-

to-side, up-and-down rambling of the train was a far stretch from my Tempur-Pedic. On a positive note, the train was clean, but I was getting increasingly sore from being cramped and we hadn't started trekking yet.

Morning brought more amazing landscapes — local villages, rice farms and oxen-drawn vehicles. Eating turned into a major event. When the train stopped at a town, masses of people selling food swarmed the windows. Bargaining was mandatory. Our military friend argued with the vendors not to charge us the tourist price, which obviously was way more. Usually I am careful not to eat too much from the streets early in a trip to allow my body to adjust to the local germs. However, this time we didn't have much of a choice. With a full belly of IDK1 (I don't know) and IDK2, I took a huge nap and spent the rest of the day staring at the beautiful countryside. Sadly, when the sun went down there was no more free entertainment. We were restless and ready to get off the train; enough was enough. Fortunately, by 8:30 pm we got to Myitkyina where again our hotel was clean and quaint. There was electricity and even a TV. Knowing this was the last taste of civilization, I downloaded my photographs and topped off my batteries so they would be at full strength going into the trek.

The next morning I leisurely took a warm shower and savored what would be my last clean feeling for over a week. Revitalized, we wasted no time and went for a walk through the Myitkyina market. It was one of the best I have seen anywhere. The range of food and wares was astounding. The harsh sun was blocked by an abundant array of colorful umbrellas covering baskets of food and spices. There were also an abundant number of dead things. Fish, meat and hooves of familiar and unfamiliar animals were plentiful.

After our market experience we met up with our guide, Ohn Lwin. For breakfast he took us to his favorite noodle place. Taking a quick inventory, we did some last minute shopping as it seems one can't plan ahead for everything. Usually when you hike, you go from plane, to train, to car, to foot. Oddly, I felt we were going in reverse since we now had to take a plane to get to Putao, basically the last village connected to "modern" Burma.

You never know what to expect when getting on a plane in a third world country. The airport didn't even look as substantial as a bus station. Just a small set of seats. However, when we were called to board, we found the "real" airport building behind the waiting area. To our surprise, sitting on the runway was a shiny jet plane. Thankfully, the flight to Putao was direct and quick. We had a quick dinner before hopping in a jeep to be carried to our adventure. How many people can you fit in a jeep? Well, in Putao, at least 14. Amid much laughter the porters were loaded on a scrap of bumper at the back end. It was a crazy ride. Unfortunately, I didn't get to see much sitting, or more accurately, hanging off the back. As we drove kids gleefully ran alongside the jeep. It seemed that just seeing a jeep was a treat. They tried sprinting to keep up as we drove backward in time.

Back in Time

We stopped at a hut where we would stay the night. The floors of the huts were made of thick, solid wood planks and the house's overall construction far exceeded anything I expected. Equally impressive was the size of the hut. Quite roomy for a hand-planed, do-it-yourselfer. As we settled in, we attracted a covey of kids. Kirk and Nancy outdid themselves and were totally prepared to interact in ways I never contemplated. Kirk pulled out postcards from home as well as a picture book of Burmese animals. The kids were fascinated. Kirk pointed to an animal and said its name in English. The kids responded in Burmese. Nancy followed by breaking out a wildly colored super ball and series of tops for the kids to spin. Even without a common language to communicate, we had no problem playing with the children. Having no props, I resorted to a childhood skill of whistling various notes through cupped hands. Sounding more like a shofar (a ram's horn used in a Jewish ceremony) than a whistle, the kids tried so hard to mimic me. Puffing away on their tiny thumbs, to their disappointment they barely eeked out anything audible. I didn't know how to tell them it took me over a day to learn how to play my first note. Deciding I wanted to teach them something they could achieve, I resorted to third grade humor and taught them how to make a farting noise under the arm, this brought many laughs. Next we graduated to thumb wrestling.

It wasn't until the following morning that Nancy pulled out the magical slinky from her bag. While it didn't walk down the steep outdoor steps of the hut "without a care," the locals found other ways to amuse themselves with it. One old, barefoot man gleamed with the joy of a child as he let the slinky drop to the ground and bounce back up. At first the kids were scared, but eventually they warmed up to it and were amazed.

We started our trek with a massive entourage. This included ourselves, our guide, a military escort, 20 porters and 4 live chickens we called "breakfast," "lunch," "dinner" and "snack," hanging upside down from a bamboo pole. Very quickly the road shrunk to a path and then withered to a tiny trail. Bamboo culms reached skyward, over 100 feet. Much secondary growth and a few mammoth trees filled in the landscape. You had to be careful, though. If you raised your eyes from the trail to look around, the trail just disappeared into the brush. While it was hard to see the distant mountain that was our ultimate destination, at times we got a small preview of the mountain peaks as we entered a clearing. While lunches usually consisted of a bowl of Ramen noodles, the cook threw in generous portions of flavorful, fresh vegetables which made the meal quite satisfying.

Invisible Attack

Shortly after lunch and a little bit down the trail we were attacked! Sand fleas assaulted us from all sides, lunching on our elbows. They put the American no-see-ums to shame. It wasn't long before we were covered with tiny, blood-blistered bites. Our discomfort was interrupted when a huge yellow and black snake slithered across our path. Normally quite bold, I was not

so brave as to chase after it to get a photo. We were truly experiencing the joys and hazards of a jungle trek in Burma. While the trek pace seemed very slow, slower than it should be, we eventually got to the first village beyond the road. These huts were more of the style that I expected. They had thatched roofs and bamboo floors. The whole scene looked like it could have been a Gilligan's Island set. Surprisingly, they actually had a light in the hut that was powered by a car battery. We repeated the drill of books, tops and heard a knock. "Who could that be?" we asked ourselves. We could have guessed all night and never would have expected who popped up at our door. Christmas carolers! The gleeful revelers regaled us in our wintertime favorites, here in the tropics under the persimmon trees.

As we became more friendly with Ohn Lwin, he started to open up. He had a definite resentment toward our military escort, a "know-it-all." At this point we hadn't had much interaction with the man and couldn't draw much of a conclusion for ourselves. It was so seldom we questioned whether or not he ditched us. He was clearly not keen to hike. I could totally see him sacking out in a village and waiting for us to return. When he finally reappeared we wondered what government restrictions he would impose.

My sleep was dream-filled and not with pleasantries. One bad dream rolled into another. At one point I woke up in the hut and was still dreaming. The hut crawled with gnarly rats everywhere. It was clear I was a little nervous about the trip. When I finally did wake up, I was in pain. My now bright red elbows swelled from the sand flea bites and were burning intensely. Nancy had a similar reaction. It hurt like hell.

The next day's hike was an easy one, long but level most of the day. We passed through three villages that were similar to the one we stayed. The most intriguing aspect of the day were the many suspension bridges. Swaying in the wind, they were flimsily constructed with rattan and bamboo hand ropes, v-ing down to support a walking path of a thin series of wooden planks a few inches wide. Strung across a river, each bridge looked like it could never hold your weight, let alone the combined weight of you and your pack. I am happy to report, they held up just fine. The easy pace led to a mostly carefree walk during which my jovial mood contaminated Kirk. The frivolity was much to Nancy's disapproval. He now sings "Bravely bold Sir Robin goes forth from Camelot..." along with other quotes from the movie *Monty Python and the Holy Grail*. Much to the pleasure or dismay of my friends I have the ability to instantly memorize and recite comedies. Nancy was just lucky I didn't switch gears into quoting *Trading Places*. She kept saying, "Ok, Jeff, time to commune with nature!" We all know it just meant to give silence a try, e.g. "shut up!"

You never know what to expect from meals in a foreign country. You have even less chance to predict your menu when trekking in a third world country. Burma was no exception. We were served fresh fruit from local trees grown by the villagers. Tangelos, grapefruit and persimmons may not have been indigenous, but we weren't complaining. It was a delightful change from freeze dried trekking food. Dinner was equally amazing as we were served a pork curry. Surprises continued at every turn, as the next village had hydro power. It was of course limited, but most huts had a single light bulb to provide light at night. I passed out at 7:30 pm and slept until the roosters called us to arise at 5:30 in the morning.

Machete Cut Trails

The next morning we woke early to the melody of monkeys chattering in the distance. There was a surprising lack of wildlife along the trail. Anything that moved was hunted out of existence to feed the local villagers or to supply the insatiable Chinese markets. The occasional bird and sand fleas were all we got to see, or unfortunately feel. At first our hike was easy and we made good time on the flat, well cut terrain. It wasn't long before we stopped for lunch. However, we weren't the only ones partaking. We became lunch again as the sand fleas repeated their assault.

While our meal was the usual fare, the afternoon hike was not. This was probably the least groomed trail I ever walked along. The trail was barely existent, even after the lead porters hacked and slashed at it with their machetes. Its incline was incredibly steep and a never-ending series of branches hung dangerously low for a non-vertically challenged 6'2" trekker like myself. I was amazed I didn't smack myself into a concussion. The good news is we only had an 800m / 2,600' vertical climb. Our pace clearly slowed, allowing the incessant sand fleas to continue their harvest of our blood. We were really trekking in the jungles of Burma now!

When we arrived at camp at three in the afternoon, we were ready to relax. The campsite was shockingly civilized. A large bamboo floor was constructed with tarps pitched over head as a semi-permanent structure. We greatly appreciated the luxury and settled in for the afternoon. This was especially true when the rains came and we were sheltered without having to retreat into our tents. While we waited for dinner, a small flock of Hornbill flew by, their unwieldy, colorful beaks leading the way. However, that would be it for wildlife on this trip. With all the commotion, we didn't notice the absence of the clucking of our friendly chickens. It wasn't until dinner was served that we realized they were no longer with us. Dinner was top notch that night as the fresh meat was a welcome addition to our diet. Afterward we tried to kill time, as there was very little to look at deep in the jungle. We became bored quickly and given the gain in altitude it was getting cold at night, so we retreated to bed for an early evening.

The next day brought a new challenge. The scheduled hike was five and a half hours with no potable water. This meant we needed to carry whatever water was necessary for the day. We also wouldn't be served lunch until we arrived at the next campsite. While there were a few scenic overlooks along the way, it continued to be difficult to see much other than the trail directly in front of us. Heaved up tree roots, covered with moss, made for an unsettling obstacle course filled with visions of twisted ankles. The problem with having lunch at 2:00 pm was that left little time before dinner. This wouldn't be an issue if we could push dinner back, but the sun set at 5:30 pm, so 5:30 pm became a strict dinner time. We wanted a real authentic Burmese trekking experience and we were getting it. As our fatigue grew and our minds began to wander, a new debate began as to how fast we could descend so we could spend an extra day in the village of Ziya Dum. However, we had to be very careful about overextending our hiking time on any given day. If we didn't get to camp by nightfall, the treacherous terrain of the hunting trail would leave us with no place to set up camp. Needless to say, it would make for a very dangerous night.

Once in camp, Nancy absorbed herself with technical difficulties related to her flashlight, while Kirk and I entered into a long discourse about the quality of a good burp. Was it duration or depth of sound that mattered most? The mind does tend to rot quickly in the jungle. Fortunately, our debate ceased with the distraction of Shegee (Giant in Burmese) our very tall porter, constructing a fire from some very wet wood. He was a real pro, getting the fire started in no time. Truth be told, he had a secret. A solid steel, crank-driven air blower that he used to first nurse and then fan the flames. Kirk and I both immediately added it to our shopping list upon our return to Yangon.

Each day along the ever-disappearing hunter's trail seemed more and more treacherous. Every step required extreme focus to avoid ending up on our asses from the wet leaves, muddy terrain or root-laden paths. At times the trail degraded to following a series of muddy footprints. The angle of ascent was incredible, sometimes we pulled our bodies up two to three feet per step. Danger just wasn't underfoot; we also had to watch for low branches that could knock us silly. Along the way, the terrain varied greatly, with danger the only constant trait. At one point I put my hiking pole through what I thought was the ground that turned out to only be moss-laden tree roots. One slip and it would have been a very long slow trip back for the porters to carry out my crippled body. There would be no helicopter rescues. Unlike most treks whose trails contain switchbacks to reduce the steepness of a climb, this trail just went vertical. When there was no way to walk up, logs with notches cut into the side were laid up against the mountain so that we could climb straight up. The highlight of the day was when we were immersed in a giant forest of rhododendrons, the long glossy leaves as the only legacy to what must have been spectacular summer blooms. We finally made it to what would be our last camp site, our base camp. While there were thoughts of continuing on and to reach the summit of Mt. Phon Khan Razi, the clouds told us not to try. I can't say we were disappointed.

Having left the villages behind, we milled about our camp and noticed most of the porters didn't have sleeping bags or blankets. One would think that the cause was financial. Part of it was the expense of a sleeping bag, but why not carry a blanket? It turns out the reason behind their frigid nights was that they preferred not to have the extra weight and would rather suck up the cold.

Kirk lent me *Beyond the Last Village*, a book about Alan Rabinowitz, who only a decade earlier was the first Westerner to explore this area. While the region was still pristine, uncontaminated by western industrialization, the Chinese had sadly done their damage without us.

On to the Ice Mountain

Our summit climb exceeded expectations. We started early, about 6:30 am, trying to beat the clouds. This was the only day where I felt I wanted to walk quickly, so I could see the sites before the weather rolled in. Ohn Lwin had another porter join in the front, while he took the rear. Everyone else, except the military escort, stayed in the camp.

This was great because it allowed me to forge ahead. I dubbed our porter the Trekinator. All he did was trek. Blink and, like a rabbit, he was 50 yards ahead. Our fast pace was rewarding, because the best view of the valley was actually before the sun peered up over the horizon when mountain peaks were just shadowy sentinels in the soft morning light. I waited for Kirk and Nancy to catch up so I wouldn't be too far ahead and then went onward. Once we crossed the snow line all those East Coast winters paid off. With better balance as we went up and up, I held my own with our speedy porter. Reaching a summit, untouched since the last snowfall, was a exhilarating experience. The snow wasn't just devoid of footprints, but formed in a unique crystallized pattern. We took a few obligatory, summit photographs including a "hero shot," one without your shirt on, as Kirk would call it. It was a tradition that didn't grow past this trip as it was easy to do at 3,500m / 11,480', not so easy at over 5,000m / 16,400'.

We headed down and it sucked. I can't say enough how much it sucked. Normally down is quicker and easier. At least it usually isn't as strenuous. However, the footing was so bad we were all slipping, sliding and jamming our knees deep into their sockets. Normally you would mitigate the terrain by allowing your hiking poles to absorb the abuse. The ground had other ideas as it sucked up one pole and then the other. Again, our trek required amazing focus. Each and every step needed total concentration. Our time descending ended up being equal to our time up, two hours in each direction. If we had ended the day there, it wouldn't have been that strenuous. However, we wanted to spend more time in the village of Ziya Dum, so we trekked another four hours down to our previous campsite. Tired as hell, knees screaming, we descended endlessly to our destination.

The next morning I started off the day with an icy jolt when Nancy shook my tent like a bear. All the freezing moisture shook down upon me. If that wasn't enough, when I was sitting at the table she poured boiling water from the teapot on the floor right near my ass. It was a less than auspicious start. As the day progressed my knee started aching. Fortunately, everything else was holding together. The hike wasn't that bad. After starting at 8:15 am, we hiked until 2:00 pm and stopped for lunch. Everything after that was flat. I actually kept up with the porters; however that did me little good because we still had to wait for Kirk and Nancy. As the day went on I started to feel better and better, but Nancy and Kirk were feeling a bit whipped. One of the hardest parts of trekking in a group is managing everyone's pace. Unlike a race, you don't want to leave your buddies in the dust.

We made it to Ziya Dum with a bit of daylight left. So in the fading light, I decided to make myself human and shave at least down to a goatee. Combined with a baby wipe bath, I was almost presentable. After a bit of reorganizing, I was now ready for the more enjoyable and relaxing portion of our trip. I am sure the porters wanted to enjoy it as well. It slowly dawned on us as we'd see each porter on one balcony or another that they had many girlfriends in the village. No wonder they were happy to

return. Apparently the portering trade has its advantage. Nancy was sick and could barely talk. What had begun as a meddling cough was exacerbated by 4°C / 40° F nights next to fire pits in the huts where the smoke rose but didn't quite escape through the thatch roof. Nancy had also managed to be stung by a bee for the first time in her life as we clustered on a log for a photo. "Wanna see my bee bite?" became her new mantra.

December 26th, Christmas Day

We spent the next day in Ziya Dum. For some reason their true Christmas holiday is on the 26th. Given that we were a day early, we decided to stay for two days. Remaining in one place had a lot of advantages. The most obvious is the rest to our bodies. My right knee was pretty sore. Nancy and Kirk both seemed equally worn down. The less obvious reason for staying was the growing comfort the people of Ziya Dum developed with us. It was a treat to watch the rethatching of the roof of a house. It was amazing to see how quickly they removed all the old forest grass and then knotted the new thatch back in place on a skeleton of horizontal poles. To our surprise we found out many of the men working spoke English. The owner of the house proudly showed us all the plants, fruits and spices he was growing on his property. I tried to get one little kid, who had a rare glass bottle, to play but he was too shy.

As I explored the village, I went down to the river and watched the porters wash some of our clothes. As I was about to leave, a young girl and her younger brother came down with a five gallon water jug to fill. After taking some pictures of her and showing them to her I felt we had built a little bit of a bond. After she filled the jug, I gestured an offer to carry it up the hill. She seemed to agree, so I grabbed it and I lugged it up the hill. Simple things like clean drinking water are taken for granted in the States. If we had to carry all our water uphill, I'm certain we would conserve more than we do. As I walked, I expected her to check back to see that I was still carrying it, but I guess she trusted me, because she never glanced in my direction. When we got to the top of the hill, she gestured to let her carry it and off she went.

I continued my exploration by wandering up to the church area where a few kids gathered. A few turned into fifteen as I started to play with them. I almost burned an entire camera battery showing them pictures of themselves. Wanting to save the last of my precious power, I went back to my old bag of tricks and tried to teach them how to whistle and I added making funny hand gestures including the Spock "Live Long and Prosper" sign.

I returned to our hut for lunch and then went to wash my hair by the river. Head and Shoulders never felt so good. See-ing some kids playing on a nearby hill, I wandered over in their direction. Many of the kids were from the same group I met earlier in the day. Upon recognizing me, they tried to whistle through their hands as I had taught them. One boy was even successful.

I was distracted by a sound that was out of place. Was that music I heard playing? I had to investigate. As I got closer to the source, I saw a huge mega phone-like device on a building. So I walked nearer, hoping someone would ask me in. They did and it was then I saw the stereo! The owner of the house came out and was very happy to have a stranger visit. Turns out the stereo was hooked to an old cassette player and wired into a hydro-powered socket. The setup definitely appealed to the tech geek in me. The owner was the pastor and spoke in broken English. He introduced me to his kids and pulled out a chair for me to sit. I showed him pictures I had taken and gestured to get a picture of everyone. He was very excited. He told me about Christmas

in his country, or at least his village, and invited me to service the following day. Gleaming with pride, he gave me a preview tour of the church. Outside we passed a table and benches where villagers created bamboo Christmas ornaments.

On the way back a water buffalo blocked my path. Circumnavigating around it led me to the shy "bottle boy" I met earlier. "Pamre," I said and he responded by inviting me to participate in a new game, "water buffalo." He and his brother made horns out of their hands and we acted like the stately beasts of burden stampeding around. Eventually I left and headed home, but returned after fashioning a paper airplane from some spare journal pages. While bottle boy laughed at it, he wasn't anxious to take it and try. It often takes a lot of exposure to get them to try anything new. I made a mental note to bring a Frisbee on a future trip!

The Hunt that Wasn't.

The next day started with a visit from the pastor, donned in his traditional Rawang tribal dress, for a bit of a culinary exchange. For a treat, he brought us popcorn. We introduced him to peanut butter and blackberry jam. Unlike many other cultures where an individual wearing authentic clothes would demand or expect payment for taking his photograph, he was excited and proud to have his picture taken. Even his equally, ornately dressed daughters joined the photographic mayhem.

A commotion ended our session as apparently the Christmas sacred cow hunt was about to ensue. To me, mind you, I am not much of a hunter, I didn't grasp the challenge of hunting a slow moving, fat cow. One man pulled out an ancient flint lock blunderbuss. After a few hours and four booming shots, we still had not seen a dead cow. I wanted to follow them with the camera, but they didn't want any pictures taken. Interestingly, they didn't want the government to know they had a gun. Sounds like our worlds aren't very different in that regard.

Having failed in bringing down the cow, next came the chicken hunt. Thankfully, this time they used just a crossbow. The wily chicken darted around the yard as one shot after another whizzed by. Then the chicken made the mistake of coming out in the open. Bamm! The arrow pierced right through the neck. Supposedly the arrows were poisoned, but it didn't seem to affect the chicken as it flew off into the scrub, with a stick protruding from its neck. After an hour of looking we couldn't find it. Clearly they needed a trusty Labrador Retriever to assist.

For less exciting fun I made more paper airplanes and showed them to the kids. They loved them, greatly preferring the distance plane to the loop-the-loop one I constructed. Some kids immediately got the hang of it, while others struggled. One kid waited until an older gentleman showed him how to use it. It was all great fun.

My hands got bit by more sand fleas. Bastards! My pinkies swelled up so much it was hard to bend them. I didn't dwell on it too long, because as I fumbled with my fat fingers, a dead cow was carried by. I guess they got it with the last shot. My pudgy fingers were less than efficient at getting my boots laced as I rushed to chase after it. By the time I found where they took it, most of it was butchered. The head was still intact sitting next to what looked like a liver. From there I checked out what was happening at the church. In front of the benches they loaded the area with hay as additional seating. I chased some of the kids around and then left them laughing and screaming to get cleaned up for the festivities.

During dinner two little girls came to the house. They stared at us for a long time and wouldn't eat anything we offered. I put our electric lantern by them. They were fascinated. However, this was just the beginning. Next, we downloaded pictures as they watched. Then it hit me, I had a video camera in the computer. I turned it on them so they could see themselves live on the tiny laptop. They were mesmerized beyond movement. Shortly after they left we headed to the church service. At first, it was like any other service, but in their tribal language of Rawang, not even Burmese. So we couldn't even get a translation. Then it morphed into an amateur talent show night, very amateur. Nancy and Kirk couldn't take it, nor the sneeze-producing hay, and cut out. Of course, they called me to the back of the room to tell me they had to leave. This forced me out of my nice warm spot, leaving me freezing in the rear. I stayed to the end and when it was over an unknown sense of urgency overcame the porters. As they rushed me to leave, I couldn't get my light on and tripped. I crushed my camera and broke my flash; better my equipment than my head!

The next morning one of the cute girls from the service came over for breakfast. We joked with Ohn Lwin translating that I was looking for a girl friend. She laughed, but thought her father might not agree that a Jewish boy from New York was her ideal suitor. Having time to relax led to more conversation. Ohn Lwin mentioned he would love to travel, but interestingly had no desire to see Thailand. "Oh, too much sex," he said. It was interesting how different cultures could be even though they were so close geographically.

Back to Civilization

The hike halfway back to Putao was easy and uneventful. Our only issue was when we got to town. The hut we were staying in was unbearably smoky. Not wanting to offend, I didn't say anything. That's when it's good to have Nancy on the trip. She had no problem getting us another house. Unfortunately, in order to breathe we seemed to have embarrassed Ohn Lwin a bit.

We got up early for the last day of our hike as we were all anxious to get back to relative civilization. It was cold as hell out, but we didn't care. A Swiss entourage was also in the village and as they disembarked with about 40 people I could only wonder how trekking would forever change this fairy tale, village life we experienced. As we started down the trail Ohn Lwin signaled for me to walk with the porters. I figured it would be a fun challenge to keep pace with them for a bit and wait for Kirk and Nancy at the first nice overlook. My porters had a different plan. I think they could smell home, because the porters took off like bats out of hell! The porters must have assimilated into the Trekinator family, because they just kept marching. There was no obvious place to stop and I didn't recognize anything. Jungle tends to look like jungle after a while, so I just kept pushing forward. I started to feel that it wasn't a good idea to stop. I worried that I was so far ahead that the wait would be long. I could just imagine my nerves rattling as I sat alone, staring down an empty trail, so I marched on. We went two hours before they finally took a break. Shegee pounded my chest in approval for my ability to stick with them. So, all in all, it all worked out well, at least for me; because just after we stopped it started to rain. The guys made a make-shift tent using my walking poles and a plastic sheet. I waited about an hour for a wet Kirk and Nancy while sipping a warm revitalizing cup of tea.

After lunch we went for the home stretch. Needing to poop, I sensed the joy of a real toilet and decided I would wait until I got back. It's amazing how important bodily functions seem when out on the trail. We finally returned to Upper Shangaung where we had started 12 days before. A jeep was waiting for us, but unfortunately it was an open air jeep and it was still raining. For an hour and a half we suffered shivering cold totally exposed. When we finally arrived at our "hotel" it was another disappointment. It was the old British HQ or barracks from the 1930's, grungy and broken-down, no shower or western toilet. The toilet had a tank, but was still a squat toilet, so there was no reward for my patience. We gave the porters their tips. They seemed very happy. Dinner was excellent as any change from the standard food was welcome. Sleeping was another matter. The fungus-laden barracks just made our skin crawl. We slept in our sleeping bags on the bed, dreaming back to the relative cleanliness of our tents.

The next morning, bright warming sun greeted us as we headed out happily to the open market. They had all sorts of items for sale, including a pair of children's Philadelphia Eagles sweat pants. Who knew the Burmese were E A G L E S – Eagles fans!

As we were waiting for the plane, I decided to have one last walk around. As I turned the corner, this peaceful town turned into an all out game of Kung Foo fighting. Drop kick to the left of me, kids flying in the air to the right and sticks whacking at each other in front of me. It sort of reminded me how dogs play, seemingly vicious, but full of innocent fun. I think it could have gone on all day, but an old, irritated woman came charging out from behind the hotel. I didn't understand her mutterings, but the kids certainly did. Two seconds later they had all scattered and my last photo op of the trek was over.

The trip back to Yangon was far easier than getting there as we flew the entire way. My room was different and appeared cleaner, or it was just my perception after weeks of grime. We went to dinner at an Italian restaurant; we had enough Burmese food in the last three weeks. The pasta I got was fine, but the "sausage" turned out to be a hot dog. Still, eating at a table, with

AC, real napkins, imported beer and chocolate cake for dessert never tasted so good. It cost a whopping eight dollars.

I woke up early the next day and attempted to clean and assess the damage to my equipment while I waited for Kirk and Nancy to get up. In addition to everything else I burned out my surge protector. It was just one more thing to add to the list of destruction. After breakfast we went to the zoo. It was originally built by the British and was fairly expansive. Most of the animals were kept in reasonable open-air accommodations. They had most of the standard exhibits as well as vipers, rhinos, strange birds and a tiny deer the size of a dog. Most of these were indigenous to this part of the world. Probably the coolest aspect of the zoo is that you can get really close to the animals, including the ability to feed some like the hungry hippos. Afterward, we headed back to meet up with Nancy's old friend and his daughter for dinner. We went to a fancy Thai place that served hot spicy foods, even by my standards. The dinner for all five of us, including a few beers was around $20. One could live here well for some time quite cheaply.

The next day started with a shopping trip for Kirk and I. We both bought the fire starter Shegee used, but were disappointed to discover it was made in China. We told Ohn Lwin that we would cook dinner for him. Shopping was a challenge, since we didn't speak the language. On the menu was a pasta and sauce dish. The one western food store had pasta and then we went to the streets to haggle for veggies. Four eggplants were a dime. Then we bought a bunch of onions and two bulbs of garlic for a total of 50 cents. We assumed we were being ripped off because we were American. Ohn Lwin later told us that the price was right. We obtained the rest of our ingredients without a problem, except ironically for the red hot chilies. Next we went souvenir shopping. We went to a lacquer shop, but I got mostly hardwood products. A bit hypocritical considering we are so concerned with the forest, but they were cheap and gorgeous. This abruptly changed Kirk's mood, which in turn concerned me. "The world is doomed," quipped Kirk. "If someone as enlightened as you is willing to buy wood products that are from unprotected forests, what hope is there?" His statement was on the mark and dramatically changed my future outlook towards what I purchase and its impact on the environment.

After shopping we joined Ohn Lwin and Nancy to get a massage and a haircut. "We'll get one for you, our treat," I offered our trusted guide. He declined with a giggle, indicating that it tickled too much. He was quite the sweet man, apparently very shy, and seemingly knew a bit more than he was telling us. So we went to the Olympic Hotel. Its huge pool and Olympic diving board gave it its name. It seemed strangely out of place, but we wanted relief for our sore bodies. As we entered, we weaved through endless corridors flanked with rooms filled with young women. With over 200 women each performing over 400 massages a month, this was no small operation. It quickly became readily apparent why Ohn Lwin was not interested in a massage; it appeared more than just massages were offered. Fortunately, I was with Nancy and Kirk so I assumed we wouldn't have to deal with the less legitimate form of their business. We signed up for an hour and half of what felt like Thai massage with extra stretching. Ohn Lwin stayed in the room translating and what parts of the conversation we understood were quite amusing. She referred to me as Shegee, the only word I understood as it was our porter's nickname as well. It meant giant. She then said, "It was a shame you are leaving, you could stay with me for free." Good thing I was leaving. Sadly, all the girls came from villages and work all but one day a month. So if it wasn't a strange enough experience, we continued our odd journey by requesting haircuts. The salon was filled with attractive young women preparing for a "fashion show." They wore dresses that were not characteristic of Burmese fashion, but much sexier. We could only imagine what the fashion show actually entailed. We left and headed to Ohn Lwin's apartment. By Burmese standards his apartment was upscale. It had two bedrooms and 24-hour electricity, but it wasn't the least bit up to western standards. We had to cook on a single, very slow burner, which proved to be a challenge. In the end the meal appeared successful, as he enjoyed our culinary masterpiece.

Our last experience before leaving was dining at the Dolphin Seafood and Show restaurant. The show consisted of Burmese girls singing songs in English and Burmese, complete with coquettish flirting. You were supposed to put feather boas on the girl you thought was best. Again, I wondered what was the implication of being the best. Each girl accepted the paid-for boa graciously and wore piles of them by the end of their song. It was all too cheesy, even for me. So, after paying less than a dollar a beer, we headed back to the hotel to pack and prepare for the long flight home.

Epilogue

Sadly, at the time I under appreciated the amazing trek through the unspoiled land of Northern Burma. After each subsequent trek, my experience in Burma grew more special in my mind. Now having completing all ten Great Treks I hold it as one of the most unique experiences. Unfortunately, you can not easily follow in our footsteps, because after seven years the unexposed land we ambled through no longer exists. The constant exposure of trekkers to this sheltered region changes the dynamics of your interaction with the villagers. You can still enjoy a trek in Northern Burma, but if you are truly adventurous seek out a similar, unspoiled experience and add it to your list of great treks.

Kirk's Corner

It was March 2004, and I just returned from Costco—the "super warehouse" shopping experience. Just the week before, I returned from my third visit to Burma. Having visited the mountain temples of the Himalayas, the religious temples of Buddha and the temples of shopping made my trip to Costco much more poignant. Costco isn't much different from Wal-Mart, Target or any other large department store with the display and quantity of goods stacked to the ceiling warehouse-style fully embodying our country's raw consumer power and desires. It is America's "Cathedral of Consumerism." But it is just a store and there is nothing wrong with a little shopping, right? After all, everybody all over the world goes shopping everyday!

So, why did this feel so strange? Why was I attracted and repulsed at the same time? How is it that the same person, me in this instance, is subject to the allure of a 62-inch flat screen HDTV and at the same time treasuring memories of, and longing for future adventures to a far away village in Burma? A village where it is a two-day walk to the nearest store. Can these seemingly mutually exclusive forces, a desire for conspicuous consumption and want of a simpler pre-industrial village life, coexist in the same mind? Will the cognitive dissonance of such opposition rip my brain in two? Perhaps the fact that I am living, breathing and writing this is a proof of sorts, that, yes, it is possible to live in these two worlds at the same time; in fact, maybe it's even somewhat normal.

Let us go back in time, literally and figuratively. In December of 2003 I abandoned the Chicago winter and high-tailed-it over to Burma. The trip was an opportunity to embrace a simpler way of life with the village people of Burma. I was longing to get away from internal combustion and our material-oriented world. However, just to get to Burma itself is an exercise in conspicuous consumption. The two international / intercontinental flights required to just get to Yangon, and all the fossil fuels burned for such purpose would be ironic enough to end this conversation right now.

Entering the Burmese time machine is always a good adventure. You can go back in time more than one hundred years quite easily. Many people live a pre-industrial, pastoral life. Of course, things are not always as they seem, they want what we have. They want more "stuff," from water pumps, to radios to light bulbs, but most noticeably they want more internal combustion.

Although Yangon, previously named Rangoon, is the former political capital it is still the time machine capital of Burma. It has a decaying tropical colonial feeling, a contrasting hint of an Asian Tiger style new economy and a wealth of Burmese-style Buddhism including literally hundreds of temples and thousands of devout worshippers. There are dozens of early 20th century Chevrolet buses, packed with people, which somehow still keep running after all these years. Most defining are the endless number of small shops and neighborhood markets. All of these elements spill onto almost every street and sidewalk making for an interesting bazaar, and bizarre, atmosphere that can often overwhelm the senses, yet I still find completely alluring.

Nancy, Jeff and I spent our time in Yangon doing a little sightseeing, and most importantly, making the preparations for our trek. What did we do? We went shopping of course! We were going to do without any shopping for over two weeks while trekking in far northern Kachin State.

In its own Orwellian way Burma is developing fast, but it still has a long way to go. However, on each successive trip I make, there is a new wrinkle to Burma's erratic progression. Two years before, on my I first visit, everyone in the countryside traveled by oxcart, or if one was rich and in a hurry, they traveled by horse cart. Now the country roads teemed with Chinese-built tractors towing trailers jam-packed with market goers and farmers taking their goods to and from market. They are really loud, polluting and annoying but, hey, they get people and goods to and from market faster. Even though I would definitely NOT go as far to say that "time is money" in Burma, because in Burma it is really not. Everything moves at a glacial pace in its own strange way.

The Burmese time machine mixes years and eras together into one technological and cultural stew. You can visit ancient tea shops with open-fire-brewed tea served while sitting in little wooden chairs on a dirt floor with a very large and out of place stereo speaker blaring some bad Burmese rock and roll covers. Similarly a village without indoor plumbing, paved streets, sewers or even proper garbage pickup, has all the villagers huddled around a DVD player watching MTV-type music videos or a pirate copy of *Saving Private Ryan*. Oxcarts, steam trains, colonial buildings, cells phones, DVDs and the Internet all come together. It is the History Channel with all shows mixed into one.

The villages we visited could only be reached by foot. Everything coming in or out travels by two or more legs, by man or beast. This fact really highlights the basic nature of our materialism and all our cargo. It is also a reason for the lack of such trappings of the locals. While they don't want carry and cart large quantities of stuff, the villagers do marvel at our cargo and desire the same.

Although Burma is generally associated with hot tropical climates, during our trek it was near freezing at night. Gathering around the fire is a daily and nightly ritual of the villagers, we welcomed taking part despite the oppressive amounts of smoke permeating all of our clothing, possessions and even our skin. However, where there is smoke there is fire, and where there is fire there is heat, and when you are really cold, heat is a very good thing. Interacting with villagers and contemplating our material discrepancies while huddling around a fire continued through our trip. Few other places offered the kind of immersion that a village trek in Burma provides. It's just this kind of experience that encourages my mind to explore the "what ifs" of our lifestyle in America and the West. What is the justification of our dependence on fossil fuels and their use for internal combustion to support our extravagantly, wealthy lifestyle? The mind can spiral almost out of control. So continues this life of a thinking traveler. A life of endless comparisons of culture, religion, lifestyle and material wealth. These questions in themselves can be reason enough to make the journey.

Having arrived safely back home, both from Burma and COSTCO, I am truly a man mired in the material world flux. After having such a dramatic experience overseas, part of me cries out to try and share or explain what I have seen and the dramatic differences in lifestyle. Despite the perspective I gained, I have not abandoned my material possessions and moved to an Amish village, but I still have resisted the 62-inch flat screen TV. Time marches on. People are busy. At a bare minimum, of course, time is always just time; time to work, time to visit family and friends, of course time to shop and occasionally time to travel to the ends of the earth and ask why?

KACHIN TRIBAL VILLAGE TREK

Ziya Dum Village

Thet Pin Gyi Camp

Kan Tauk Myint Camp

Pho Khan Razi

Taung Chay Camp

Awat Dum Village

Wason Dum Village

Upper Shangaung Village

Lower Shangaung Village

N

Step back in time along ancient stone paths created by the Inca to transport men and material. Immerse yourself for four days in fog-laden trails where the discerning eye may spy many of the 500 species of orchids. Along the way pass snow-capped peaks, lush cloud forests, ancient culture and some of the world's most famous archeological ruins. Your trek culminates waking up to sunrise over the famed stone works of Machu Picchu, enigmatic ruins built over 500 years ago. Hewn on top of a mountain, this beautiful city's mystery and beauty captivates all who behold it. It's popularity has soared in recent years and sometimes it can be downright crowded with 500 people per day entering the trail.

Fundamentals

Days Trekking: 3-4 days	**Approximate Elevation Change:** 1,600m / 5,250'
Distance: 45 km, 28 miles	**Price Range Independent:** N/A
Max Elevation: 4,200m / 13,780' - Dead Woman's Pass	**Price Range Outfitter:** $450 - $600
Starting Elevation: 2,600m / 8,530'	**Challenge Level:** Moderate

When to Go

The main trekking season is from May to September, with April, October and November also providing reasonable trekking. However, as with most popular treks, during the high season the trails are quite crowded.

Guided vs. Independent Treks

A guided tour is required for all trekkers, although some of the more aggressively independent trekkers may find a way. While there are many companies available for hire in Cusco and it is easy to find one that matches your budget and level of comfort, you must book in advance. Reservations at the more reliable guiding companies fill up quickly. A multitude of porters are available for hire so take a load off and give a job to a local. A porter's weight is meticulously monitored at the starting point and along the trail, as Peruvian law is careful not to overload their young men. The load maximum is 20 kilos / 44 pounds so plan accordingly.

Access / Local Information

The access city is the charming town of Cusco. A myriad of travelers' services are available in all ranges of price and quality. The town square is beautiful and the surrounding villages and ruins keep you occupied for very interesting, exploratory side trips. Cusco is accessible from Lima by flight or a grueling bus journey. It is also accessible from La Paz by bus or a bus and train combination. From Cusco the trail head is accessed by train, private bus or public bus.

Difficulty

The main trek is a four-day, three-night adventure. There is a shorter three-day, two-night version, although we strongly recommend the longer version. The trek can be challenging. Trudging up Dead Woman's Pass on the second day can take a toll. It tops out at 4,200m / 13,770', so some acclimatizing is helpful. It is likely you will have spent some time in Cusco, to help your body adapt. However, climbing is only one of the issues. The descent can also be troubling if there is a lot of precipitation, because the trail can get fairly muddy and slippery. In addition, the stone paths can brutalize your knees when descending so make sure you strengthen your quadriceps and hamstrings in the months prior to your trip.

Orientation

The Inca Trail and Machu Picchu are located in the Central Andes of Peru. Lima is the capital and the major arrival point for international travelers. La Paz, Bolivia, is closer but does not have the same number of flight connections. A quick flight to Cusco from Lima puts you at the jumping off point for the Inca Trail.

On the Trail with Jeff

After returning from Burma, the seed of walking the ten best treks in the world was sprouting. It was a rough year during which I lost three friends. While everyone at the funerals said life is short, no one lived up to their pledges to work less and change their life. Well, no one except myself. My priorities abruptly changed. While I wouldn't have described myself as overly materialistic, there was definitely a strong part of me that enjoyed the finer things. However, seeing my friends die unexpectedly weakened the old adage of "the person dying with the most toys wins." This was strongly reinforced when I watched half of my house submerge under water after 12 dams broke upstream. With ten minutes to save what was important from my downstairs, I lost nothing of sentimental value. Instead, I lost everything of monetary value, with the damages totaling nearly $100,000. These events all led to a new philosophy. I wanted to die with the best stories and memories. For me, the path to these stories was to hike the world's greatest treks.

Having the life of an academic and no longer focused on a consulting career, I took every opportunity I had to travel. This created a new difficulty for me. Who was I going to travel with? My relationships with women usually didn't make it long enough to plan international excursions, and while these trips were not as expensive as people might think, a companion needed a certain level of financial resource, a desire to see far off lands and cultures, the fortitude to handle the issues of third world travel, the ability to take time off from work, as well as a reasonable level of athleticism. When I decided to head to Peru and hike the Inca Trail during a break in between school quarters, my friend and former teaching assistant Matt Dormond topped the list. He had all the qualifications, except perhaps for carrying a few extra pounds around his middle. I gave him a training program and he dropped some weight, but possibly not enough. Time would tell.

As we headed south, I shifted gears from follower to leader. In a way I felt like a cheater. I was now on my third "trip of a lifetime" and had barely any experience trekking in the U.S. or along any less grand trails. I guess it didn't bother me too much as the lure of the world's treasures pulled me back on the trail. We flew from Philadelphia to Lima, Peru, and directly on to Cusco, the primary access town for the Inca Trail. It was perhaps one of the great surprises of the trip. Perched at 3,400m / 11,200', Cusco was the capital of the Incan Empire from 1200 - 1532. The nearby pre-Incan ruins of Sacsayhuamán are impressive in stature and mystery. Like many ancient constructions there is much debate about how the Killke people could build the monument with so little space between the stones that you cannot slip a piece of paper between the cracks. However, for me it was the Spanish influence from the 1500's, which was infused with traditional Incan style, that forever placed Cusco close to my heart. Spain's unique display of grandeur in the Plaza de Armas is bounded by La Compania de Jesus Church with a picturesque fountain drawing your attention to the center. Whether eating in one of the many restaurants around the plaza or sipping tea while gazing across to the church, one could spend hours captivated by the architecture.

We spent a few days acclimatizing in Cusco, before rising to start our trek at 4:30 am. We completed some last minute packing and hopped in a cab to meet the group of ten trekkers with whom we would share the trail. Of all the Great Treks, this was the only one where I formally hiked with a group. We were quite the menagerie, an award winning author and his wife, two students, a French couple, a BBC executive and his wife and ourselves. We were as matched as the passengers aboard the Minow on Gilligan's Island. After early morning pleasantries were exchanged, we were on our way by 6:00 am.

I snoozed most of the ride to the trail head with the exception of a quick stop for breakfast, a fogged out view of the Sacred Valley and a stop in a local village for last minute provisions. A small grass-roofed market allowed for the last minute pickup of fresh fruits or vegetables sold from canvas tarps or small stands. From there the cab took us to highway marker 82, where the trek began. We had to sign in at the park entrance, which was a sea of porters and hikers. Unlike many treks, on the Inca Trail the porters are strictly monitored as to the limit of weight they can carry. This greatly increases the number of porters and creates quite a chaotic scene for the start of what should be a tranquil hike.

Along the Paths of Ancients

The start of the hike was a wide trail with the Rio Urubamba roaring to our side. It's a good thing the trail was wide, because even though they limit the number of trekkers, there was a ridiculous number of people ambling about. I felt like I was in a crowded park instead of a multi-day trek into nature and history. What a stark contrast to the sparsely travelled trails in Burma.

Although my trekmate Matt and I were carrying a heavy load, the burden of my ever increasing array of photographic equipment, we walked quite comfortably. This led to a quicker pace than I thought wise for Matt, but he wouldn't hear of slowing down. After all, "this feels great." With no shortage of rocks, there were plenty of natural benches when we needed a break. You had to keep close eye on your snacks though, as the local goats and dogs were quick to snatch up your dietary delights. Judging from their healthy coats they were successful more often than not. Our effort stayed pretty consistent all the way to lunch as we passed terraced farms, local huts and a few stone ruins in the distance. This was partially due to the slight drop in altitude as the start of the trail was at 2,600m / 8,580'. Lunch was served in a huge tent and by trekking standards was simply incredible. After a bit of a break we pushed on. However, our gentle, even terrain was replaced with a steep incline. Matt, on his first significant trek, struggled a bit, but made it through well considering we were camping at over 3,000m / 9,840'. Our arrival in the large, very active, campsite barely went noticed.

Dinner again was excellent, although Matt didn't get to enjoy much of it. The overexertion on the climb combined with the altitude knocked him for a spin and he skipped most of dinner. It just meant more dessert for the group. A jello-like substance with cinnamon was quite a tasty treat. Matt caught a second wind after dinner, so we played cards in the tent and called it an early night. However, the night would be far from over. Whether it was the food, the water, the altitude or the exertion we could not say, but in the middle of the night nature called Matt in an urgent way. "Open the tent!" Matt called out as he fumbled with the tent zipper in the pitch black.

Having a 200+ pound smelly hiker rambling around the small confines of our tent was unsettling to say the least. The thought of him not getting out in time was even more disturbing. Fortunately, he escaped the confines of the tent before it was too late. I fell back asleep quickly only to be woken by the unnerving gnawing sound outside the tent. While we were using a tent provided by the tour company, the thought of something chewing through our tent did not sit well. Of course, the thought of going outside and challenging whatever it was didn't sound any better. After shuffling around enough, whatever it was decided there were better grazing grounds elsewhere and left us alone. Other than Matt's mid-night trips to the outhouse, the rest of the evening passed in quiet slumber.

Dead Woman's Pass

The next day, breakfast exceeded expectations. We had pancakes, real light, fluffy pancakes, unlike whatever it was they served on Everest. There was also bread and oatmeal among other assorted treats. We would need it, because the second day of the trek was the hardest of the four days. Our goal was to make it over Dead Woman's Pass at 4,200m / 13,770'. While I was comfortable with the thought of going that high, it would be higher than Matt ever hiked.

It was a long, slow journey up. Between the fog and clouds, there weren't many highlights, just lots and lots of people. I was definitely missing the ever present spectacle of the Himalayas. Still there were interesting views at our feet. When we reached a part of the trail where the stones were like giant pavers bordered with lush, green foliage and a rippling waterfall at it's edge, I stopped to take some pictures, hoping it would give Matt a chance to progress ahead at his own pace.

At this point I was still learning my photographic craft, so after permuting through every possibility I could think of, I started to search for Matt. Unfortunately, it didn't take much to catch him. Selfishly, if the weather were better, I might have been tempted to trek ahead, but as there were absolutely no views, I didn't have to test whether I was a good trekmate. Matt and I continued together. He was really struggling even though we paced ourselves well behind the group. To his credit, he never lost his sense of humor. It was a pleasant change from the sisters' viscous banter up Mount Everest.

By the time we got to the tea break, everybody else was shoving off. We rested a bit to recharge and then headed up the final steep climb to the peak over 300m / 984' above us. Looking up the trail, I went into coaching mode. "Let's break it up into 10 pushes of 100 vertical feet at a time. After making good progress on the first couple of pushes, Matt suffered. Sweaty, with labored breathing, climbing 100 vertical feet at a time wasn't going to get Matt to the top. So we divided the rest of the climb into small 10m / 33' vertical segments. This was the first trip I took a GPS and it's altimeter came in handy. Matt was sucking air attempting to get oxygen to his burning hamstrings. Our progress was deadly slow. However, we kept gaining altitude. Finally, we could see tiny specks of people standing at the top of the pass. While enthusiasm said, "let's make it in one last push," we had to continue to break it into small segments of progress. After what seemed like an eternity Matt was one tired, hot, sweaty boy, but he had completed the hardest part of the trek.

Instead of taking in the view of the surrounding snow-capped mountains, ham that Matt was, he took a few hits of oxygen from our guide's bottle. While I didn't think he needed it, he did seem to feel a lot better after a few tokes. Perhaps there was something else in the bottle that I didn't know about. Sadly, our view continued to be obscured by incessant clouds. So we relaxed and pigged out on the food we were carrying. Our guide Alex asked for a photo of himself, because for as many times as he led groups he had very few. It seems that the lack of respect for guides was fairly universal.

After a long rest, we started our descent. One good thing about being slow, at least on the Inca Trail, was that the hordes of people had already passed by and the path was a bit more secluded. The only people hiking around us were those who didn't prepare properly. Struggling along the trail, guides towing them along, the tired and injured ambled nearby. The descent did not seem as bad as I thought as the intricate, stone path progressed gradually. Still, it did beat the hell out of my knees and back. The stone steps, while giving the appearance of being a tame and well groomed trail, proved quite jarring to the joints. After an endless journey down, we finally saw the campground. It looked like a city of tents, but to our tired bodies, it looked perfect. Fortunately, we got there in time for a late lunch. Chicken, veggies and tea refueled us nicely.

Our contentment didn't last long as the campground chilled quickly once a cold fog rolled in. Tired and without much to distract us, I led a group stretch and then meditated by myself for a bit until dinner was served. While dinner was as good as always, it was our guide's special surprise that was the highlight of the meal. He brought rum mixed with a fruit-like juice and introduced us to the game "Be on the Happy Bus." A category was picked and then everyone had to name things in the category without repeating. If you repeated or couldn't come up with an answer, you had to drink. The problem was that we all wanted to drink to stay warm. It made for great fun. After the booze was gone, the crowd dispersed and we all went to bed.

On to the Ruins

Given the previous day's difficulties, Matt and I hit the trail super early. This gave us a head start and allowed our pace to be rather pedestrian as well as allowing us to walk without feeling like we were on a street in New York City. We moseyed along nicely all the way to the first set of ruins, Runkurakay, before the pack engulfed us once again. The humble stone ruins were nondescript in comparison to the those that would follow. However, it made as great a resting spot for us as it had for the Inca messengers centuries before. Still, for all the hype about the Inca Trail, these were the first set of ruins that were even remotely interesting. This was especially true once we hiked above and looked back at it's unusual double walled semi-circular architecture.

Sadly, just as Matt was doing better, another member of our group now suffered with an ankle swollen like a melon. Eventually, I talked him into using one of my hiking poles. Damn proud Britt had put off surgery so he could participate in the hike. We walked, well he hopped, from one set of ruins to another. Terraced walls built up to the main chambers of the ruins, while the translucent fog set a wonderfully eerie tone. Now this was what I envisioned when I heard about the Inca Trail.

With no useful light to worry about from a photographic standpoint, I decided to hang back with our injured friend. Given his lack of experience, I thought it wise to keep him company. Matt on the other hand was feeling invigorated by the denser air of the lower altitude. With a boyish splendor he charged ahead without a care in the world. "Take it easy!" I yelled, which had about as much effect as telling an elementary school kid to slow down on the way out the door for summer recess. As I strolled along the trail, small, colorful birds darted in and out of the brush. Matt beat me to the campsite by quite a bit of time, but then paid dearly as he conked out again. It was a shame because this campsite was equipped with a restaurant and showers.

Destination: Machu Picchu

We awoke the next morning with great anticipation. After three days of hiking we were just a short walk from peering down upon Machu Picchu. Instead of riding directly up to the gate as many tourists do, we would have the satisfaction of hiking down to a sunrise view from above Machu Picchu that was promised to be breathtaking. While many of the grand views were

blocked with dense fog, by keeping an eye out along the trail, I spotted dramatic pink, white and yellow orchids blooming in the nooks and crannies where the exotically colored plants could attach themselves. The bird life was even more vibrant, all setting the stage for our entry to reaching the Gateway of the Sun.

Finally we reached the last check point. Anticipation grew as we patiently waited for them to usher us through. Sadly, the weather did not cooperate and we were once again greeted with a fog bowl. The city was totally enveloped in low hanging clouds. Beautiful certainly, but given our vantage point, photogenic it was not. We descended down to the ancient city and wandered for hours through its stone structures. Unlike some of the smaller ruins on the trail, Machu Picchu was an expansive series of stone structures that truly deserves its reputation. Almost as plentiful as the tourists were the friendly and not so friendly llamas. They walked around acting like they owned the place and indeed they did.

Epilogue

Having finished the Inca Trail, I realized I should have made this my first trek and not a walk after two of my favorites. It's perfect for a beginner, lacking experience. The regulation and guidance provided significantly simplify the complexities of international trekking leading many to consider the Inca Trail to be one of the best treks in the world. The huge crowds, mundane trail and bad weather didn't compare with remote world of northern Burma. Sadly, I left feeling this trek did not live up to my expectations. For me, the Inca Trail was about the fun I had along the way as well as the destination. Machu Picchu itself is truly amazing and more than exceeded the hype. When I look at the trip as a whole and add in the Cusco experience, it is a trip well worth taking.

Kirk's Corner

Although Jeff's trip to the Inca Trail was not one of his favorites, I feel the Inca Trail is a truly top notch adventure. The list of the great archeological sites of the world include the Egyptian pyramids and temples of the Nile Valley, the Parthenon of Athens, the Roman Forum, Angkor Wat in Cambodia and Pagan in Myanmar. All are superb destinations for those interested in grandeur and history. However, none of these sites offer a meaningful trek to the destination. In contrast there is one great archeological site nestled high in the mountains offering an approach by trekking through the heart of one of the world's greatest mountain ranges, following footsteps on a trail carved in stone by the masons of one the world's great empires. That site is of course Machu Picchu and the trek is the Inca Trail.

Your first stop along the journey to Machu Picchu is Cusco, a fantastic ancient Incan and Spanish Colonial city. It blends this heritage magnificently. Historically, culturally and as a travelers resource center, Cusco does it better than most trekking gateway cities around the world.

One of the frequently cited drawbacks is that the Inca Trail is popular and it is being loved to death by thousands of trekkers every year. On the flip side, there is a limit to the number of trekkers per day that are allowed on the trail. Plus, you can always hang back from the throngs, let them rush ahead and have the trail all to yourself.

Well-Managed Experience

Once on the trail the advantages of the Peruvian trekking organization readily become apparent. All trekking on the Inca Trail must be with a guide service. This essentially puts all the trekkers on the same footing by standardizing the experience. An often overlooked benefit is the enhanced access to the history and culture. It also promotes employment for locals as guides, cooks and porters. The specified itineraries sometimes can be restrictive, but at least it keeps the flow of trekkers moving forward in a more orderly fashion. In addition, the Peruvian government has fended off commercial interest on Machu Picchu very well for a poor country. It has outlawed sightseeing over-flights, stopped a helicopter landing pad and resisted urges to build trams and hotels on-site. I highly appreciate and applaud these efforts and you will, too. The tight restrictions also set a strict weight limit for all porters. This promotes proper care and treatment of your porters and stops abusive practices for overloading porters which happens on many other trails.

Awesome Andes

The Andes are perhaps the most underrated mountain range in the world. How can you beat rugged snow-capped peaks rising out of the Amazon River Basin. Keep in mind this is the second highest plateau in the world, the highest being the Tibetan Plateau. The Peruvian Andes contain 30 peaks over 6,000 meters. If you are lucky you will have some clear weather to appreciate these snow-capped giants. As you finish the trek and again cross over the Urubamba river, be sure to marvel that the torrent of water rushing by is some of the farthest headwaters for the Amazon. From these lofty peaks, as the crow flies, it is only 200 miles to the Pacific Ocean. However, this water has something different in mind, instead it makes its way through the Amazon River Basin on a 4,000 mile trip to the Atlantic Ocean.

Ruins, Ruins, Everywhere

From the challenge of summiting Dead Woman's Pass and visiting the many smaller ruins you pass daily, there is plenty to see and discover on the trail. Even the stones beneath your feet are rich with history as most were carved or laid by the Incas themselves. Excitement builds every day as another ruin is passed. Overlooking the terraced fields of Llapactapa and climbing to the carefully perched egg-shape ruins of Runkurakay are all worthy of respect and awe for both their age and location. Knowing, however, that the granddaddy ruin of them all is at the end of trail keeps up your morale and increases your desire to push forward.

Grand Finale

There are few physical introductions to great ruins more dramatic than trekking through the jungle after several days on the trail to a viewpoint overlooking Machu Picchu. Your first glimpse comes just as the first rays of sunlight fall upon the ruins. In fact, ruin may be the wrong term, the stonework itself, made without metal tools is superb and astonishing in its precision and durability. Much of it is in the same condition as when it was created hundreds of years ago. The seams of giant stones cut within millimeters of precision fit together absolutely perfectly. All in all, I thoroughly enjoyed my trek to Machu Picchu. If you appreciate history, mountains and trekking you'll enjoy the spectacular journey amidst the ruins of the great Inca Empire.

INCA TRAIL — MACHU PICCHU

N

km 82

Wayllabamba

Llulluchapampa

Warmiwanusqa

Paqaymayo

Runkuraday

Sayacmarca

Phuyupatamarca

Winay Wayna

Inti Punku

Machu Picchu

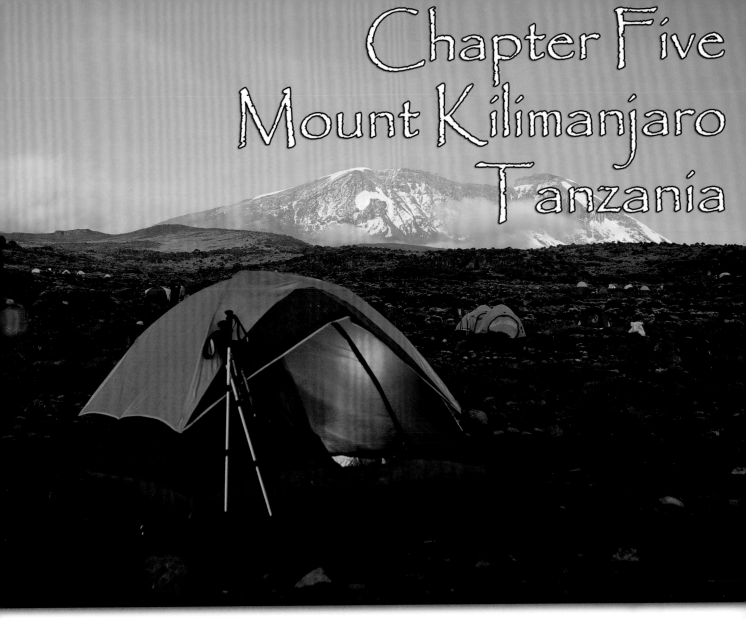

Chapter Five
Mount Kilimanjaro
Tanzania

The free-standing snow covered peak of Kilimanjaro towers above all else in Africa. With numerous routes to the top every would-be mountaineer can find their path to summit the highest peak in Africa. Whether you choose the "Coca Cola" route and sleep in huts, the more traditional route and camp in tents, or choose a technical approach with cramp-ons and ropes, the peak of Kilimanjaro is attainable by any fit individual with an iron will. Climbing 4,405m / 14,452' you'll pass through dense jungle, barren wastelands and a sunrise framed in a breathtaking glacier. Upon completion you can reward yourself with a safari into Africa's national parks where the sights, sounds and smells of lions, elephants, giraffes, are just a taste of the variety of life unshackled by zoos and man's contamination.

Fundamentals

Days Trekking: 6 days	**Approximate Elevation Change:** 4,405m / 14,452'
Distance: 100 km / 62 miles	**Price Range Independent:** N/A
Max Elevation: 5,895m / 19,340'	**Price Range Outfitter:** $1,100
Starting Elevation: 1,490m / 4,888'	**Challenge Level:** Difficult

When to Go

There are two seasons in which there is likelihood of dry and reasonable trekking conditions. The first season is from January to mid March with an alternative season from June to October. However, to travel to Africa and not join a safari is a sin. While any of the national parks are spectacular in their own right, why not time your trip to coincide with the migration of the wildebeests. The stampede of countless animals is an experience that should not be missed.

Guided vs. Independent Treks

Climbing Mount Kilimanjaro is tightly regulated. You must go with a guided group.

Access / Local Information

The main access city is Arusha, Tanzania. From there your trekking company drives you the 130 kilometers / 80 miles to the start of the trek.

Difficulty

There are many challenges to reach the summit of Kilimanjaro, but with care and proper preparation it is an achievable and exhilarating accomplishment. The single most obvious challenge is the altitude. Climbing to almost 6,000 meters is a laborious, lung-straining task. It is the highest walkable summit in the world. Compared to the Everest Base Camp Trek, you are rushed up the mountain at twice the pace of elevation gain. However, it is just a walk with no technical climbing required. So, if you are fit and handle altitude reasonable well you should be okay. The second issue is staying healthy. Even though we were very careful, we still managed to have intestinal problems. We were not alone, so be careful and carry good medications!

Orientation

Mount Kilimanjaro is located on the northeast border of Tanzania, 320 kilometers / 200 miles south of the equator. While most people climb the great mountain from the Tanzanian side, situated within Mount Kilimanjaro National Park, it is also possible to climb it from the Kenyan side as well.

On the Trail with Jeff

On my trip to Kilimanjaro I was once again playing the leader role. This time my travel companion was my neighbor Chuck. In his mid 40's, father of three girls, he got infected with trekking fever when I returned from Everest with tales of adventure. While he truly wanted to head to Nepal, he "settled" for a summit trip to Africa's rooftop.

Following a recommendation from Kirk, we set up our trip with Bobby Tours, a local company in Arusha, Tanzania. While there are many groups we could have joined, we chose to set up our own private expedition. First we would climb Kilimanjaro along the Machame route and then we would cap our African experience with a week-long safari through the Serengeti. Cutting out the middle man saved so much money that our private tour was cheaper than most group excursions.

Landing in the dark, we didn't get much of a fix on our surroundings. Peering out of the hotel van, we observed the outline of a shanty town. Small shacks by the side of the road, few lights and people wandering everywhere gave us fear when imagining what our hotel might look like. We were pleasantly surprised when we arrived at a clean hotel with a pool in the back.

Definitely beyond acceptable by third world standards, it was simply, but tastefully decorated with marble tiled floors and a friendly staff. Given our long trip we didn't spend much time exploring. Instead, we passed out quickly.

The next day we wandered around the hotel grounds until it was time to head to Bobby Tours. To our surprise, the hotel backed up to a golf course. We pondered what other surprises would be in store for us. When the van arrived, we quickly piled in, anxious for the details of our adventure. We travelled past more shack-like homes until we arrived in the more modern structures of downtown Arusha. Upon arrival tour owner Bobby asked us if we would mind if his brother-in-law Jae-Mul joined us. Jae-Mul was an interesting guy from the United Kingdom who was aimlessly traveling around the world for some time. Usually he didn't respect regulations and snuck into parks, but given his relation to Bobby, he promised to hike Kilimanjaro on the "up and up." He was definitely a loner, and we were unsure if he would stay with us for all of the ascent.

We met our guide, Simon, a very tall and powerful man with a gentle and calm disposition. He walked us around the town and through the markets. "It is perfectly safe, as long as you are off the streets before dark." "Wonderful," I thought. That was certainly one prediction I wasn't going to put to the test. Simon took us for African BBQ sausage, it was quite flavorful, but I worried if eating from the streets would cause us intestinal distress. We heard almost as many stories about people getting sick climbing Kilimanjaro as from drinking the water in Mexico. We lazily ambled through markets filled with small animals sold for meat and lots of beans as a staple of their diet before heading back to the hotel for our last good night of sleep.

The next morning we awoke and honestly, I don't remember the bus ride at all. Chuck says I slept through it, which is probably true. I didn't miss much, though, as Chuck said we wound along a dirt road with a stream of lush vegetation and huts along the way.

We arrived at the start of the trail by a series of control gates. While we were on one side of the gates, a multitude of street merchants were selling last minute supplies, hiking poles, bandanas, shirts, pants, you name it. They were waving it in our faces trying to get our attention. Much of the equipment wasn't even new. Often the equipment was stuff given to guides at the end of the trek and then resold to the next group of trekkers. What a racket! In general, I always try to avoid buying equipment on the trail, Chuck forgot bandanas and there were at least ten people willing to sell him many more than he needed. At least they couldn't break on the trail, or could they?

Once Chuck's transaction was completed, we started along the day's 18-kilometer trip through the rain forest. The assault up Kilimanjaro was extreme from an altitude perspective. Starting at 1,490m / 4,888' we would climb to 5,895m / 19,340' over 6 days. That's an average of over 730m / 2,400 vertical feet per day. This was far more than the Everest Base Camp Trek that kicked my butt. Although I had more experience and was in better shape, I was still concerned. On our first day, we had to climb almost 1,500m / 4,950 vertical feet. Chuck, unlike the others I set training programs for, worked out religiously. Primarily training as a runner, he was used to a quick pace and set an aggressive one once we hit the trail. In contrast with all of my previous treks, the porters actually trailed behind us. Granted they had a lot more weight than we did, but they were far more acclimatized to high altitude hiking. This really concerned me. The porters generally knew what they were doing, did we? My pulse immediately rose to 176. While I knew that was the upper limit of a pace I could sustain, I conservatively requested of Chuck that we slow down. There was no need for mountain bravado here.

The crowded trail was surprisingly well groomed, framed with timbers and run-off chutes for excessive rainwater. While not overcrowded like the Inca Trail, groups of slow trekkers tended to clump together making passing difficult. When the trail climbed uphill, they would slow to a painful crawl.

As we got to the Machame campsite it started to rain, then pour. OK, I guess I owed Chuck a debt of gratitude for getting us off the trail before it started. Unfortunately our porters were nowhere to be seen. Thankfully, there was a guard hut that we could take shelter in until they arrived. After an hour of waiting,

the porters appeared. The campgrounds were a site to see, an endless littering of tents. I greatly underestimated just how many people were on the trail and hoped it would thin out as we climbed. Making the best of a crowded situation, we set up our tent far away from everyone else and then focused on dinner. We were again very concerned about the safety of the meals, not wanting our summit hope derailed by something as simple as hygiene. While we meticulously filtered our own water, we were at the mercy of our guide, porters and cook for the cleanliness of our food. Dinner seemed safe, cooked potatoes, veggies, some mystery meat, with an unpeeled mango for dessert.

Beyond the Masses

Given the crowded site, I slept amazingly well. As we ate breakfast I started to have some intestinal distress. Given the amount of time since dinner I felt it couldn't be dinner and it was too soon for breakfast to be feasting on my system, so I hoped it wasn't anything serious. While not the best of ideas, I took an Immodium and hoped for the best.

Once we started down the trail, I was already feeling better. Chuck and I agreed to walk slower as the jungle faded away and the trail became more rugged. We went up, straight up. Unlike the previous day where all the porters seems to dawdle, the porters and ourselves got an early start. This left the hordes of slower trekkers behind us. It was great, with the exception of a few late-starting porters passing us, the trail was comfortably empty.

The foliage and flowers were incredible. Simon simply called everything an "Alpine" flower. He noted they came in two varieties, pink and white, not even recognizing they were different species. Yellow wild flowers were prolific, as well as a ton of variegated green and white plants. We definitely felt the void of understanding about the flora and were constantly disappointed with the level of knowledge Simon possessed about the surroundings. Still, it was hard to be angry with him as he was extremely caring about our well-being and seemingly competent with regard to the trail and mountain, two important factors in a guide.

Our progress was excellent, reaching 3,790m / 12,500' in altitude in 2 hours. We were thinking there wasn't much of a climb left un-

til the trail ended at a pretty intense rock scramble. Getting over it made me feel like a kid. Once on the other side we crossed a valley and found the Shira campsite at 3,840m / 12,670'. We were feeling particularly strong and it only took us three and half hours. Our early start and solid pace allowed us to beat the daily rains. From the campsite we got our first views of Kilimanjaro. Desolate and devoid of any kind of village life, we relied on Simon for knowledge. Frustrations grew as we could not even get simple questions answered. To add salt to the wounds, Simon sent us on a wild goose chase to officially sign in to "the book." After circling around for an hour, it turned out the registration book was at the campsite. Of course, on the way back to our tents, the rains came. Thanks, Simon. Late in the evening the skies cleared for a glorious view of Kilimanjaro in the late day light. Illuminated in the distance the summit looked much more than a few days hike away.

Kilimanjaro's Revenge

That night I slept great and awoke feeling better and stronger than the previous days. Again we got an early start and headed

up a well groomed trail. The slow steady climb into the bright sun provided us great views of the barren but snow-capped peak of Kilimanjaro. The day before we were politely asked by Simon to wait for him as it would look bad if we got to the campsite before him. So today we walked with Simon. The pace was sluggish, but tolerable. It was actually good to proceed at a slower pace as the stunning views motivated many photo breaks along the way.

Midway through the day, the clouds rolled in about the time Simon redirected us to a side tour via the lava tower. We were currently at 4,420m / 14,500' and the detour, which is taken by less than 10% of the people, required climbing to 4,660m / 15,280'. From an acclimatization perspective this was an excellent idea. Hiking higher and sleeping lower was always a prescription for success. As we climbed, our lungs were challenged by the lack of air. Our effort wasn't rewarded though, because when we reached the "tower" there wasn't much to see. An unimpressive bland rock formation rose above us. Perhaps in different light it looked more appealing. Before shifting gears and heading down, we had a quick snack of some refreshing carrots. As we descended, we were quickly surprised by how treacherous the trail became. The rocks seemed to have been scattered about from an ancient volcanic eruption. While amazing in their geological assortment, they were hard to appreciate because they were covered with very slick ice. Just as Chuck and I cautiously slowed up, Simon transformed from turtle to jack rabbit. Cursing under our breath, we wound down the trail passing dramatically different foliage. Surprisingly, there were giant cacti like trees and lichen. Soon we reached the Barranco Camp 3,950m / 13,035', sitting below an ever closer Kilimanjaro.

Feeling great, we decided to change our plans and push forward without the extra day of acclimatization. We figured the faster we got off the mountain the less chance we had of getting sick from GI issues. However, no sooner did we make our decision then problems struck in "River City." Chuck just got "the runs" in a major way. Never one to complain, he claimed to feel fine. We had dinner and then it was my turn to run for the outhouse. It had to be the damn raw carrots. We cursed our lapse in judgment!

Skipping a Day

I woke the next day and praised the mighty gods of Cipro, a hiker's all-purpose antibiotic. I felt completely fine and Chuck was holding his complaints to himself, which was easy to do as each day the views of Kilimanjaro improved dramatically. From the time we left camp until about 10:00 am the low hanging sun lit up the mountain. Deep blue skies accented the stately mountain. We started hiking down with a dip from 4,000m / 13,200' to 3,950m / 13,050', but it didn't last long. Before us was a sheer cliff called the Barranco Wall. Having purposely avoided any technical climbs, it was the steepest, most exposed ascent I have ever climbed. While it was the closest thing to a technical climb in any of the ten Great Treks, it was basically a long vertigo-inducing rock scramble. Like a chess master, I plotted my steps a few moves ahead while locking my attention to the sheer cliff, ensuring that three points of my body were in contact at all times. As a child I was almost thrown off the Statue of Liberty by my rowdy camp counselor, so I had no love for heights and narrow footholds. However, the hype of the wall turned out to be much more than the reality and we made it no worse for wear.

After a few minutes of walking Simon suggested we take a short cut. Why is it short cuts never seem to work out? After all that effort climbing up, we went straight back down into the "Gorge of Eternal Peril." I keep waiting for the old man from Scene 24 of *Monty Python and the Holy Grail* to come out and ask me three questions. By the time we reached the bottom, we actually dropped lower in altitude than we started. Once at the base, we had to climb right back up. Talk about spirit breaking. Surprisingly, the thought of the climb was worse than it actually was. So, in almost no time we were returned to 4,156m / 13,750'. We trailed along the ridge for a while and then started significantly ascending.

Immersed in fog, all around us was a barren wasteland of scattered lava rocks and nothing else. It was not the least bit appealing from a hiking perspective and it was made worse by the onslaught of hail. Simon said we were about an hour from where we would stop for lunch. We walked 45 minutes and then Simon declared, "45 minutes to go." Ugh, par for the course, though, with Simon. We eventually got to Barafu Camp at 4,550m / 15,015'. It was our final campsite during the ascent. We were alone in the cold. Exposed and without shelter, we huddled next to a rock in an attempt to lessen the swirling winds and froze until the tents arrived.

Getting there early did have one big advantage, we were able to scope out our campsite by a bunch of boulders that at least blocked some of the wind. Once our tent was assembled, the sun heated it up just enough that the temperature was tolerable. We took a much needed solid nap, ate some plain potatoes for dinner, purified some water and then napped for the next four hours before our midnight ascent to the summit began. The big question was whether to try to go down into the crater or not. I wanted to go, but Chuck was still quietly suffering. Our bond was quite strong and frankly, I couldn't see leaving him to go in search of further adventure. We had to play it by ear.

Onto the Rooftop

At midnight we were promptly awoken from a less than satisfying sleep. Having never started a trek in the middle of the night, I didn't know what to expect. While intellectually I understood there were reasons for this, it didn't feel smart. To top it off there was no moon, so it was pitch black. Mental note, when planning a hike up Kilimanjaro, plan it for a full moon.

We decided not to be proud and allowed Simon and one of the porters, Mysothiri, to carry our day packs. Of course my pride ended with my camera, which I carried myself. Freed from the weight of my tripod and other items, I felt energetic. I hoped this would continue until we reached 5,150m / 17,000' or so. From there I figured I could trudge up the rest of way on sheer will. Again only time would tell.

After quickly weaving through camp, we bumped smack into the back end of a line of lights. It was completely surreal. Faint head lamps serpentined up the mountain as the hikers plodded along the switchbacks. We started almost last, which was good and bad. If we had started earlier, we would have reached the top and froze waiting for the sun. However, being in the back of a slow moving herd, wasn't much better. It was hard to get warm, because we weren't moving fast enough to raise our pulse. Passing was next to impossible, as the trail really didn't allow for it. So, we followed the hikers in front of us on the slow march up. As we did, we noticed one of the porters didn't have gloves. Since I had two pairs, I gave him one. Amazingly, he didn't wear them. He just put them in his pockets saying they would make his hands colder.

Distressingly, one by one hikers stopped dead in their tracks. Before the sun cracked the horizon their bodies were filled with exhaustion, their hearts filled with despair and their eyes filled with frozen tears. It was hard not to get disheartened as the body count piled up. Would it be us next? Buddhist discipline came in handy. I reminded myself not to worry about the goal, but the steps to reach it. Methodically, we tried to focus only on putting one foot in front of the other. This was easier than usual, since there was nothing to look at but the feet in front of us.

I watched the GPS altimeter mark our progress as we rose from 4,545m / 15,000' to 5,150m / 17,000'. I was still feeling pretty good, but that wouldn't last. Like participating in a marathon, you just don't feel good from 20-26 miles no matter your fitness level. At over 17,000' you're not going to feel like jumping for joy. We counted our blessings that we ditched our day packs. We would have struggled much more if we hadn't. Jae-Mul was hurting bad, significantly more than ourselves. However, we knew he wouldn't stop because he was doing this as a tribute to his friend who committed suicide.

While I was in mid-trance, the next thing I heard was Chuck hurling. Throwing up is one of the signs of altitude sickness and I was now second guessing skipping the acclimatization day. I didn't know how much I could trust Chuck's imploring statements of well-being. Always a person who wants to please, I wondered how much suffering was hiding behind his forced smile. As it turns out, while reviewing my notes for this book he admitted to me a secret. Two days before the summit attempt, he had severely sprained his ankle and kept it to himself. Chuck down played his condition stating it was just after he drank and claimed it was the Gatorade. Given that he pledged that he had none of the other signs of altitude sickness, I agreed to march higher.

So, on our sorry group crawled up the mountain. We marked our progress by 75 vertical meters / 250' at a time. It was slow, painfully slow, but better than my ascent with Matt on the Inca Trail. As the night dragged on, we continued up the mountain. Each of us feeling better or worse at different times. Jae-Mul and I had previously reached a little over 5,450m / 18,000' before, so we knew what to expect. However, when we passed 5,115m / 18,200' I was on new, higher ground. The game of expectations was wide open. Trouble struck again when our porter Mysothiri begrudgingly turned back with altitude sickness. At about this point I started pondering, "wow, maybe I need a new hobby."

Things felt a little better when we reached the milestone of 330 vertical meters / 1,000' to go. I couldn't imagine how mind-numbing this would be without the GPS to mark our progress. At this point we all knew we would make it, it was simply pacing and mental fortitude. I hung with Chuck, but Jae-Mul was fading badly. To play it safe, Simon went back with him. While Simon wasn't the most intellectual guide in the world, he one of the most caring I've experienced. The problem was he had most of my camera equipment, but at close to 5,490m / 18,000' your brain doesn't work fast. He faded out of sight and with it my hopes of getting good sunrise photos.

We reached the peak, and it was cold beyond my wildest imagination. It was easily the most frigid I have ever felt. I thought the peak of Kala Pattar (Everest Base Camp Trek) was bad until this. Still the sky was starting to illuminate with a myriad of shapes forming in the distance. First and foremost, the view of the glacier was breathtaking. I pulled my outer gloves off and pulled the camera out from inside my jacket. In the dim light, I needed my tripod, but I didn't want to miss the fleeting seconds of perfect pre-dawn light. So I took a few shots, cursing myself that they would be blurry. Fumbling in the cold to get my gloves back on, as soon as I did the sun popped out. Off the gloves came to get new photographs that I was sure wouldn't equal my standards. When the gloves went back on for the second time, Simon appeared. Off came the gloves for a third icy blast and I got reasonable images. Unfortunately, the cost was the loss of all the feeling in my hands.

Chuck was waiting patiently ahead and I didn't want to tarry, so I packed up quickly and moved on. We took pictures at the peak, some with his Century 21 flag. Talk about not leaving your work behind! We got someone to take a few quick pictures of us and then headed down banishing any thoughts of going into the glacier. We were just too damn cold.

Now, if you are thinking descending would be a simple task, you would be wrong. We had to drop 1,200 vertical meters / 4,000' on a steep trail covered with loose ankle-twisting shale. I ignorantly expected we would simply head back down the path we came up. I was wrong, this was a different route entirely. I was never very good on the down to begin with, my knees were aged from far too many miles. They certainly were no better after hiking all night to 5,895m / 19,340'.

For the second time in a few hours I dragged my body farther than I thought possible.

There's not much to say about going down other than it was three hours of completely thrashing my body. Chuck looked great, he clearly enjoyed the descent more than the climb, but our pain was the least of our problems. Simon hadn't brought water, so he was drinking ours and we were running low. We made it back to the Barafu Camp parched, but that was not the end of it. We had another 1,500 vertical meters / 5,000' to descend. So our total for the day was 1,240m / 4,100' up and 2,760m / 9,100' down. Now faced with taking a nap or being responsible and filtering more water, you can guess we took the nap. To my dismay, that left us with only 3/4 of a quart of water to get down.

Again we dragged our bodies onto the trail, but at least this decent wasn't as steep. It only took us 2 1/2 hours, albeit 2 1/2 completely dehydrating hours to reach the Mweka Camp. We camped a mere two-hour walk from the end of the trail. That was very comforting after a never ending day.

There was one final complication. By the time we headed down, we were more or less brain dead. We started the day at 12:00 am with the sun rising at 6:30 am and neither of us were alert enough to put on sunscreen. We got fairly lucky considering the possible consequences. My hands got red and my lower lip was burned but otherwise, I escaped pain free.

That night dinner did not sit well. I was afraid that beating my body to death from effort and dehydration my resistance would drop and it did. Chuck was still not eating, maybe I should have just eaten energy bars. Either way I woke up at 4:00 am and had to make an emergency run to the outhouse.

I went back on the Cipro and skipped breakfast. The final descent was just what we needed, an easy, soft dirt trail with a steady, gentle grade down. We dropped the final 1,515 vertical meters / 5,000' in about 2 hours. When a woman in flip-flops with a little kid at her side appeared, it was a sight for sore eyes. We knew we were close.

Once down we were accosted with the mobs of people shilling shirts, hats and a ton of stuff we didn't need. Chuck seemed compelled to buy from them. It was one time he couldn't please everyone as there were an endless number of merchants all selling the same stuff. Simon asked for Chuck's hiking poles and to my dismay he gave them to him. My guess is they probably went for sale at the next day's hike.

After the Mountain, the Adventure Continues

Pulling out of the park, we relaxed on cushioned seats until we were snapped back to reality as we passed a freshly flipped car with wet blood dripping down the windshield. Our laissez-faire attitude abruptly changed and we strapped our safety belts on quickly. The drive back was slow with many stops to drop off porters. Before reaching the hotel in Arusha, we stopped at Bobby Tours first and picked up our luggage. To my relief, everything was safe. We then moved on to the hotel where we made ourselves human again. A shave and shower did wonders to remove the week of pain. Next on the agenda was a trip to a cyber cafe where I had hopes of downloading the Super Bowl. Mind you, this was in the days before Sling Box and I had an elaborate setup staged so we wouldn't miss the game. It was uploaded to my server in chunks, but I couldn't get access. Apparently my friend set the security settings wrong. After some technical wizardry, I was able to reset the restrictions, but had lost too much time to download the entire game. I settled for the last 20 minutes and saved it for later.

After the cafe we were supposed to meet the driver from the hotel, but he was nowhere to be seen. Apparently we mixed up the location as he was just around the corner. Meanwhile, everyone was our "Friend." "Remember me?" They all tried to pretend we had spoke before. It was an interesting angle to get you talking. Of course, this led to a discussion of how we should buy Tanzanite from them. My response should have been, "Oh yes, I remember you, where is the $10 you owe me from yesterday?" Luckily we found the driver, before it got dark, and had a great dinner.

It was great to be back in our hotel, get a good breakfast and to be clean. Mysothiri was supposed to meet us so we could print photos for him and the other porters, but he didn't show up and best we could tell he went back up on the mountain. Instead, we met up with Jae-Mul. He promised to take us to a school for orphans and the really poor. We got a quick bite to eat and headed to the school using real local transport. A large, low class mini-van, with the fare collector as well as other people hanging from it. For the most part it was a very efficient system. However, every so often someone didn't agree with the price declared by the collector and an argument ensued. Of course, we knew this would happen with us and it did. Jae-Mul refused to overpay and they finally settled on a lesser amount. This required us walking the last few hundred yards ourselves, but it wasn't worth the hassle to negotiate further. The "town" was a loosely connected bunch of farms and shanty shacks.

We wound our way around and out of nowhere a school appeared. It was pretty impressive. A few complete buildings, some buses and a lot of construction. We met the founder/director and she told us the story of how she started donating money to causes. Her generosity was contagious and others donated as well. Unfortunately, many of the causes abused the funds. Someone was willing to donate the land, so the school spread from there. They had quite the organization. They tested kids to make sure they had the potential and double and triple checked that the kids were significantly in need. Their hope was to educate the kids and have them stay in Tanzania to become their future leaders.

We hitched a ride back with the school's PR guy, got cleaned up, and headed to dinner with Jae-Mul. He invited us to the "club" that was just for Indians. We met some of his relatives and their friends. They were quite a group. It was Saturday night and they were out drinking and eating while their wives were at home. The club was tucked away in a far off corner of town. The drive over was a bit frightening as we had no idea where we were going or how to get back. Chuck was still feeling pretty bad and I was just getting better, so we called it an early night.

The next day we started our safari, which is a must if you are going to climb Kilimanjaro. We took eight days, but if you are limited on time you can see plenty. Visiting Ngorongoro Crater, the Serengeti and numerous national parks we saw it all; cheetahs taking down gazelles, lone rhinoceroses standing proud and stupendous stampedes of wildebeests and zebras migrating over 500 miles. As we travelled, in a jeep thankfully, the pains of the climb dissipated and we lost ourselves in the adventure. We couldn't have asked for any more.

Kirk's Corner

In contrast to Jeff's trek up the Machame Route, I hiked Kilimanjaro via the Marangu Route, also known as the Coca-Cola route. I'll tell you, there was no Coca Cola and it was no picnic. It's not a technical climb. However, getting above 19,000 feet is never easy and that's what I found out on my expedition on Kilimanjaro.

It's the Journey - The Grueling, Arduous Journey

My personal trip to Kilimanjaro started in my imagination many years before – you know – Hemingway's, *The Snows of Kilimanjaro* and so many *National Geographic* specials with Kili towering over the African plain while lions, elephants and zebras tramp about. The physical manifestation began in Capetown, South Africa, in June of 1994, having just chucked my job and bought a one way ticket to Africa to find out how the other 80% of the world lives.

Two and a half months later I was standing nervously at the Marangu Gate at the base of Kilimanjaro. I got there by working my way north from Capetown through the deserts and savannahs of South and East Africa to bring the trip to its hopeful culmination at the peak of Kilimanjaro, the rooftop of Africa! Our expedition numbered eight climbers from five different countries: Nigel was a Brit who also quit his job to do a bit of traveling. Andrei was a quiet young bloke from Norway. Canada was represented by the high-strung traveler, Annie, who was always talking about shadow puppets from Indonesia or something about the "amazing" masks in Mexico City. In retrospect I really appreciate her enthusiasm and having since seen the Mayan death masks of Mexico, which are really "amazing," but at the time her over-enthusiasm was a bit too much.

Few climb Kili without going through Arusha. To get there we had an overnight drive from Dar es Salam. This road was the most ruined and rutted I had ever ridden. This forced us to proceed very slowly. In fact, we were going so slowly that bandits carefully and quietly hopped on the back of the truck in the dark. They climbed the small ladder to the roof and began throwing off equipment in order to steal it. Greg, the assistant driver, heard the slight shuffling above and popped the roof hatch just in time to see the "perps" jump off to escape. We drove back. Greg had the courage to go rummage in around the side of the road in the underbrush and managed to find our camp stove and one of our tents. When I returned 10 years later I was impressed to see a beautiful paved road recently built with Danish engineers. It now must be one of the best roads in East Africa.

From Arusha we made our way to the small town of Moshi to coordinate our expedition. After a day and a half of preparations we set off from the base camp at about 6,000 feet. In a human frenzy at the trail head, our leader selected three assistant guides and eleven porters from the frantic mob of desperate job seekers. The porters, of course, carried most of our personal gear which required four porters, food stores required another four, and their own blankets, clothing and food which added a final three. Plus we had two guides; Modesto and Chris, whose main role was coordinating the lodging, porters and leading us for the "assault" on the peak on summit day.

The first day was about a five-hour hike through the rain forest to Mandara Hut at about 9,500 feet. The huts essentially consisted of little A-frame wooden structures, which slept about 8-10 people in bunk-type beds. It wasn't enough that we were gaining altitude and the trail became steeper. The previous night was miserable – it felt like I had a case of giardia.

The next morning, besides high fever and chills, as I tried to get down some breakfast an urge, "the urge," overcame me and I dashed toward the outhouse. Needless to say I didn't quite make it. After feeling completely overwhelmed by cleaning up this lovely mess, I set out on the trail mostly hiking solo as my case of an "over functioning bowel" continued. I was forced to make sporadic dashes to the woods or behind rocks. It was raining, the trail turned to mud and I felt miserable. However, I vowed to be the sickest man to the top of Kili! I finally relented and took some "plug you up" drugs and continued my trudge upward.

The third day was more grueling and provided us a steep eight-hour hike to Horombo Hut at over 13,000 feet. I felt a little better and the weather was much more cooperative. Nigel and I teamed together for the day's hike. In order to avoid altitude sickness the Tanzanian motto is "Pole - Pole" (Polay - Polay) which means slowly - slowly. It was suggested that one could regulate their speed by only breathing through one's nose. It didn't make sense and my climbing buddy Nigel and I figured we really needed to maximize oxygen consumption. We decided to breathe as hard as we could through both mouth and nose in order to get as much of the precious O_2 to our brains. It was a long day and we arrived at Kibo Hut just before sunset.

After a brief dinner we scouted our view of the summit route. We saw the trail switchback up the mountain from Kibo to the rim of the crater just shy of 19,000 feet. We all hit the sack early. The combination of altitude sickness and a long day's hike made sure just about everyone was exhausted. However, I laid in bed for quite some time with butterflies in the tummy, wondering and worrying how the summit attempt would go.

It takes about six to seven hours of hiking to reach the rim. Almost everyone leaves about midnight in order to be there for sunrise. For the die-hard summiters it is another 200m / 600' and 2 hours of hiking from the crater rim to the true summit. Half our expedition set their goal for the rim, no small accomplishment. Nigel, Annie, Andrei and myself were attempting the true summit. We woke up at midnight. Putting on about every stitch of clothing we had we left just after 1:00 am. Two of our guides, Modesto and Chris, went with us. It was an incredibly steep climb through loose gravel (scree). Annie fell behind early and took guide Chris with her. The trail was hard to follow in the dark, but Modesto knew the way. There were several groups ahead of us and we could see the small light of their torches (British speak for flashlights) winding up the mountain side.

As we followed the switchbacks up the mountain we took occasional rests where we basically lied down on our backs and choked down as much air as we could. After one prolonged rest, Nigel and I waited for Modesto to give us the go ahead. We waited and waited, not too anxious to start climbing again. Finally we called over to Modesto who was lying nearby, "Modesto, Modesto?" There was no reply. We called several times. Louder and louder we called. No one was energetic enough to get up and walk over to Modesto. So we lay on our backs and contemplated what was wrong with Modesto. At one point, we even thought he might be dead. That finally motivated us to crawl over to him and we were, of course, relieved that he was still alive. However, he had been sleeping and was clearly disoriented and exhausted. He claimed he was fighting off a malarial recurrence. It was clear, though, the altitude was getting to him as well. He was determined to lead on, however, we felt there was no way he should continue. The day before we had run into a couple of guys who had to turn back because their guide became so sick that they needed to practically carry him down the mountain. We did feel Modesto could make it down on his own. Since there were many more groups coming up the mountain, we insisted and sent him to camp.

After Modesto turned back Nigel, Andrei and I continued unassisted. It was rather difficult finding our way with only flash-lights. All the rocks seemed to look the same. We eventually made it to the rim of the crater and were just in time to watch a dramatic sunrise come over the clouds at about 7:00 am.

After taking in this spectacular site, we all discussed our options for heading up to the true summit. We were all pretty exhausted at this point, Andrei decided against going, but Nigel and I had no intentions of turning back without getting to the true peak. We trudged on hopeful of making the summit. The remaining glaciers of Kilimanjaro surrounded us in 100- to 200-foot cliffs with the volcanic crater below us. It is a surreal environment.

Without a guide we were a little challenged. The altitude began to take its toll. The trail was not especially difficult but every breath and step was taxing. There were times when I felt I couldn't take one more step. I laid down at one point and it was only Nigel's consistent prodding and shaking me that got me back up. I would have been quite content to nap their indefinitely, perhaps even to my death. We thought maybe another snack might revive us. I had eaten so many candy bars for energy that I could hardly stomach another and it turned out they were frozen solid anyway. My water bottle also froze and in attempting to open it, it shattered into pieces. I really began to wonder if we could make it to the top.

We continued on very slowly. Our perseverance finally paid off, we pulled ourselves to the summit at 8:42 am August 17th. We promptly collapsed. It was sometime before we gathered enough energy for some photographs. Nigel had figured out that we were the highest people in the world at that time. Our competition in the Himalayas was grounded due to the monsoon season; Mt. McKinley in Alaska, as well as the Andes, were sitting at about midnight to 2:00 am, so no one would be on the peaks. After the photos and another short rest we were able to gather enough energy for the return trip. Despite our exhaustion we somehow made it back down to the crater rim. The sun was hard at work and the temperature had warmed up to a near civilized level, just above freezing. With the kinder temperatures and the descent in altitude our bodies recovered some energy. We had made our way to the rim and now we needed to descend all the way back to the second night's campground. The only good thing about climbing a scree slope is that you get to go back down. If the conditions are right you can basically moonwalk your way down which involves running with giant leaps and soft "powdery" landings in the scree. My father once told me about a similar descent of Mt. Fuji when he climbed there in the 1950's. It is heart racing excitement and you feel as if you are flying down the mountain.

Once we finished with the scree we still had to drag ourselves many grueling miles back to the Horombo Hut. No more flying, just trudging on for what seemed like an eternity. But the exhilaration from having stood on the peak of Kili sustained me down the mountain. To stand on the rooftop of Africa was the realization of a lifelong dream and inspired me to experiment with moving from the trekking world into the climbing world. I will never forget persevering to the summit through difficult circumstances and the jaw dropping beauty of watching the sunrise from above the clouds in the freezing cold of the crater rim.

MOUNT KILIMANJARO TREK

Shira Camp •······ Lava Tower •

Kilimanjaro Summit •

Machame Hut • Barranco Camp •

Barafu Camp •

Mweka Camp •

Rau Camp •

Machame Gate •

Mweka Gate •

Rau Gate •

Chapter Six
Torres del Paine
Chile

Chile's Torres del Paine is the "classic" Patagonian trek offering towering granite peaks, valleys surrounded by 360-degree panoramas of mountains, glacial views stretching to the horizon and incredible fields of wild flowers. More than any of the other Great Treks, Torres del Paine offers a vast assortment of ecosystems, climates and experiences. It's a highlight reel of nature at its finest. There are options from day hikes, to the very popular short "W" trek, but to truly take in all of its splendor the complete route should be circuited.

Regardless of the duration of your trek there are many starting points. Trekking the circuit can require as few as eight days, but it took us eleven. Regardless of the season, the weather is quite unpredictable and patience is rewarded. Hasty trekkers miss the best views, settling for partial glimpses at the towers, valleys and glaciers. Instead, taking your time allows the views to ripen under the proper weather conditions. There is simply no comparison to seeing the towers under the rays of the early morning sun versus the often gray, clouded over, muted views of a midday trip up.

Fundamentals

Days Trekking: 8-10 for the complete circuit, 5 for the "W" trek	**Approximate Elevation Change:** 1,175m / 3,850'
Distance: 120km / 75 miles	**Price Range Independent:** $100 + food and transport
Max Elevation: Just under 1,220m / 4,000' (Gardner Pass)	**Price Range Outfitter:** $1,800 - $3,000 for the W circuit with refugios
Starting Elevation: 45m / 150' (depending upon location)	**Challenge Level:** moderate (with an Outfitter), difficult (Independent due to pack)

When to Go

Prime trekking season is from December to late March. While this is indeed when most people trek, the weather during this period is still unpredictable. A well-planned trek allows extra time for weather slowing down your progress. There are many stories of difficulties traversing the Gardner Pass and we were stalled for a day when the next campsite was flooded after torrential rains.

Guided vs. Independent Treks

The trek around the circuit is clearly marked and there is little need for a guide. Unlike other treks there are no porters to help you with your load. However, there are guides and many options for the less hardy traveler. Many people stay at the refugios and/or the Hosteria Las Torres and day hike to the primary sites with their belongings being carted by horse.

Access / Local Information

The traditional way to reach the trail head is to travel through Chile, landing in Santiago, then flying to Punta Arenas and taking a bus to Puerta Natales. One more bus from there takes you to the park.

While you can buy many last minute items you need in Punta Arenas, it is quite easy to find any supplies in Puerta Natales. Try not to buy your food and perishable supplies in Santiago, because the airline charges you for excessive baggage if your checked luggage weighs too much. This can somewhat be avoided if you fly to Punta Arenas shortly after you arrive in Chile. Check with your airline for their exact rules.

Interestingly, while Punta Arenas appears to be the more modern city, the Internet access was better in Puerta Natales.

An alternative way to get to the park is to fly through Argentina. You can fly to Buenos Aries and then take another flight to El Calafate. From El Calafate you can catch a bus to Torres del Paine. We couldn't confirm if this stopped in Puerta Natales along the way or was a direct bus. Going through El Calafate was more quaint than Punta Arenas and if you plan to add a trek around Mount Fitzroy, it is more convenient.

Difficulty

Your effort level on Torres del Paine depends largely on the weight of your pack and the weather. If you hike with a organized group and get lucky with the weather, the trek is easy to moderate. However, if you are completing the full circuit, tenting it and carrying all of your supplies, the trek can be difficult. You need to have the luck of a lottery winner to escape without some bad weather. When it rains the trail can be muddy and very slippery. Too much weight on your shoulders also takes its toll as the days go on, so plan carefully according to your fitness level for the best experience.

Orientation

Torres del Paine is located in the southernmost tip of South America on the Chilean side of Patagonia. It is approximately 100 kilometers / 60 miles north of Puerta Natales.

On the Trail with Jeff

Our journey around Torres del Paine was just one of four treks I scheduled for the winter of 2006. Having taken the quarter off from teaching, I planned to get the most out of my time away from work. Unfortunately, I had surgery to remove a piece of glass from my foot a few months prior to my trip. For a month beyond the operation I was given strict orders that I couldn't bear any weight on the recovering foot. This left me in a huge physical deficit and only a little more than a month to prepare for my trek. A wise man would scale back his plans, but no one ever said I was wise. Instead, I ratcheted up my therapy and prepared as best I could.

Who Speaks Spanish?

My flight landed in Santiago, Chile, slightly before Kirk's. Waiting around for your friend to pop out of customs always seems to take longer than expected. Anxiety wreaks havoc with your stomach as you hope all is okay. I filled my time trying to read whatever Spanish I could decipher with my incredibly poor high school language skills. As I saw the familiar black mop of hair come through the gate, my joy turned to fear as he was empty handed. No luggage was in sight. Losing luggage on any trip can be a nightmare, however, losing your tent, sleeping bag and other camping equipment is devastating. "Good thing your Spanish is better than mine," I joked. Kirk looked back at me inquisitively, "I thought you spoke Spanish?" Damn. Clearly we hadn't spoken about speaking. What else did we forget?

Fortunately his bags came a day later and we were off on our version of "Planes, Trains and Automobiles" to reach the far southern end of Chile. While Kirk and I had a rough plan to complete the circuit in ten days, we were unsure of how realistic it was given the dramatic and fast changing weather conditions. I donned a new role, one with which I wasn't very comfortable. I was no longer the strongest hiker, but the one that could be a liability. My fear was tempered a bit knowing I was traveling with Kirk and that I could rely on him for help if needed.

The route to Torres del Paine was certainly not a straight path. We navigated many buses to reach the access town for Puerta Natales and then a final one to the park. The roads were heavily under construction in the oddest of patterns. Instead of working on one contiguous section, they paved small sections at a time. We hopped on and off from smooth highways onto cinder roads and back again. After countless repetitions of this, the bus finally let us off at the catamaran to take us across the lake and start our trek.

The boat took us to the trail, letting us off at 6:30 pm. While normally a bit late to start a trek, we were so far south that the sun set close to 10 pm, giving us plenty of light to walk. We didn't pass a soul all the way to camp and enjoyed the cloudy, comfortable climate. Upon arrival at Campamento Italiano, the campsite looked a bit somber, maybe because the light was fading, but we didn't dwell upon it too long as we had a tent to pitch. Frustratingly, we found no signs indicating that the water was safe, so we added iodine to our drinking water as we left our filter in the access town to save weight. As we prepared dinner, we realized one of our many mistakes. We both forgot bug spray. Of course, one only realizes one forgets bug spray when there are plenty of bugs snacking on your unprotected skin. After cooking, eating and cleaning up we got to bed late, at least for us, 11:30 pm. This meant we had to sleep fast as we wanted to get up for sunrise.

Indecisions Abound

Our second day was a complete mind-fuck. We got up to what looked like perfect hiking weather. While it wasn't super bright out, the sun was shining and we started our hike about an hour or so past sunrise. To keep our load light we left our equipment in the campsite. The trail followed the path of the river Frances and was a bit challenging, but any struggle was forgotten taking in the glaciers dropping down from the mountains with the river roaring at their base. We clipped along for about an hour until we were engulfed in a complete fog bowl. Within minutes the sky went from relatively clear to pea soup. Kirk suggested that we turn around so we could be in a better position the next day for more pristine views when the weather hopefully improved. It sounded reasonable, so we headed back down the trail we had climbed halfway up. When we arrived back in camp, we packed up immediately. However, as we were about to leave we glanced back at our aborted attempt and noticed the weather cleared. "Let's go back up," Kirk suggested. Frustrated, I was now adamant about moving on. I didn't want to end up going in circles. So we headed to the next camp, which was over 20km / 12.4 miles away.

The trail was bordered with pristine lakes. Again we walked alone as we were behind the pace of trekkers who left before us. At one point we stopped for a break and saw a slew of condors circling in the distance. It was a shame that you couldn't put your tent along the lakeshore, but they were very strict about campsite regulations and for good reason. The park was kept in great shape, no litter or contamination was anywhere to be seen.

We stopped at Albergue Los Cuernos, a refugio along the way, hoping to buy a quick lunch. No dice, as they only served breakfast and dinner. So we did as any self-respecting trekker does to help save time, we loaded up on what we could buy. Unfortunately, that was junk food, cookies and chocolate bars for a whopping $10. Fueled on a sugar high, we made pretty good time. The trail as a whole was easy, however, in places it presented challenges, the largest of which was a small river crossing. Trekkers amassed at its bank hypothesizing as to the best route across. After much debate, it was decided. There simply was no good route. On the bright side, while it looked like it had clouded over again in the valley we just left, we enjoyed relatively good, clear skies with no wind. With a heavy pack and 21° C / 70° F temperatures I was sweating buckets. Still, with lots of hydration, a little Gookinaid (an electrolyte drink now called Vitalyte) and salty peanuts, I was feeling pretty strong. My feet hurt from the atrophy of the last few months, but the surgical spot was hanging in well. Kirk struggled a bit the second half, but we both maintained a respectable pace. We even felt good enough to detour around a lake to see what kind of birds were crowded on its shore. Unfortunately, our effort went unrewarded as they were common geese.

The test of our wills came when we reached the next refugio and campground at Albergue El Chileno at 7:30 pm. We were both exhausted. We could stay at the refugio, or walk another hour to the next campground, Campamento Torres. If we stayed there, we would be in a better position to see one of the highlights of the trip, the granite monoliths called the Torres (Torre De Agostini, Torre Central, Torre Norte, and Torre Monzino.) While they looked dismally gray during the day, they were best seen at sunrise when they are lit to a fiery, red flame by the early morning light. We decided to buy dinner at the refugio, soup with mystery meat, chicken and rice for the main meal, and a dessert for $16. It tasted great, but then after walking as hard as we had, my shoe probably would have as well. We talked to a nice British couple who thought that all you needed for energy was chicken soup. Perhaps that's true if you stay in the refugio and someone else carries your load.

Fortified with our meal, we decided to head to the closer campground. At first we made good time and saw the 1/2 hour sign within 20 minutes of walking. However, as it started to get dark, we were seeing no signs of camp. The darker it got the farther we seemed from camp. After what felt like an eternity, we finally arrived. There was no roar of the river as in the past camps, as this site only had a tiny stream for a water source. Fortunately it was drinkable, but a new problem emerged. Finding a campsite that late in the day was a big challenge. All the prime and even the less prime spots were taken. The only sites left were on an angle, so we slid quite a bit during the night. Given how tired we were, we really didn't notice much.

Mountains of Fire

What a loud campground! While most people were getting up early to see the sunrise, loud, ignorant campers were yapping away as early as 4:00 am. As we grumbled in the tent, I felt something crawling on me. I jumped! Kirk jumped! The tiny mouse jumped! It was exactly what we didn't need to start the day. Fortunately, we had hung our food as recommended because of critters in the campgrounds. It didn't seem like many people heeded the sage advice. Maybe they should have.

We got up quickly and hit the trail in total darkness. Considering the distance we walked the previous day, my legs didn't feel too bad. Kirk felt strong as well. At first we made good progress meandering around in the dark, but then we lost the trail, we totally lost it. About the same time my legs just died. Uphill, out of shape, with my tripod, camera and lenses, battling boulders and scree was just too much. Kirk marched on blazing an insane path. I followed, but slowly, having to take breaks. As the sun began to rise, so were my frustrations. I was not used to worrying about "making it." While I pushed, I tried not to push too hard as it was dangerous in the dark on the treacherous terrain.

Finally I arrived with the majestic towers in front of me and just in time. The sun rose over the horizon and lit up the massifs with the vibrant, fiery reds seen in the postcards. Looking back toward the sun gave an equally beautiful silhouette of the other mountains. It was all anyone could ask for. The glorious spectacle lasted a scant ten minutes. It was amazing how dramatically different the towers looked just a few minutes after showing all their glory. The advice was correct, if you want to see the towers, you must get up there before sunrise. Many trekkers hiked up later in the day and if they were lucky they caught a gray glimpse of the towers in between the clouds. It's like seeing a Broadway show in Idaho. In contrast, we reveled in our sights with another group of trekkers, perhaps 30 people had marched up for the sunrise, and then headed back down.

Given the amount of hiking in the past 24 hours, we decided to take a recovery day and revisit the towers again the following morning. We slept through the entire afternoon, until we finally arose to walk back to the refugio for dinner. It took quite a while to be served. Dinner was a crepe-like meat dish whose ingredients I never quite figured out. The menu in the refugio should have been named for Henry Ford. He used to say, "You can have a car in any color you like, so long as it is black." Likewise, their was only one choice of meal for dinner each night.

Feeling more relaxed, we actually took notice of the world around us. It was a little scary. We were out in this amazing wilderness, yet it felt like we were in a lodge in Colorado. While people weren't dressed to the nines, the amount of "show" clothing seemed out of place in remote Patagonia. You have to wonder what progress will bring to this place in 20 years.

Again we arose at 4:00 am to catch the sunrise. Sadly, the show was nowhere as spectacular as the previous day. With nothing to compare it to, those who were there for the first time thought it was pretty awesome. We waited around for a bit, but after a brief glimmer of hope, the skies clouded over. So we headed back down, ate breakfast and started a leisurely waddle down back to the valley.

Pay No Attention to the Man Behind the Curtain

We had only intended to walk to the campground near Hosteria Las Torres, so we took our time. Hordes of people were coming up in large groups on the main trail. Most were not trekkers, but day hikers, many of whom were coming from the $200/night hotel at the base of the trail. One dude was even hiking with a full umbrella, maybe a good call considering the weather patterns.

We made great time down the trail and reached the "high end" hotel in three hours. As weird as a high-class hotel seemed on a trek, we were more intrigued by a nondescript, little store outside. We bought three small sandwiches, an apple, a banana, an orange, a liter of orange juice, a liter of peach juice and potato chips for a total of $11. Turns out the potato chips won for the most calories per gram of any food we ate, making it the perfect trekking food. It was a shame we didn't know the degree to which we could resupply on the trail. Besides appealing to our culinary tastes, we could have saved quite a bit of weight by buying supplies along the way.

We debated staying there for the night, but I wanted to push on an extra seven miles to recoup the lost day. Hell, we ate great and it was barely 1:00 pm with 9 hours of daylight left. So we headed down the trail. Almost immediately my legs told me it was a mistake, but there was no turning back. Now we were off the main circuit and on the optional back portion of the trail. The first two hours were fairly mundane, where the path transformed from a narrow hiking trail into something more fit for a four wheel drive. We thought maybe this was the reason this part of the trail was optional.

As we progressed, the land opened up and the remains of a forest fire were evident. Nature is powerful, though, and much of the land was in recovery with wildflowers and ornamental grasses everywhere. A beautiful, aqua green river snaked silently in the valley we were approaching. In contrast to the previous raging rapids, this silent serpent moved with an incredible current, but no sound. The picturesque nature of the trail continued to improve with a gigantic field of daisies stretching before us as far as the eye could see. We stopped for a water and rest break, feasting on the sight. While "as the eye can see" is a catch phrase often applied as an exaggeration, be assured there was no visible end to this field. It reminded me of the poppy field in the *Wizard of Oz*. We walked for miles in the ever present company of infinite daisies. Our dream was turning into a nightmare as it seemed the trail would never end. Finally, we got to a river, but alas, there was no bridge. After looking around, another trekker from the other side of the river signaled that there was a bridge downstream. We assumed we were home free. We were wrong again. Amidst the daisies were streams of mud that engulfed our boots and legs if we were not careful. An paltry number of small logs were intermittently placed as unstable footholds. One slip and we would be doomed (as one guy we met at the next campsite found out - quite the muddy, stinky mess he was).

Who'll Stop the Rain?

We continued past the predicted 7-mile distance, past 8 miles and finally saw a sign, 800m / 1/2 mile to camp. According to the GPS it was 1,000 meters, but who was counting; OK we were. The campsite was a fee site, $7 per person, but that meant a shower. The grounds were still in the field of daisies making for an incredible backdrop while we did our nightly chores. We cooked dinner, cleaned up and got ready for bed just as it started to rain. While the campsite was the prettiest so far, it was also the most exposed. We hoped, in vain, it wouldn't rain long.

While the rain continued, I slept like a baby. One advantage of the Torres del Paine Trek is you never climb higher than 1,200m / 4,000'. So unlike other hikes, you can actually get a good night's sleep. By the time we woke, the rain stopped. We cooked breakfast and slowly broke camp. While we did, a pair of foxes came by and ran through the daisy field. It was the perfect accent to one of the best views we had from a campsite.

The next section of trail was fairly easy, but at 20km / 12.4 miles in length, we were in for a good bit of walking. Before we left we found a scale and weighed our bags. A mistake indeed! Mine weighed in at 68 lbs, and this after already consuming a few days of food. Kirk's weighed in at 53 lbs. We think it may be off by 10 lbs, but that's still a bit more than I planned to carry. Of course, now when I walked I felt every ounce of the "68" pound bag.

The trail was quiet, with very few trekkers. For the majority of the hike we walked alone through the meadows of green grass littered with spherical clumps of yellow flowers. Eventually the few trekkers on the trail clumped together and, unfortunately at the worst time. We came upon a tree filled with foot-long, green parakeets. As I quietly pulled out my camera, a group a trekkers came up from behind. The birds felt surrounded and flew away. Shortly after, as we progressed down the trail, we saw a sole condor flying relatively close. However, he must have spotted our growing group, because he gently rode the winds in the opposite direction.

After a bit more trekking, it clouded in again. We were teased periodically with partial views of the glacier-covered mountains just behind the clouds. With a few miles to go, it started to rain and we played one of many iterations of "should we or shouldn't we." Not sure how far we had to go, we pulled out our rain gear just in time for it to stop. We thought we were in the clear until about 1/2 hour from the campsite, the skies just dumped on us. We ran to Refugio Dickson next to the campsite and it didn't take us long to decide to pay $25 each to sleep inside. Staying dry and not setting up a tent in the downpour seemed a no-brainer. The flexibility of deciding where to sleep and how long to stay at a location was an unrecognized bonus. Treks like the Milford Trek in New Zealand do not offer such luxuries. Good weather or gale-force winds on Milford you are forced to move forward every day. The weather continued to live up to its unpredictability as shortly after paying, the sun peered out. We both looked at each other wondering if we had just wasted our money, but we didn't wonder long because, in Patagonian fashion, just as quickly as the sun appeared the skies closed back in and a downpour ensued.

We falsely assumed as long as we were staying in the refugio we could buy dinner. It turned out you had to order a full hot dinner a day in advance. So much for total flexibility. We tried to wait the rain out so we could cook outside, but instead ordered what was permissible on demand, two bowls of soup and a few cans of the worst tuna ever. Instead of white solid chucks of fish, it was all scraps of the darkest meat. Luckily, there was no shortage of beer, so we filled up on liquid carbs.

In contrast to the cool, wet campsite, the refugio was really hot. Warmed by a quaint wood-burning stove combined with the body heat of way too many trekkers escaping from the soaked campground, it was uncomfortably hot. Still we were not complaining, at least not until a bunch of British girls tried to turn the refugio into a Santiago disco by blasting Spanish club music throughout the rooms. The dynamics of this refugio were completely different from the one we had dinner on the main trail. Everyone here was a circuiter and no one was wearing show clothing. Some of the women, including the two British girls, were trying to scam a free room. None succeeded initially, but the dancing girls were not giving up easily. They went with the cook to another building/tent. We could only imagine what price they would pay for a roof over their heads. All these issues were relatively minor compared to the news that came in on the radio. The next campsite was submerged and everyone there was huddled in the guard shack. In addition, the trail beyond the site, through the infamous Gardner Pass, was probably closed. Our mood turned somber as we debated whether we would be forced to wait a day, two days or three days? Who knew. After all, in Patagonia nothing is predictable, except for the irregularity of the weather. At some point we figured we might have to give up and head back, but we had a few days to play with and hoped for the best.

A few times during the night it sounded like it stopped raining, but that was the mountain pixies playing with us. By morning it was still pouring. We had no idea what to do, so we hung out for the day. It was already flooded behind us and we knew we couldn't go forward, so we stayed put. A few brave souls moved forward by midday, we wished them well but weren't willing to take the risk. From the radio reports, it sounded like the pass was traversable, just a muddy mess. Supposedly the next campsite was still flooded, and with the rain still coming down I wanted to move on the next day one way or the other. One guy said, "You are supposed to be able to experience all four seasons in Patagonia in a single day." However, right now we seemed to be only experiencing spring! On a bright note, at least the disco music had stopped. Tensions were rising though as whatever they played was at eardrum piercing volumes. At one point another trekker lowered the volume on the radio and without hesitation a local just raised it back up. Finally, I shut it all out with a good midday nap. When I woke up around 5:00 pm, the rain had stopped. We bought a pound of pasta from the refugio and some sauce for dinner. As you might expect, the rain started again after dinner.

Up and Over

Given the degree of noise, I actually slept great that night. We woke up at 6:30 am to blue skies, absolutely stunning views of mirrored lakes framed by the snow-capped mountains. It was finally time to push toward the pass. The goal for the first half of the day was to get to the Campamento de los Perros, the previously flooded campsite. Normally we would stop there and rest for the push up the Gardner Pass, but we hoped to do a double trek that day, assuming our legs held up. It was amazing to see what a difference the weather made.

On the entire way to Campamento de los Perros we had great weather. What a delightful change! The hike was fairly easy and we were treated to great views of Glacier de los Perros and the lake of the same name just below it. With icebergs floating in the lake and washing up along its shoreline, it seemed the perfect place to stop for lunch. It was a tad out of the way, but worth it. The view was great, we were out of the wind and relaxed in total solitude. After lunch we continued to the campsite, which was dark and damp, but had a great view of a pond that reflected white daises and the mountain above.

Most people coming in were continuing on to the Gardner Pass, others already tired from the day and called it quits. We had heard so many fearful stories: "winds so strong you cannot stand up, steep impossible descents," etc. We respected the challenge of the pass, but were feeling very strong after a full day's rest. Given the weather was still good, although getting a bit cloudy, we decided to push through the pass.

As soon as we did, it got tough. The trail was steep from the get go and really, really muddy. We were warned a few days earlier that we would see a lot more mud and, fools that we were, laughed when we didn't initially find the trail that muddy. This must have been what they meant. A blessing and a curse, there were tree roots sticking up above the soup. While we could easily trip on them, they also gave us a place to land without sinking into the grimy abyss. We finally got on drier ground, but it was no less stable. It was a steep climb of slate and scree. To top it off, just as we exited the forest the rain returned. We were second guessing our decision, but had no choice at this point but to push forward. It was fairly warm out, 16° to 21° C / 60° to 70° F, which meant that either we could be rained on by the elements or rained on inside our jackets by sweat.

Fortunately the rain stopped and we got a good look at the climb up the Gardner Pass. It was quite the climb, 915m / 3,000' of elevation gain on the day, up to 1,220m / 4,000' in altitude. As we climbed the wind got stronger and stronger. The owner of the hostel we stayed at in Puerta Natales had suggested we travel the circuit clockwise, instead of counter clockwise as we

were, so that the wind would be at our backs. Good thing we chose not to listen to him. We totally lucked out. The wind was blowing in the opposite direction it usually does and was at our backs for the complete ascent.

We got to 1,070m / 3,500' and the skies looked clear, at least for Patagonia. So we started up to the pass. The wind was fierce, but was actually helping push us along. All in all, it was quite a reasonable climb. My foot wasn't hurting in the least, even after eight hours of hiking. I was feeling great. One couldn't ask for a better view with Grey Glacier to our right dropping off into a lake. They said you would get quite a rush coming up the pass and having the glacier materialize in front of you. They were right, it was mesmerizing. The glacier trailed back to the horizon with mountains dotting the landscape.

Our luck would change, though, as the path down to the campsite was more treacherous than the way up. It was a complete mud bath. We could see ass prints of those who slid down before us, but the warnings didn't help much. Our butts added to the collection. Eventually we got to the campground, after a rude drop in altitude and then a climb back up. Very few people were staying there, which was a wonderful change from Refugio Dickson. We set up our tent, made dinner and watched the sun set over the glacier. That night most people were tired and sore, so everyone wished each other an early good night and hit the hay.

We got up at 7:00 am to watch the morning light. While it brilliantly lit the mountains, it hadn't yet illuminated the glacier. So we had a quick breakfast, caught the light over the glacier and then headed to the next camp. It was supposed to be 305m / 1000' lower, and depending upon what you read, it was anywhere from a 4 to 6 hour walk. At first we didn't make any progress going down, just up, down and back up again. However, along the way our constant companion, Grey Glacier, entertained us with great views.

The "treats" of the trail were the rickety ladders, flimsily held together, that we climbed and descended. At first they were quite nerve racking, especially with heavy packs on our backs, but we got used to the feeling of nearly falling off. As we passed the first campground, Campamento Guardas, we detoured a bit to a viewpoint along the face of Grey Glacier. We were able to see the blue ice, deep chasms, icebergs, the lake and mountains surrounding it. We could have easily sat there all day, but it was only supposed to be an hour to the next campsite. We hightailed it down the trail and with the exception of one more photo stop, pounded it out in a little over 30 minutes. I was starting to feel like my old self and began to contemplate doing a 20-mile last day without the pack.

Since there was a store at the campsite, we pigged out on soup, pasta, rice, cookies and of course, hmmmm, more beeeer. A shy American trekker named Tristan decided to eat at the refugio. He came back shocked. When we asked him how it was he said, "Horrible, I had to talk with people!"

We were all trying to stay up late to try to see a comet around 11:00 – 11:30 pm. That would have been awesome, but fatigue won and I passed out. The next day there were conflicting reports about the comet. Some people said they saw it, while others said they didn't due to the clouds. Perhaps people didn't know what a comet looked like?

Walking on Ice

We awoke at 8:00 am the next day and got ready for a ice walk directly on Grey Glacier. We took a small boat to a larger one, which took us along the face of the glacier, up close and personal. The light blues and whites of the glacier contrasted with the deeper blues in a seemingly random yet patterned formation. It surprised me how different the glacier looked close up as the boat coasted ever so close to the icy behemoth.

Our group of twenty did not look the most athletic, but the walking on the glacier was fairly pedestrian, so it didn't matter much. When my foot first stepped onto the glacier I thought I was still on solid land. That illusion was broken as soon as I hit the "ground" with my ice axe and saw we were actually walking on a living wall of ice. We walked around for four hours, using the ice axe and crampons, sticking to the stable, safe areas. Usually glacier walks require everyone to rope to each other in case you accidentally step on snow with a hidden crevasse underneath. However, there is no fresh snow on the glacier, so we were allowed to amble freely.

Walking on the glacier gave us a completely different perception of it. It was similar to the difference felt by those who view the Grand Canyon from the top versus those who descend to the river and see all the canyon's majesty from a completely different perspective. While the glacier is an impressively beautiful sight when seen from a boat or the trail, when walking on it one gets the feeling it is alive. Strong water currents rip under the icy surface intricately cutting rich blue caverns. Even though it was relatively safe on Grey Glacier, peering into a crevasse to see the underground rivers did cause a bit of apprehension.

We had a "lunch," which was just a snack. You would think that for $130 day trip they could provide you with a real meal. However, we were quickly distracted as the next agenda item was ice climbing. I thought it wouldn't be that cool, especially based on the lackadaisical pace of our group, but it was a rush. The guides screwed in a single carabineer up high and lowered a rope through it for safety. One of the guides stayed at the bottom pulling up the slack in the rope in case you fell. Then you climbed by kicking your crampons into the near vertical ice and following it by two swings of your ice axes. You then shifted of your weight by rocking your hips forward into the "sexy position," as the guide liked to call it. It was just as the mountaineering book I was reading described it, okay, other than missing 6,100m / 20,000' or so of elevation. The goal was to get to the top and kiss the carabineer. If you didn't you had to kiss your guide. I went second and reached it, but it was much harder than I expected. About half of the group made it and then it was a hurried walk to catch the boat back to the campsite.

We pulled out a few tricks for dinner. Sure, we had pasta again, but this time we added chicken soup to the mashed potato mix to help break the monotony. Yes, we were desperate for a change in food variations. We went to bed and set the alarm for midnight, hoping to see the comet. When the alarm sounded at midnight, once again the skies were clouded over. However, I woke up at 2:30 am and out of a half opened eye saw it blazed across the horizon, taking up about 1/5th of the sky. Tiredness beat out my photographic bug as I was way too exhausted to take photos. Kirk stepped up and got out of the tent to take a few shots.

Play it Again Sam

We woke up and it was a chilly 9° C / 48° F. To me it felt a lot colder. Two Canadians disagreed and started the day with a dive into a glacier-chilled lake. Instead of following them, we headed out on the trail. The walk started out with an unexpected climb of 180m / 600' before coming back down. There were not a lot of great views along the last seven miles of trail, but at this point it felt more like a mission to complete the circuit than to take in every possible sight. As we progressed, the number of trekkers increased dramatically. Most seemed like they were on their first day, clean, smelling of deodorant and with energetic smiles. It was a great feeling to reach the sign post at which we started our trek ten days earlier.

During lunch we debated going back up the valley we traversed the first day when we got fogged out. Of course, as we debated it the rains returned. Undeterred, we decided to return to Campamento Italiano by day hiking the last bit and leaving much of our equipment in the tents. We made great time and the sky started to clear as we ascended. After retracing our previous steps for one and a half miles we finally hit new ground. It seemed exceptionally cold as the wind whipped in our faces. However, as we climbed we could see the circle of mountains forming around us. The sky became blue just as we reached our viewpoint. It was absolutely awesome. The view couldn't truly be captured in a picture. The complete 360-degree panorama was lit by a bright sun shining down upon mountains silhouetting the valleys and aqua green lakes. We stayed for a bit and headed back to camp as we still had a long way to the catamaran. When we returned, I was extremely happy that my foot had healed and I felt much stronger than at the beginning of the trip. Unfortunately, I passed my bad foot karma to Kirk as his feet took quite a beating.

Epilogue

As I ponder back through the treks, Torres del Paine keeps rising to the top. The amazing diversity, flexibility and lack of altitude can't be matched. Where else can you experience so much and barely reach 4,000 feet in altitude? No frigid nights, lung sucking climbs or bouts with GI issues. Instead, glistening glaciers, endless wildflowers and birds big and small fill your days.

Kirk's Corner - Patagonian Trekking the Argentine Way

As Jeff and I prepared for our trek in Torres del Paine we decided to make preliminary excursion into Argentina to get a taste of the Fitzroy Massif deep in the heart of Parque Nacional Glacier (pronounced Glassy-er) and see if it was a worthy alternative to Torres del Paine. What we ultimately found was an excellent trekking region with a multitude of options and some fantastic scenery. Here is how it went down:

Patagonia is the earth's southernmost continental region outside of Antarctica. The severe and rapidly changing weather reminds you of this fact on a consistent basis. We stepped off the bus in El Chalten, shouldered our packs and took a few steps directly into a fierce wind and cold rain. The temperature was slightly above freezing but I'm confident the wind chill was decidedly lower. As the bus rolled away Jeff and I looked at each other despairingly. It is times like this when you wonder, but dare not speak, "why the heck am I doing this?"

We stumbled a few more steps before examining our surroundings. Surprisingly, on this dusty road at the edge of the ramshackle town there was a little restaurant. It looked deserted, but we were desperate for a little shelter and perhaps some hot food before we ventured into the bitter elements for the next several days. We were both pleasantly relieved when the entrance door was unlocked and the kitchen was open. We settled in for some hot soup and short respite in final preparation for our journey.

Ultimately, all good things must end as did our little lunch. We again shouldered our packs and set forth on the road directly into the howling headwind and the cold rain. The road quickly turned into a trail and ultimately the trail headed steeply uphill and entered a forest. With twisted, old trees and clouds swirling through the branches, this forest spookily resembled Tolkien's Mirkwood. We spied a break in the forest and were expecting and hoping for a viewpoint of the valley floor below. Instead of the vista we received natures' baptism, horizontal sheets of rain in our faces. Perhaps the Fitz, as we called it, wouldn't be such a great substitute.

The wind held steady and we climbed higher and got colder. I dreaded setting up a tent in such conditions. We were both surprised that as we neared our campsite the weather broke in our favor with the rain subsiding and the wind calming down. After getting camp set, we chased a coyote and a large white throated caracara around the camp in efforts to get some close-up photos. After some food we were finally feeling relaxed and ultimately, the clouds started to clear revealing a impressive view of the setting sun and swirling clouds on the Fitzroy Massif. Quickly the "why the heck am I doing this" washed away leaving only feelings of satisfaction and awe.

We speculated that night which would be the norm: the awful wind, rain and cold or the spectacular evening sunset. In the morning we had our answer, it was perfectly sunny and for a brief few moments the massifs were lit with a fiery red paralleling the great Torres del Paine. We scrambled uphill on the trail, over the ridge and continued down to Laguna De Los Tres with shimmering picture-perfect reflections. We took full advantage, snapping one photo after another. We returned to camp with the weather still holding. In the afternoon we headed to Lago Sucia, an impossibly beautiful lake, with hanging glaciers plus an astounding waterfall. The tone was now set. We set forth over the next four days into some of the most amazing mountain scenery that Patagonia has to offer. Each view was as beautiful if not more so than the last. Sunrise was absolutely breathtaking as it illuminated the peaks in an orange glow, fantastically reflected in Laguna Torre.

We finally finished our trek right back where we started. However, everything about the dusty road in the ramshackle town suddenly seemed a lot neater and brighter, and we were certainly much happier. We celebrated with a couple of tasty micro-beers.

We had hoped for a decent warm-up to prepare for the Torres del Paine Trek. Ultimately, what we found was a destination in its own right. Argentina brings together hospitable people, charming towns and some fantastic trekking amidst some of the best looking mountains that Patagonia has to offer.

The gateway to the region is El Calafate, a charming mountain getaway where you can catch the bus to the frontier and trailhead at El Chalten. While there are at least a dozen trekking route variations, ours took four days, hiking and camping along the base of the range. This allowed us daily penetrations to selective viewpoints and lakes deeper in the park. We didn't have time to enter the Rio Electrico Valley. It is noted for even more stunning scenery.

So pack your bag and make the journey to the Argentine Patagonia, or if you are already headed to Torres del Paine extend your trip into the Fitzroy region for more fantastic Andean trekking.

TORRES DEL PAINE TREK

N

Puesto Seron

Campamento Torres

Torres del Paine Lookout

Albergue El Chileno

Hosteria la Torres

Los Cuernos

Catamaran

Refugio Lago Dickson

Mirador Frances

Campamento Britanico

Campamento Italiano

Refugio Lago Peñoe

Campamento Los Perros

John Gardner Pass

Campamento Paso

Campamento Guardas

Campamento Lago Grey

Glacier Grey Hike

Chapter Seven
Annapurna Circuit
Nepal

There may be one trek that has it all: snow-capped peaks of the world's greatest mountain range, steep rice terraced valleys, active villages along most of the way reflecting two major ethnic cultures, hot springs, holy pilgrimage temples, high mountain passes and much more. It is a trek of epic length, but offers many options for shorter, but still rewarding journeys. This trek is none other than the Annapurna Circuit.

While Mount Everest often captures the general public's eye, the trek around Annapurna is often considered superior to the shorter Mount Everest Base Camp Trek. As a circuit Annapurna offers another advantage in that you don't have to double back. You start at a much lower elevation 820m / 2,700', but still attain high alpine altitude maxing out at 5350m / 17,550' on Thorung La Pass. From a mountaineering perspective, Everest garners attention for its dangerous summits, while Annapurna proves to be a much more formidable mountain to climb with one person dying for every two who reach its summit.

By following the complete circuit, starting in Besi Sahar and ending in Naya Pul, you experience the delights of the many villages, encounter numerous temples, ecosystems and wildlife. Every day you gain impressive views of some of the most famous mountains in the Himalayas: Annapurna I through IV, Dhalguiri, Machu Puchari, Nilgiri and Gangapurna. By walking around them, you experience multiple views of each massif.

The Annapurana circuit is continuously evolving, but the one constant is its status as one of the world's greatest treks. One of the most popular variations from circuiting is to fly into Jomsum and trek back. The second most common is to trek into ABC – The Annapurna Base Camp – also known as the Annapurna Sanctuary. The bottom line is that you can't go wrong in trekking in the Annapurna region.

Fundamentals

Days Trekking: 15 - 21 days	**Approximate Elevation Change:** 4,530m / 14,850'
Distance: 248 km / 155 miles	**Price Range Independent:** $300 - $700
Max Elevation: 5,350m / 17,550' - Thorung La Pass	**Price Range Outfitter:** $1,500 - $3,000
Starting Elevation: 820m / 2,700'	**Challenge Level:** Difficult

When to Go

The prime trekking seasons in Nepal are fall and spring. Fall in Nepal is October to early December and the spring season runs from mid March to mid April. Fall offers clearer skies and more crowds on the trails. Spring presents a greater possibility for dusty or hazier skies, but also gives you a chance to see the spectacular Rhododendron trees in bloom. Be aware that starting your trek too early could result in a shortened trek as the Thorung La Pass could be closed.

Guided vs. Independent Treks

Trekking around Annapurna or to Everest Base Camp provides the same options whether you hike solo, with a guide and/or porters. Anecdotally, it seemed there were more independent hikers on Annapurna. However, the benefits of hiring a guide and porter are equally true on this trek, if not more appropriate given the longer duration. Days and days walking have a way of wearing you down. Why not make life simpler and easier by hiring a guide and porter?

Access / Local Information

Kathmandu is the gateway for most Himalayan treks. See Chapter Three, Everest Base Camp for more information related to Kathmandu. The start of the trek is the village of Besi Sahar. It can be reached by a local bus from Kathmandu. Some might prefer a tourist bus to Pokhara and then a local bus to Besi Sahar, however, the local bus was not overly inconvenient until it got close to Besi Sahar. Many locals hop on and off there, but whether you take a tourist bus to Pokhara or not, you'll still have this experience.

Difficulty

The trek around the Annapurna mountain range is not an easy one. While it is the third highest trek in terms of maximum altitude, the Thorung La Pass is a long push at high altitude. Unlike Kilimanjaro or Everest Base Camp, if you get in difficulty in the middle on the pass, there is no simple escape route down. In addition, the pass is often covered in deep snow making it impossible to traverse. Train hard to prepare for the rigors of this trek. Also, give yourself extra days if acclimatization is needed or weather slows your progress.

Orientation

The Annapurna Himal lies about 140 kilometers to the north east of Kathmandu near the resort-like village of Pokhara. The entire massif and surrounding area are part of the 7,629 km² Annapurna Conservation Area which is the largest protected area in Nepal. The trail winds around the massif following the Marsyangi River in the east and over Thorung La to descend into the Kali Gandaki. In fact, the Kali Gandaki Gorge is considered the deepest in the world from the peak of Dhaulgiri 8,167m / 26,788' to the river bed at an elevation of 2,520m / 8,266'. The Annapurna Base Camp trail drives directly into the heart of the range for a unbelievable 360-degree Annapurna experience.

On the Trail with Jeff

By the time I was ready to start the Annapurna Circuit I had returned to the top of my trekking game. Having just completed Mt. Fitzroy, Torres del Paine and a trek back to the Everest region called Gokyo Ri, I was in shape and acclimatized to altitude. It was indeed a luxury. Unfortunately, it came at a cost. Before my Gokyo Ri trek some of my camera equipment was stolen, but I had enough backup equipment to make due. I only had to replace a lens and hope nothing broke as I ventured around Annapurna. Unfortunately, instead of enjoying my time between hikes, it was spent futilely hassling with the police to get an official police report which was necessary for me to process my insurance claim.

My guide for this trip was Padam, Kirk's guide from my original Everest trip and my guide for Gokyo Ri. With his help dealing with the police we still had a little time to be tourists and he took me to the Pashupati Temple. The holiest Hindu temple in Kathmandu, it exemplified the "Circle of Life." They have both cremations and weddings going on simultaneously. Both ceremonies were heavily attended, at least if you counted the wild monkeys darting in and out of the structures.

We tanked up on good food at a local Indian restaurant in Padam's neighborhood, enjoying Tandori chicken, real chicken, not scraps of meat like we are served on the mountain. We also had garlic naan, curry and cokes. After the incredibly satisfying meal, I went with Padam to select the porter. The choice of porter was key as I wanted to move quickly. If the weather was cooperative, my improved physical condition could allow us to cover a lot of ground quickly. If we moved fast enough, I hoped to add the Annapurna Base Camp Trek to our itinerary. This was very ambitious, but we've already established I am not sane. We went to a guiding company Padam knew and interviewed porters. We were very clear about the pace and distance we wished to cover each day. I am not sure they believed me, but as Padam would say, "What to do, what to do?" So we hired an enthusiastic, young porter named Seba and ventured off to finish our chores.

Last Day and on Our Way

To get to the start of the trek, we took a local bus to Besi Sahar. It was full of all the pains of a local bus: bad seats, frequent stops, and delays caused by haggling locals negotiating a ride for a few kilometers. It reminded me of a larger version of the buses in Tanzania. We passed one non-picturesque village after another. As we got closer the villages got dumpier and dumpier. Although larger than the other villages, Besi Sahar looked just as bad.

We had a nice dinner with a Spanish trekker and his guide. After dinner we went to my room and watched a bad movie on my laptop, at least it passed time. After the movie I went right to bed and slept great, as we were under 900m / 3,000' in altitude.

First Day of the Trek

I got up around 6:15 am and was ready to roll. We had breakfast and were on the trail within an hour. The beginning was inauspicious to say the least, it was a dirt road where commuter buses outnumbered the trekkers. While the trail was full of Nepalese, it was nearly void of trekkers. During the entire day we passed only six.

As a whole, the trek on the first day was not that magnificent. No ocular fest here. The villages were dreary, broken down and had little charm. This is a huge contrast to the first day of the Everest hikes or even the poor villages of Burma. I hoped it would improve, it had to. In addition, another growing problem was the speed of Padam and our porter Seba. We hadn't walked more than four hours at low altitude and Padam was unable to match what I considered a comfortable walking pace of just over five kilometers / three miles per hour. We got to the proposed destination before noon and I definitely wanted to continue to walk through a few more towns.

We had lunch at a town called Bahum Danda and Padam and I decided we would continue farther. We met another guide and a bunch of Israeli girls who decided to follow a similar plan. However, as they left Seba was nowhere to be found. Finally, after impatiently waiting for two hours, I decided to run down and find him. I went all the way to the last rise and there he was plodding along. I explained our plan and his tersely-toned response was a question, "Where's Padam?" Unable to communicate effectively, I ran back up to Padam and we waited for Seba.

Seba was definitely odd. On one hand he seems very honest and caring and on the other hand very stubborn. He told us, "This is how fast I walk and if you don't like it to get another porter." I had never experienced a porter who was anything but humble and hard working. We didn't overload him with weight. In fact, I was actually carrying quite a bit of weight myself, thereby lightening his load considerably. He only agreed to carry our bags to the next town. At least that kept us moving and we could decide what to do there.

Once on the trail it started to pour. I wasn't too happy that I wasted all the good weather waiting. We hid out at some family's house where we found the Israeli girls and waited for it to stop. After half an hour the rain ceased and we decided to head to the town of Syange. It was grungy, but at least it had electricity. I really wanted to go farther, but we worried about Seba and called it a day.

The Israelis picked the same town and guest house to spend the night. The hustle and bustle were a stark contrast to the solitude of my Gokyo Ri trek a month before. It was a culture shock to have so many trekkers in one place. I hung out with a sole German girl named Sandra and the few girls from Israel, but in the end we called it an early night.

We cut our goal back for the next day to Bagarchhap, because that was as far as Seba was willing to agree upon. We desperately needed to find another porter. He even barked at Padam that it was Padam's responsibility to ensure his safety. While this is true, we were very clear about our intended pace before we left Kathmandu. Was I being unreasonable? I didn't think so. What a change this was from the great porters I had on my previous treks.

On to Bargarchhap

All night I heard the rain coming down hard on the roof and kept hoping I was wrong. I tried to tell myself that maybe the sound wasn't rain, but a nearby river or waterfall. After all, the rain couldn't possibly be coming down that hard. After thunder echoed through the valley, I found myself hoping it was the police practicing exploding bombs like on Gokyo Ri. Eventually, I got up and looked, but it was still pouring out. So much for the early start, at this point I was hoping for any start.

By 9:00 am it cleared up enough for us to brave the trail. Padam talked to Seba again and apparently came to an understanding. He was free to leave if he wanted to, however it wasn't that simple. Faced with the reality of being fired and other possible repercussions back in Kathmandu, Seba backed off and agreed to continue. I didn't like the tension, but didn't know what else to do. The compromise they agreed to was that Padam would now carry his sleeping bag as well as his personal belongings instead of Seba carrying them for him. So to make it easier for Padam I agreed to carry my laptop and batteries. Padam volunteered to carry it all, but Padam was sick before we began and I didn't want to overload him.

We finished breakfast and headed out. The river we followed roared fiercely as it was fed with the runoff from many tributaries and waterfalls trying to wring out from the storm. The path was rocky, slippery and still non-picturesque. As we walked we did at least pass a few guest houses that looked newer and more on the level with that in the Khumbu Valley (Everest Region).

We stopped for lunch at the town of Chamje. Given our slow progress and the weather, we cut our goal back to reach the town of Tal. After lunch we had some brief spots of sun and the landscape began to improve with deep cutting rivers ripping through the valley carving gorges right through the rock. It was particularly impressive when two rivers cut through the high stone walls and came together into a single confluence. I hoped we put the worst of the weather and dilapidated towns behind us.

Contrary to my wishes, the sun disappeared and the cool gray clouds returned. It was a shame as we were so close to the snow-capped mountains, yet they were barely visible at the base of the valley. They tried hard to peek out behind the clouds, but they weren't succeeding. Padam looked at them and worried, indicating they shouldn't be covered in snow. As we walked a dejected group was headed down. "It's closed, too much snow," answering our question before we even asked it. While it was obvious they were talking about the Thorung La Pass, I was unsure what they meant by "closed." Did that mean they were stopped by the administration from going or that it was just difficult to go through? If we had a large enough group breaking the trail, would that work? I didn't know and hoped we wouldn't have to make a difficult decision.

We got to Tal and to our surprise Seba was only a half an hour behind us. Padam ripped into him, in a slightly friendly tone, and told him he could do better. I think he did just fine. The town of Tal was built on a sand bank next to a river that clearly rose higher than its current level. I wouldn't have wanted to be there when it did. These guest houses were more pleasant than those before, which was odd as we were getting farther and farther away from a main road. In contrast to the stone-cut buildings in the Khumbu Valley, these were cement constructions with etchings in them to make them look like bricks. Happily, they had electricity here, so I was beginning to be hopeful I might have power for the rest of the trip.

The best laugh of the trip so far was when the three Israeli girls showed up. One came in like she was in charge of the place, trying to figure out if it were to her standards. The modest guest house owner told the girls they were full, even though they weren't. Apparently, Israelis had a reputation for being loud, bossy and messy. Bravo to this Nepalese woman who wasn't willing to sell out. Quieter Israelis, Lior and his ex-girlfriend showed up. They were certainly an interesting choice of trekking partners. Interestingly, they were showed available rooms.

Dinner continued to be the identical fare as the previous night's. Oddly, all the menus were basically the same within a region with nearly identical prices and variety. As we just entered a new district, I was hoping for a change in menu. After dining with Lior and his ex, we ended up in a heated discussion about the Holocaust. They argued that the Holocaust was different than any other genocide. I have always had a problem with this thought process. I, for one, find all genocides equally unacceptable and find the lack of concern over other genocides a failure of the Jewish people to truly understand the meaning of "Never Forget." For the record I am Jewish. We also got into another discussion about Jewish people buying German products. It certainly wasn't a boring night and one of the experiences I enjoy most about trekking.

Where to Today?

I slept great, nothing like a heated political debate to help you settle in for the night. While waiting for breakfast the Swiss were ripping on me for being American and stating that I was the cause of the rain. So it seemed like the political banter was not yet over. They were laughing at how America was just beginning to be concerned about the environment. I tried to explain to them not all Americans had their head in the sand, just the current administration.

It was still raining when Sandra headed out. We tried to get Seba to start before us, but he refused to leave without us. It seemed he didn't trust us to follow him. He was clearly safer starting ahead and having us catch up to him than leaving him walking behind alone. His actions continually perplexed me.

So, we started out and Padam immediately fell way behind. Walking alone, I was not happy. My mood didn't improve as it started to rain and rain hard. A miserable cold, soaking rain that I thought couldn't get worse. Oh, but I was wrong. Hail was then added to the equation. About this time I reached a fork in the path I remembered Padam telling Sandra to take the high road, so I did. Up, and up, and up I went until I noticed that way down below there was a bridge to cross the river. I was on the wrong trail. So I headed back down and found Padam running up to catch me. As we got on the right trail it rained even harder, so we stopped in a small village to grab some tea. As we got started walking again, we found Sandra in a tea house with the front courtyard completely underwater. We agreed to walk together, but after going up a bit I was starting to pull away. I told her and Padam I would head up to Bagarchhap and order lunch for us so we could save time and possibly still reach the village of Chame. One aspect of trekking in Nepal that I now fully appreciate is the ability to flex your schedule as the weather and your progress requires.

Padam neglected to tell me an important detail, most of Bagarchhap was washed away in a flood. I blew right past the remnants of the town, never even realizing I was passing through a town at all. I ended up in a lifeless village called Danaque before I was told I had passed what was left of Bagarchhap. I ran back to find my would-be lunch dates and happily found them coming up the road. Padam quickly realized that I missed the town and had continued up the path. We ordered lunch in Danaque and watched not just the rain come down, but many downhearted trekkers. It seemed like many people were being held up at the top of the trail just before the pass and finally gave up hope of getting through. By 1:30 pm we had finished lunch and decided to continue. Padam sent Seba first, and this time he actually listened. After a short bit we realized our folly as the rain that was coming down in buckets here would clearly be coming down as snow up on the mountain. The sobering reality was that there was no rush to get up because we would just have to wait. The reality didn't sit well with me, but as Padam states again and again, "What to do, what to do?" It was an expression I would hear all too often on our trip. So, we decided to turn around and regroup. Unfortunately, Seba was up the trail from us, so I ran up after him. He was quite confused

by my explanation, but was certainly happy to be turning around once he understood my intentions. We decided there was no harm in waiting a day. As we hung out, more and more people were descending. Some told us that trekkers were stuck in Manang and that they weren't able to go up or down. So at least our temporary hold seemed like the right decision.

On to Chame, Again!

The next day things started to turn for the better. Being superstitious, I put on my favorite bandana, which I usually wear at the start of a trip for good luck. It had belonged to a dear friend, who unfortunately passed away of brain cancer. By taking it on each trek, I felt like she was coming with me. Clearly, my transgression was the reason for the bad weather. Seba headed out first, then Sandra and then us. We quickly caught Sandra on the first big rise and continued at a good clip. Confusion soon ensued. Hordes of people were marching down, each with a different story: two meters of snow, one meter of snow, the police turning people around, four days sitting in Manang, white out blizzards and waist deep snow. Pick your poison, if any of them were true, our circuit of Annapurna was done. However, the cynic in me, or optimist depending on how you look at it, always felt that when everyone follows one course of action (take the late investors in the stock or real estate market before they crashed) that it's usually about the point that fortunes reverse themselves. With everyone giving up, I hoped it meant that when we got up the trail it would be clear for us to pass. When we reached a guard post, Padam checked and 38 people had already come down by 10:30 am.

As we walked, we hopped on and off the "new road" they were building. At the time it was just pieces of dirt roads they hoped to connect into a single road to Manang. At first it sounds horrible and that the trek would be ruined. However, I have to say that every time there was a choice between the old trail and the new road, we opted for the new road and I can't say I was upset at the prospect of walking on a gently sloped path for a while. The problem would arrive when the cars started traveling it.

As we passed through the town before Chame, I noticed a sign for phone service. It was the first phone I saw in days. Not one to call home on treks, I had started dating my girlfriend Jennifer shortly before my winter travels. Wanting to still have a girlfriend when I returned, I tried to call home when I could. This turned out to be a wise move, as Jennifer is now my wife. I talked for about four very expensive minutes before it cut out. Apparently expensive does not equal reliable. They were unable to reconnect me.

We made it to Chame twenty minutes later, with plenty of time to walk farther. However, it didn't make sense to press higher. We needed time for the previous four days of snow to melt if we had any chance of going over the pass. As we were waiting for lunch we watched people coming by in both directions. You could tell from their facial expressions which way they were going; hopeful expressions on the people going up and disgust on those in retreat downward.

The guest house we chose turned out to be the best one so far in Annapurna. We were in the lap of luxury. First, we had nails in the walls. You would think all places would provide a mechanism to hang your clothes, but none so far had anything. Then, to our delight, our room had two light bulbs, we would actually be able to see at night. To top this off, they brought burning embers from the fire into the dining hall to heat it up. All of this cost just one dollar a person per night. After a quick lunch, that a local dog was eyeing quite hungrily, I went out to watch a bunch of local kids playing street cricket. I introduced them to Guinness beer via my promotional Frisbee that I carried. See, I learned something since Burma. They were amazingly adept with it and enjoyed it immensely. We played for a good hour and without speaking a single word to each other.

I tried calling my girlfriend back, but the phone wasn't being very cooperative. Padam negotiated a much better rate, so if I could connect I could actually talk without it costing more than the entire day's expenses. Finally in mid dinner, they reached her. Padam rocked. I didn't even realize he shushed the room so I could hear better. Way to go Padam!

After dinner we all watched *Wallace and Grommit* in the dining hall. The guest house owner's kid watched as well. Seems they are quite universal characters. When the movie was over, we headed to our room to get some much needed sleep. The noise level from the room next to us was unbelievable. However, I wasn't called the "Geek of Sleep" in college for nothing. I passed out until 6:00 am the next day.

On to Pisang

We woke the next day to clear skies again, and hoped our luck would hold out. After a quick breakfast, we all headed out quickly by 8:00 am. I assumed Padam would go with me, but he wanted to go slow even though he said he was feeling better. He claimed he didn't want to get to the next town early, because it would be "boring." As I feared, when we started, I broke away even though I was still only averaging just over three miles per hour on a trail that was basically the unfinished road. The trail was wide, with a gradual incline, and had no snow, except where there was the remains of a huge avalanche, making it an easy walk. The only difficulty was later in the day when it got quite windy. So, I drafted behind a porter that was carrying a load over one meter wide and over two meters long. I felt bad for him, but my scrawny frame wouldn't have blocked much wind.

Shortly after I reached a town with a tea house and decided to grab a cup of tea while I waited for Padam. When Padam caught up we pressed on after a few minutes; it seemed like I could always come up with a reason to get going quickly. Today's reasons were to avoid avalanches, get on the snow before it turned slushy and wet, and of course the traditional, I wanted better light for my photographs.

Right after the break, the trail turned really slick. It was covered in "Snice," as I call it, half packed snow and half ice. So, we continued together, but at a much slower pace, taking care not to fall too many times. While the trail degraded, the views improved dramatically to the more traditional mountain panoramas that I expected to see in the Himalayas. I could definitely see skipping the first couple of days when the road is completed and just starting in Chame. After about an hour we came upon another very quaint village whose first establishment was a bakery. Since it is a good idea to support the locals, and having nothing to do with the sweet, aromatic smell pervading the air, we stopped for cinnamon rolls and tea. Seba even joined us. It was the first time I felt like we were a team since the first night.

After the snacks we trekked on to the town of Pisang, going the entire way without passing a single trekker. It was a quiet and wonderful walk, even though we had a strong headwind blasting in our faces. When we got to Pisang, we picked a guest house that was a bit older, hoping to avoid the loud crowds. Padam said it's not as nice as it once was, but it seemed fine. Apparently other people had the same idea as the guest house filled up quickly, but it seemed like a much quieter group. Dinner was crowded and we had to wait for everyone to get served before we did. While waiting, I finished *A Walk in the Woods*. It was quite disappointing. The author, Bill Bryson, declared himself a thru-hiker even though he didn't finish the Appalachian Trail! Given the frustrations I was battling, I burned the book in disgust. At least it lightened our load. There were no Israelis staying at the guest house. Apparently some showed up, but were turned away. It's quite interesting to see how their behavior causes a clash in cultures between them and the Nepalese.

On to Manang

I fell asleep early, but couldn't stay asleep. Perhaps I wasn't as acclimatized to the ever increasing altitude as I thought. Breakfast was also a bit late, so we didn't hit the trail until 8:15 am. Unfortunately, fifteen minutes made a big difference. A few huge, slow moving groups were in front of us, and with the trail narrowed by snow, it took almost two miles to get by them and into the open.

The walk itself was uneventful, but gorgeous, with views of Annapurna II, III, and IV, as well as Gangapurna. The trek started at a cool 0°C / 32° F, but within an hour the "oven" of reflecting snow was cooking me and all my jackets came off. My thermometer now registered over 16° C/ 60° F. This changed, though, as the last stretch of the walk was directly into the wind and was quite cold. Regulating body temperature was a constant battle that required lots of removable layers to stay comfortable.

Padam accompanied me for the majority of the walk. First he claimed he wanted to keep pace with Sandra, but after he left her to walk with me he claimed, "my legs don't work," and faded badly. Seba was even keeping pace with him. Padam apparently didn't understand the concept of lactic acid and the fact that charging back to catch me put him over his anaerobic threshold. Seba on the other hand had come a long way. He was more responsive and friendly, later in the trek Padam told me he explained to Seba, the night before leaving Pisang, if he did a good job I would probably give him a generous tip.

Just before we got to Manang, we got to see the vultures of Nepal up close. With about a two-meter / six-foot wingspan, they are imposing birds. We stopped in Manang, which is one of the more elaborate towns on the mountain. The bakeries were as good as you will find this high up and the guest houses

were comfortable and clean. For this reason most people stay there for a day of acclimatization. However, at only 3,500m / 11,500', I felt it was too low to acclimatize. Due to our slow rise in altitude, later would be better. I think since it's the last real town on this side of the pass, people wanted to enjoy it. I certainly did. Given the cleanliness, I tried a yak burger for lunch, it was quite tasty and more importantly I had no ill effects afterward. I met a wonderful Swiss couple, who were also into photography. So we chatted and relaxed the rest of the afternoon, while eating pastries from the bakery. They were travelling the world and stayed in touch with me throughout their travels. We're even Facebook buddies now.

We also met an unfortunate German guy who tried to get over the pass with his girlfriend and guide. Apparently they were breaking trail in fairly deep snow and he just collapsed. The story varies a bit depending who told it, but the gist is that his girlfriend went down for help, but no one would go back up as evening approached. Eventually, he told the guide to go down, as "we both don't have to die." He stayed up there all night, huddled in two sleeping bags before hobbling down the next day with totally frostbitten hands. When I met him he had them bandaged and was in no mood to repeat the whole story again, so I didn't ask for a first person account.

On to Yak Kharka

We were going to shoot up close to the pass, but instead decided to split the altitude gain over two days. We started with a day hike around Manang and then walked halfway up to the town before the pass. The day hike was a quick jump up to see the lake, glacier, mountain and town from up high. It was a pretty awesome view, but tainted because the lake was still frozen.

After the day hike, we grabbed a quick bowl of soup and headed up to Yak Kharka. No news was good news, as we didn't see any people coming down because the pass was closed. Unfortunately, I talked to at least five people who were coming down due to altitude problems. This solidified my theory that people's acclimatization plans were askew. Interestingly, the guidebook doesn't say their plan prevents altitude sickness. It only prevents death from altitude sickness. Nice distinction.

As it turned out the first half of the climb to Yak Kharka strained me and I am not sure why. We passed the nice Swiss couple, hiding in the shade and not looking too well. The girl, Stephanie, suffered from food poisoning. I hoped they would make it.

As we progressed the heat was brutal. I think that's what may have affected me. I hydrated well and recovered for the second half of our walk. The snow was much worse, with LSS (Leg Sucking Snow) enveloping our boots. We made it though and Seba continued to improve in both effort and attitude. He even volunteered to carry Padam's jacket. Along the way we passed some beautiful orange butterflies, no one apparently told them winter was staying late this year.

Once at the guest house, I cleaned up and put on a fresh pair of underwear. I felt almost human. On a long trail it is indeed the little things that make a difference. I even got to try something new, sea buckthorn tea, which was just warm juice made from sea buckthorn berries. It tasted great and is supposed to have lots of antioxidants. It was a little risky as I didn't know if they boiled the water properly, but what the hell, you have to take some risks. I met a group of very kind Israelis staying at our guest house. Turns out they went up to the next town, Ledar, and were treated so rudely that they walked an hour back down the trail to our friendly guest house.

Unfortunately, I slept poorly again. I also developed a little bit of a headache. I wanted to justify it away as dehydration, but given that is a common mistake I paid careful attention to my body. I was definitely glad we decided to take an extra day to get to Thorung Phedi before going over the pass. Before I could leave the guest house, word got out that I was the "photographer guy." I guess shooting one hour long exposures at night gets people's attention. Anyway, I became the camera doctor for the guest house owner who had a camera that she couldn't get open. After showing her that covering the door with your hand when you press "open" doesn't work, she was exceptionally grateful.

To Thorung Phedi and Beyond

Once again we changed our plans and decided instead of heading to Thorung Phedi, the standard stop before the pass, we'd push another 400m /1,300' higher and sleep at the high camp. One could view this as increasing our risk of altitude sickness. However, my thought was that if I slept too high and felt bad in the morning, I would know and come down. If on the other hand I slept lower, headed to cross the Thorung Phedi Pass, and got in trouble, then I would have a huge problem on my hands. I viewed my "risk" as the conservative approach.

We got an even later start than usual, 9:00 am, but it was a beautiful day and we made good progress through the early part of the trail. However, our luck would change as the trail became quite hazardous with a steep, dropping cliff on one side of us. The very narrow ledge we were supposed to walk across was not very reassuring. I stepped in holes made by previous trekkers, not daring to skip a step as I had on previous sections. The problem was the footprints were much smaller than my feet and often pigeon-toed to an uncomfortable degree. Along the way I got behind a few guys who were really struggling with the terrain. They had no walking sticks. Aside from being inconvenient, it was a danger to themselves and me. Avalanches were a fairly prevalent occurrence and getting caught on a ledge can be quite dangerous. As I walked, I witnessed more than one rock come tumbling down and didn't want to be around if it started a chain reaction. Just another reason I like to walk by myself and out in front. I also noticed that while I walked with the group our size and noise scared away any possible wildlife sightings.

We got to Thorung Phedi in good time and took a much needed break. The fort-like guest house was filled with a pack of Germans I had heard were ahead of us. It made getting lunch very slow as there were 15 people in the group, plus porters and guides. At least one of them was quite friendly and I chatted with him about other treks as well as his experiences in Nepal.

After lunch we headed up a steep incline to the high camp and the entry point of the pass. It was a 400m / 1,300' climb and literally straight up. By doing it in advance, aside from the acclimatization benefits, it also saved us a grueling hour on the hardest day of the trek. Instead of walking up in the ice cold morning, we exchanged one extreme for another with the sun radiating from the snow in all directions. The walk up was like being in a kiln, sapping all the liquid from our bodies. We progressed slowly and tried to steadily climb to the top. Padam, Seba and I walked the closest together so far. The problem was on the way up it was so slick I felt like George Jetson on the treadmill going nowhere in the slush. Finally, we turned a corner and saw the high camp just 100 meters ahead as we went by a nearly passed out Israeli sprawled across the trail. Concerned, we checked on his well being, and he was more frustrated and tired than in difficulty, so we continued up toward our destination.

The guest house was quite different than the previous ones. The rooms had dirt walls, or as the eco-friendly would say, earthen walls. Padam thought this was great, as they would provide better insulation. Hell, if it kept us warm, I'd love it, too. Oddly, the rooms did have electricity, quite an unusual combination. There were apparently other inconveniences of high camp. There was no water source. The other trekkers were melting snow, but fortunately, Padam brought out his charm and saved me a lot of work by getting me complimentary water to filter from the guest house. They normally charge per glass or liter, but he negotiated something so we didn't get charged. Padam was an enigma. At times he was incredibly resourceful and other times irresponsible, but he was always entertaining and that counted for a lot during a long trek.

I wanted to eat early as we were going to get up at 4:30 am to get out on the pass at daybreak. So, I put my dinner order in early to try to get ahead of the 15 or so non-Nepalese guests. I shouldn't have rushed, dinner was dreadful. It was so salty my mouth felt like it shrunk to half its size. I was pucker-lipped all night regardless of how much water I drank. It wasn't just mine that was horrible, not a single soul had a positive word to say about their meal. Could they have done this to sell more water? Who knew. After dinner I went right to bed, although I couldn't sleep much. I also developed the cough from hell. I had read where mountaineers cough so hard that they can crack a rib and until now I didn't understand how that was possible. Let me tell you, they are not exaggerating.

Over the Pass and on We Go

We got up by 4:30 am and were in the dining hall by 5:00 ready to roll. Most of the guests were there, but nobody was ordering breakfast after last night's so called dinner. I guess it would be pretty hard to get a skilled chef to live at over 4,800m / almost 16,000'. Instead of breakfast, we just waited around until there was enough light to see. I didn't feel it was worth walking with a head lamp and risking slipping over a ledge. So at 5:45 am we headed out. Sadly, it was just after the German group came by. We got stuck behind them and it felt like being back on Kilimanjaro slogging our way up to the summit at a painfully slow pace.

The problem was the "trail." It was a tiny ledge cut into an ice sheet on the side of the mountain where it was very dangerous to pass. So I sat at the back of the pack until they decided to stop, you know, to breathe. Padam already fell behind, apparently having dropped and lost his water bottle. That meant I had to share mine with him. Again, just like I had on Kilimanjaro. The déjà vu was quite strong that morning. On Kilimanjaro I ended up incredibly dehydrated and had vowed not to let it happen again.

Once we ditched the Germans it was clear sailing over the pass. Padam and Seba trailed behind me, but I came upon a group of porters walking at about my pace and followed them. It was an amazingly comfortable trek, considering we were climbing to over 5,400m / 17,600'. The mountains towered above us on all sides, and while I expected blistering, cold winds it was quite comfortable. The morning temperatures when we started were between -5° to -2° C / 25° to 30° F and rose considerably as we progressed. Along the way there was a false peak, but shortly afterward we reached the sign indicating the high point of the pass. It was a glorious moment for me, as a week earlier I thought the weather would never allow us to reach this point.

However, getting to the pass was just the start of the day. It turned out that down was more difficult than the up. The trail became less trodden on the descent and it was significantly more steep and slick. It was not at all fun. I tried the best I could to step in the footprints of those who came before me, but it wasn't easy. After dropping the first 460m / 1,500' or so, and breathing denser air, I waited for Padam to catch up. When he did, he informed me, with a smile of course, that it would get a lot worse. Padam picked a bad time to be right. The way down was a brutal slip-sliding affair. I fell twice, with acrobatic flair, if I do say so myself. Padam fell many times or as Seba liked to put it, "He fell more than nine times."

We stopped at a tea house for a celebratory Coke and then headed to Muktinath, which turned out to be one of the more interesting villages on the trek. Padam wanted to get holy water from the temple there, so we walked around it, but unfortunately, it appeared to be closed. Instead, we walked into town and stopped at the Bob Marley Guest House for lunch. It was a considerable change from the high camp. We ate outside on an upper deck and I had succulent eggplant ravioli. That's what I call a proper reward for our hard work.

Overzealous hiker that I am, I wanted to pick up a day and try to still have time to make the trek up to Annapurna Base Camp. So, we headed to Jomson, a good dozen or so miles down the road. The extra drop in altitude, promise of Internet access and ability to call my girlfriend also motivated my crazy plan. It was a huge undertaking considering we already walked close to six hours through the hardest part of the trail, but the trail basically followed the "new road," so I figured we would make good time. We passed a number of scary looking villages as the road snaked along a dry river bed. We were greeted with a bird-like call. I believe you are familiar with it, although I hadn't heard this call for many days. It is called a horn. There were motorcycles scurrying up and down. It was unsettling after so long without seeing internal combustion. As we entered the riverbed, the sand-laden wind whipped in our faces at about 30 mph. I was warned about this, but thought it was an exaggeration. This torture went on for miles until we finally reached Jomson.

Once in town I thought we were done, but the town went on and on with the guest houses on the farthest end. While Jomson lacked any real charm, it was far more modern than any other village of the trek. They had satellite Internet and our guest house resembled more of a cheap hotel than a shack. It had a bathroom and a hot shower in the room, a queen size bed and the room temperature never dropped below 13° C / 55° F. Figuring it might be safe to try meat, I had a yak steak for supper. While I am sure it wasn't fillet mignon quality, it tasted as if it were.

Second Day from Hell, In a Row

I got up early to get organized, which turned out to be a good thing. Even though the guest house was nearly empty, someone above me started the day with a few harmonious Buddhist chants. The guest house turned out great for me, but was a bit of a rip off by Nepalese standards. They charged a lot for the room, 500 rupees or $8. In addition, they charged Padam and Seba for their meals, which is not standard Nepalese etiquette. However, it's a small price to pay for a working shower.

We left Jomson, and all of its amenities, by 8:00 am with a good 20 km / 18-19-mile day ahead of us. We were not sure how far we were going to go, but wanted to push far down the mountain and see if we still had enough time to add the Annapurna Sanctuary portion to our trek. We started well, and got to the first town, Marpha, in about an hour. Many trekkers skipped it, as the new road bypassed the town, but how could you not stop for the "world-famous" apple pie. While they grow all the apples locally, it was too early in the season to get fresh apples. So we really went out of our way for nine month old apples. Padam first brought me some spiked apple cider. I thought that maybe getting drunk was their plan to help us forget about the age of the apples. I guess it worked, because the accompanying apple pie tasted great.

Shortly after Marpha, Padam fell significantly behind again. His new excuses were his feet hurt, that I was an athlete and I was too tall with whom to keep pace. However, after getting into a good groove I just went about my walking until a tractor pulled up honking. It was Padam. He asked if I wanted a lift. As we discussed taking a tractor the night before, I was a bit peeved. I had stated that we could hire a tractor for Seba, but that we should walk. So when I replied I didn't want a ride, he stated that he would meet me in Lete and asked if I would like him to take my pack. Having been without my equipment on Kilimanjaro, I promptly said no and before I could say anything else, he was gone in a puff of tractor dust. I didn't even know where Lete was. I assumed it must be a small town just ahead. I was horrified when I pulled out my map and saw that it was a good 16 km / 10 miles down the road and past where we agreed to have lunch. I was totally pissed. To add insult to injury, I didn't see Seba in the tractor, which meant that any time saved would be lost when we had to wait for him to catch up.

Fuming, I stomped down the trail. There were many times I had to choose between the new road and the old path and didn't know which to pick. As luck would have it, I usually selected the harder trail. Eventually, I got to another fork, this one with a bridge. I was pretty sure both paths led to my destination, but wasn't sure which was correct. There was a sign that said "TOPA" with everything else worn away. I assumed it meant KaTOPAni, the town before the one I was supposed to meet my tractor-driven guide. Of course, the path went up and up and it eventually led to a town with no name. It was dreary with no real guest or tea houses. I crossed another bridge and could see a town map. I hoped it was Katopani. Luckily, it read Kato-pani/Lete.

After about five minutes I saw Seba. Apparently he was on the tractor as well and I just didn't notice him. There was some hope for Padam yet. A lot of my anger faded knowing he got a break. When I stepped in the guest house, everyone burst out laughing. Apparently, I got there only thirty minutes after their two-hour tractor ride. They all assumed I would arrive many hours later. I half jokingly, half seriously ripped on Padam for being a lazy ass. I told him he let a scrawny white guy embarrass him and that Nepalese men were supposed to be strong walkers. The banter went on for a bit, with Padam trying to teach me the words to slow down, "bestari, bestari." However, the other guide decided to teach me words that Padam would not, "cheto, cheto," which meant faster, faster. The rest of the trip to Ghasa was easy and the skies cleared for a rather pleasant walk.

My best laugh of the day was hearing Padam complain about the tractor ride. "It was too dusty. It was tiring because it bounced so much. It stopped too many times," etc. Then Padam had a revelation, "You know I should have given my pack to Seba for the tractor and walked with you." Wow, what a novel idea.

Interestingly, they said if I had gotten a ride in the tractor I would have had to hide under a blanket. Apparently there is a lot of resentment related to the road they were building. By giving someone a lift, they would be helping kill the lower elevation towns. The towns rely on trekkers stopping at given intervals and eating/sleeping at the guest houses. As modern internal combustion hits the mountain, people will start skipping towns and the towns the road was built to support may die. I was told if the tractor driver was caught he would be fined 10,000 rupees or beat up. Unfortunately, this is destined to happen.

On to the Hot Springs and Tatopani

Now at lower altitudes, I finally had a great night's sleep, over nine hours and I needed it. As we left town we passed many work crews on the new road. Their chores ranged from manually hauling dirt to chipping away at rocks or driving pipes to drill holes for dynamite. Halfway through the hike we passed a beautiful waterfall, so we took a break. Just after the falls, we passed another group working on the road. They were trying to roll a huge boulder down the mountain and get it away from the road. We watched for close to half an hour as they tried to leverage it with poles and flip it over. They finally gave up and all ran down the mountain for lunch. As we continued, Padam informed me he had lost his walking stick again, and asked to borrow one of mine. On top of this, he lost half the medication I gave him earlier. When we finally arrived in Tatopani, it was like climbing and reaching a false peak. The town started with a few buildings and then went back to wilderness for quite a while until we arrived in the heart of town. When we did get to town, we got caught in a Nepalese traffic jam of people and oxen. While the town was described like Thamel, with lots of open air restaurants. The comparison was certainly a stretch. To it's credit, it purportedly had hot springs. Given my experience in Peru at the end of the Inca Trail Trek where the "hot springs" were way too skanky to take a dip, I was quite leery of what they would look like. Tatopani's hot springs turned out to be significantly better. There were two slate lined "pools" and a place to rinse off before you took a dip. I soaked for twenty minutes, not wanting to soften my already abused feet too much. After the refreshing treat I went back to the guest house and had a number of nice conversations with some Americans, a Kiwi, a Canadian and an Austrian. It was a pleasant exchange with the topics ranging from the road being built around Annapurna, to Mormonism, global warming and electric cars. We hit a little bit of everything.

To Gorapani

We left around 8:00 am and headed for Gorapani. Most people were either hanging out for another day, heading only halfway there or taking the shortcut out to the town of Beni to finish their trek. I couldn't fathom people would stop now when the best view of the Himalayas is supposed to be from a morning trek to Poon Hill, only an hour up from Gorapani.

The trail started down the riverbed and was easy for a bit. However, as we reached the bend the path left the riverbed and headed straight up never-ending stone steps. It was amazing. If there was a break in the steps, it was only for a few yards and then they would start again. This went on for miles! Countering the painful ascent were some of the best landscape views of the trip. The valley we were climbing out of was lush with incredible farm land, Rhododendrons in bloom and the peaks of snow-capped mountains towering above. Slowly we climbed about 760m / 2,500' and then broke for an early lunch.

Lunch turned out to be a surprise. It was dal bhat, but dal bhat with soy beans. A nice change and a good source of much needed protein. After lunch, the pain continued with more steps and a drop in altitude equal to the morning's gain. While our journey was less than four hours of actual walking time, we took over two hours of breaks, including lunch.

At one break point, I got a can of real mango juice. It was even cold! The luxuries of leaving high altitude were an appreciated treat. However, the guest house's outhouse was something of another matter. It was the worst "facilities" I ever graced. It didn't even have a hole in the floor. Instead it had a stack of slate for you to squat on and a slide for your business to roll downhill. This was all exacerbated by the incredibly low ceiling and the fact that when I stepped on the slate it almost flipped over. At least I only had two more days until I got back to real bathrooms.

Along the way there was a sweet familiar fragrance permeating the air. At first I couldn't place it. It was hard to imagine that there was a pleasant smell overriding the odor of donkey crap rising from the trail. Turns out we entered an area with lilacs in bloom. When we got within one thousand feet of Gorapani, I decided to push it up the hill. Padam fell behind and when we met in the town he questioned how one could get faster when one is tired. I told him that his wife asked me to cause him pain. We bantered like brothers.

Gorapani is a typical Nepalese village with nothing to distinguish it from any other village other than the view. Unfortunately, as I arrived the mountain peaks were all under clouds. I met a wonderful Israeli couple and they invited me to have Shabbat dinner. Having already ordered my dinner, I ran back to eat that and then joined them for a few quick prayers, a little kosher wine and some wonderful conversation. They were such a joyous couple, I felt lucky to have met them. Their guide specialized in guiding Israelis and knew more of the prayers than I did.

Poon Hill and a Great View

I set my alarm for 2:20 am hoping to get a night photograph of the mountain range. When I woke the skies were clear and I was excited for our dark ascent. I knocked on Padam's door and he was ready to roll. A real trooper, he scolded me the night before not to go up by myself and that he would join me. We headed up to Poon Hill in the pitch black, climbing about 300m / 1,000' in a half an hour. It was so dark, at first I set my camera up in the wrong direction. Once it was set up right, I programmed it for an hour exposure. Padam and I sat, waiting in the cold. We stared up at dimly lit sky, watching for falling stars dropping from the heavens. I continually peeked at my watch like an expectant father, until finally the camera shutter clicked. The anticipation was great, as I wasn't sure if I had time to shoot again before the sun rose, so this had to work. A click of the camera button revealed, SUCCESS. The mountains were exposed fairly well and the stars circled the sky. At the time I didn't know that I should point the lens in the direction of the North Star, I just lucked out.

Bob, a German guy I met earlier, then showed up, followed by a few locals selling hot chocolate and tea. It was a rip off at a buck for a tiny cup, but much needed. So I bought a round, twice. As the sun started to warm the air, about 5:30-6:00 am, the hilltop flooded with nearly two hundred people. Hell, I didn't think I saw two hundred tourists in total over the previous two weeks. It was culture shock. However, this place is like the high points of the Torres del Paine Trek, with many people making this their sole destination from the closest point of entry. All in all, the sunrise was not that spectacular. The view was still excellent until around 7:00 – 8:00 am, so many people could have slept in instead of crawling up the path at 4:00 am. After coming down and checking out the photos, we decided to stay another day so I could attempt some shots in the evening as the views were great even a few hundred feet up the hill. Of course this required having power, which was completely unpredictable. Long exposures kill batteries. Luckily, I was able to fully recharge.

I have to return to the subject of taking care of one's business one more time. It's truly a sign you have acclimatized when you choose a squat toilet over a regular sit-down toilet due to the disgusting nature of the sit-down. Let's just say I had acclimatized. I caught a nap for a few hours in the afternoon and then my quiet guest house was invaded by a noisy group of

French people. Luckily, I was headed out for dinner with the Israelis. We cooked in their guest house kitchen, but they were very respectful of the Nepalese, trying hard not to get in their way. After dinner I headed back to my guest house to pick up my camera equipment. As I entered my one-time guest house, I sadly discovered the French turned it into a would-be discothèque. Gladly I was heading back out. By the time I returned, they had passed out.

On to Ghandruk

That night Padam dreamt he sawed off his feet. I just can't imagine what could have inspired that! The trail went through a moss covered Rhododendron forest interspersed with lilacs that gave the trail a refreshing scent. The trail first climbed about 305m / 1000' to a view equal to the one from Poon Hill. Honestly, we should have just climbed there to catch the early AM sunrise and miss the masses of people. It would have also saved us considerable time. Many of the Rhododendrons were in bloom, giving the forest a pleasant, reddish hue.

My experience with rude French people did not end, it would turn out to be my 24-hours of rude French. I spotted a French guy with a pro video camera. I complimented him, indicating what a nice camera he had. He arrogantly responded, "Yes, it is! I am French TV." Unfortunately, my French experience continued. A bit down the trail, we saw monkeys playing in the tops of the blooming Rhododendrons. Padam and I stealthfully moved to get in a good position for a photo. There were more than four monkeys up there, at least until another French group came by shouting "Look, monkeys!" Of course, that was the end of the monkeys, they all scattered. "Oh, they are running away again," shouted another of their boisterous party. No kidding! I wanted to run as well.

We did get a few more dramatic looks at the Fish Tail (Machhapuchre) Mountain, but the clouds started to roll over it. Padam said, "The mountains must be cold, they are wearing a coat." So we broke for lunch in Tadapani, a town surrounded by fifty foot Rhododendrons. Farther down the road, Padam suggested we wait up for Seba who was lagging behind. The area we were crossing had some theft problems in the past. It was a refreshing change for Padam to be concerned for Seba's welfare. Interestingly, the maps suggested group trekking in this area, a nice marketing spin. We got to the town of Ghandruk early, around 1:00 pm. There was pretty much nothing to do, so I took a walk around alone. First I stopped in the local "museum" that "highlighted" the history of the region. It had a few items, and I mean just as few, that were all kept in a single room. They had a water bottle, a milk jar and even a mouse trap. As I walked around where the locals lived, a few kids came up and asked for sweets, pens, then rupees. As I offered none, they honed in on my MP3 player. So I let each child try it for a few minutes and they loved it. They listened, danced and then fought over whose turn was next. Simple fun, that was one of the treasures of the trip and why village-based trekking is often superior to wilderness walks. Afterwards, I headed back to the guest house and ordered an early dinner as I wanted to shoot that night and get an early start to Pokhara. Dinner was awful, and that's being generous. I ordered a roast chicken and veggie pizza. Both tasted like cardboard and left me hungry, so I ordered a veggie noodle soup and hit the hay at 8:00 pm.

On to Civilization

I arose at 2:00 am to shoot Fish Tail Mountain. Some images were satisfying, except for the excessive camera noise that comes with long digital exposures. Waking up that early gave my mischievous mind too much idle time. There is an old expression, "Revenge is a dish best served cold." It is very cold in the Himalayas. I decided to get back at Padam for the tractor ride with Seba's help I placed rocks in his bag. He figured it out pretty quickly, but it was good for a laugh.

We hit the trail by 7:15 am and walked down a lot of steps. Passing some beautifully terraced farms, the trail eventually leveled off to a river. When we reached the town of Syauli Bazaar, Padam joyfully suggested we take a taxi. I would have none of it, I made my tired Nepalese friend walk the rest of the way to Nayapul. Unfortunately, the rest of the way was on a dirt road. It was shades of things to come once they complete the main road. There were lots of areas of the road that had standing puddles. Aside from being a pain and aesthetically unpleasing, it's also a health hazard as it breeds mosquitoes. Shortly, I heard the siren song of civilization, horns honking and my amazing trek was over. We took a local bus to Pokhara. It was speedy enough, but the uncomfortable seat hurt my butt that was no longer used to such comforts.

Pokhara was a pleasant change from other villages and cities in Nepal. Situated by a reasonably wide and quiet lake, it's much more peaceful than Kathmandu or its touristy suburb Thamel. We got our first real meal in two weeks at a lakeside restaurant. We relaxed while we engulfed a full juicy tandoori chicken and garlic naan. After lunch we walked around a bit, got a shave and haircut, and then went back to the hotel owned by Padam's sister-in-law. Guess who was waiting for me there? Sandra. She made it, although the group she joined to cross the pass took fourteen hours to complete the journey. We had a pleasant dinner of dal bhat cooked by the family who owned the guest house. It was much better than most of the dal bhat we had on the trail. After dinner Sandra and I visited some of the people she crossed the pass with and then called it an early night. I wished I had more time to relax there, but, alas, getting the police report for my stolen camera equipment from the start of our Nepal adventure called me to Kathmandu.

Back to Kathmandu

Getting back to Kathmandu turned into another adventure. Our bus struggled on the hills and eventually broke down about ten miles outside of the city limits. Padam and I quickly made an executive decision and got off. We flagged down a local bus to go the rest of the way. Unfortunately, after traveling about a ½ a mile, we hit a dead stop - gridlock. The traffic was awful, but we reached Kathmandu before sunset. Too late to stop by the police, I was dropped off at my guest house and took a relaxing night in the now fairly crowded Thamel.

Heading Home

After resolving my police issues, there was one last item on the to-do list before I left. I wanted a better photo of a snake charmer than from my previous trip. I hadn't seen one this time, so Padam and I headed out on his motorcycle to find one. We did, and he was very patient as I took lots of photos. After that it was a short ride to the airport for the multi-day trip home.

Epilogue

When Glenn Canyon was flooded by the creation of the Lake Powell Dam, the loss of pristine trekking trails was called progress. When the dam on the Yangtze River was built in China, flooding villages and a valley 365 square miles wide, again it was called progress. Now in Nepal the government is building roads in the Annapurna region from the villages of Beni to Muktinath as well as from Besi Sahar to Chame in the name of progress. While the construction of new roads allows supplies to reach towns far up the mountain far more quickly than the current porter/mule train system; the benefits come at a sobering cost. With the road incomplete, the dramatic contrast between walking on the new road versus the old trail is remarkable. The old trail is characterized by quiet, serene countryside alive with songbirds, monkeys and other wildlife. However, the new road is a wide flat path that often fills with mosquito-infested puddles, motorcycles and tractors. By contaminating the pristine environment, many trekkers may simply opt for another trek, one without the curse of internal combustion.

Is Annapurna doomed by progress? Opinions vary. Surprisingly, those most effected by the impact of the road, trekking operators, had a laissez-faire attitude citing that new alternative routes would open up to replace the traditional trail. Perhaps they are correct, let's hope so or the world will lose one of its unique treasures.

Kirk's Corner

Both Jeff and I had challenges with porters on the Annapurna Circuit. Although I completed this trek many years before we met, I witnessed a meltdown in the safety system, as basic as it was, that gets porters and trekkers through difficult conditions. Telling this story may help you learn about how treks can go wrong and what you can do to prevent it.

My arrival in the magical kingdom of Nepal was quite shocking. Walking the streets of Kathmandu was truly an experience likened to the Middle Ages of Europe: medieval architecture, vast open markets, wild dogs and cows wandering the streets among worshipers at thriving temples, thieving monkeys and open sewers.

Nepal is undoubtedly one of the poorest countries I have visited outside of Africa. The three primary employers in Nepal are tourism, agriculture, and a carpet and textile industry employing woman and children with nimble hands and fingers. Otherwise, the options for full-time employment are very limited. This leaves young men almost nothing to do when they leave the countryside and come to the Kathmandu Valley looking for a job. The living conditions for the average Nepalese are quite modest by anyone's standards, doctors are scarce, plumbing is rare and trash is everywhere. Despite these conditions that could easily foster pessimism and a bleak outlook, the Nepalese remain good-natured, friendly and have the desire to keep pushing on through the most difficult of circumstances. The two predominant cultural/religious influences are Hindu, pushing up from the Ganges plain in India, and Tibetan Buddhism, coming down from the mountains of the Tibetan Plateau. It all combines to create a vibrant fabric of life throughout Nepal. The other element in the mix is that historically, at least since opening its doors in the 70's, Nepal is host to travelers and trekkers who seek out this fascinating kingdom at the foot of the Himalayas.

Ultimately, the Kathmandu Valley combines indomitable people from two of the world's oldest cultures sprinkled with intrepid travelers living in a spectacular setting in the shadows of the world's highest mountains. Thus, the stage is set for a trek through some of the most majestic mountains and villages on planet earth.

I was in the same situation as many other dedicated trekkers with limited time. I had to select between the two major treks of Nepal, the Annapurna Region and the Everest Region. After careful consideration I chose the more village-oriented and culturally-rich Annapurna. In some ways I was surprised by my selection. I thought I would make a beeline for the geographic highest point on the planet, Mt. Everest.

The Himalayas begin where most other mountains end. Although not quite as high as Everest, the Annapurna mountains still dominate their landscape. I knew I would be impressed with their scope, but I didn't realize how much until I saw them up close. The Annapurna Circuit usually takes about three weeks and covers over 250 kilometers. It provides views of three of the ten highest mountains in the world, all over 8,000m / 26,240', and dozens of peaks over 7,000m / 22,960'. It more than exceeded my expectations!

In some ways I wasn't sure I would "enjoy" trekking in Nepal since I was accustomed to my traditional, more solitary North American Rocky Mountain wilderness experiences. The thought of sharing my mountain vistas and wilderness solitude with other trekkers and local villagers didn't sound appealing at first. As it turned out "tea house trekking," from village inn to village inn, was equally rewarding. There were not as many trekkers as I had expected. So, that was a real bonus. I have some very fond memories of sitting around the local family kitchen's wood-burning stove with an entire Nepalese family drinking tea, eating Tibetan bread and just being an observer of the family's interactions.

So, after eight wonderful days on the trail I found myself in the high Himalayas headed for Thorung La (La means pass). The steep climb to Thorung La was through a foot and a half of freshly fallen snow, with blinding sun, high winds, treacherous trails, bitter cold and stunning views to its summit at 5,416m / 17,765'! The fresh snow made it cold on the feet. Climbing to over 17,000' takes your breath away quite easily and several trekkers turned back. After several long and cold hours of slogging through the snow we ascended the pass. I was hiking slowly and taking lots of photography breaks. By the time we reached the Thorung La, we were some of the last to summit. I like it that way as it gives me a more solitary feeling. Atop the pass we stopped for a moment to enjoy the view and have a snack.

As we descended Padam, my guide and porter, bounded ahead anxious to celebrate with a cup of tea at a small tea house about three hours hike down the trail. It was then the situation got interesting. As many of you already know, one of my mantras of trekking is that "mountains don't care." In this case they didn't care about the three trekkers who became snow blind. This temporarily painful condition is easily prevented by sunglasses and can occur as a delayed reaction after exposure. The mountains also didn't care about the porter who went over the pass in flimsy canvas shoes and no socks. When I found him he had made it over the pass and through the snow, but his feet swelled from frostbite to about size seventeen and they could no longer fit in his shoes. He was struggling to walk along barefoot at the pace of a slow turtle.

I was stunned that he was left behind. A short way down the trail I spotted a lone trekker with a camera and a small day pack. With no one else in sight, I immediately thought that the injured porter belonged to him. When I confronted him, barely containing my anger. He immediately popped my balloon by telling me he had come up on a day hike from Muktinath, the other side from where I started.

I explained the porter's situation to the German trekker, Oliver. He agreed to help try and rescue him. There was virtually no one else around and we couldn't find out where or for who he was working. He spoke no English and we spoke essentially no Nepalese. They had taken most of his load leaving him a small pack with some cooking equipment figuring that although he was hurting, he could still make it down the pass. In the best case, they were waiting two hours below at the first tea house. After a surprisingly calm discussion over possible courses of action, our first step was to put socks on his feet and cut the top and back of his shoes to make room for his swollen feet. We had to de-lace our shoes and use the longer laces to try and keep his shoes on his feet as best we could. He could barely walk and it was literally painfully slow. Then we tried to support him with one of his arms around each of our shoulders to take the weight off his pained feet. It was no use. He could still barely walk, and it was hard to stay on the trail walking three abreast. At best it would take eight hours at this frost-bit pace.

It soon became apparent that we would not get off the mountain with the young porter on his own feet. If we wanted to be down that day we had no other choice than to attempt to carry him. Luckily he was small, about 120 pounds, and we alternated with Oliver and I switching off carrying him piggy-back style while the other carried all three of our packs. Oliver and I finally got the kid to the small tea house halfway from the top of the pass to the first lodging. There was a guide seemingly waiting, although he didn't come up the trail to help us as we struggled on the mountain. When we arrived he did confess that, yes, this was a porter on his team and he snickered a bit as to why we would help this young kid. Well, I was so upset I could hardly talk to the guy, but Oliver gave him a small, and unheard, lecture on the incident. The guide was the leader for a reputable company and was leading three western trekkers. As we examined the porter's feet, he didn't try to help and only said that the swelling wasn't frostbite, that it was caused by his shoes being too tight! He also claimed the porter sold the good shoes that were bought for him, so it was his own fault. Even if this were true, and porters do wear flimsy shoes and sell good equipment opting for simpler means, they would use a combination of plastic bags and socks to keep their feet dry and at least a little warmer when hiking through deep snow. This guide ignored his responsibility to make sure his team was properly outfitted.

At this point one of the customers of this trekking company was in tears realizing that they, in part, were responsible for the situation of their porter. One was concerned and angry and the last seemed more indifferent as if it was not his problem. Finally the guide conceded that he would hike down to Muktinath and send some of his other porters to help carry the kid the rest of the way to Muktinath. It's hard to believe the lack of concern from the trekking company for their employee. The porter would be very lucky to save his toes. I was the worst case of frostbite I have ever seen. Eventually the rescue porters came and carried the kid all the way to Jomsom where he was medevaced two days later by helicopter. My sense is the customers of this guide intervened and forced him to step up and take responsibility for the situation, although the customers may have reached into their own pockets to pay.

Annapurna is truly one of the world's Great Treks. After hearing this story you may feel that you don't want to hire a porter. But keep in mind that it is good business for the local economy to hire a porter, plus it lessens your load and helps you have a more enjoyable experience. However, when you hit the trail with a porter, either hired independently or as part of your com-

pany, make sure they are outfitted for warm dry feet and have basic sunglasses. It is true that porters sell good equipment for money, so you might be wasting your cash to buy them decent hiking boots. Instead, at least make sure they are prepared for cold and wet snow and their eyes are protected from the sun.

If you are an independent trekker keep an eye out for your fellow trekkers, too. You may want to give some friendly helpful hints, without being overbearing, that could save time, energy and help keep everyone safe and sound. My 23 days around Annapurna were an amazing experience for so many reasons, and although helping to rescue the porter added complications, it was good to be able to give a little back to Nepal which has given me so much.

ANNAPURNA TREK

Muktinath

Thorung La Pass
Thorung Phedi

Letdar

Yak Kharka

Gunsang

Manang

Braga

Hongde

Pisang

Bhratang

Chame

Danaque
Bagarchhap

Tal

Chamje

Jagat
Syange

Bahundanda

Ngadi
Khudi

Jomsom

Marpha

Tukuche

Kokhethati

Kalopani

Ghasa

Kopchepani

Dana

Tatopani

Ghara

Chitre
Poon Hill
Ghorapani
Tadapani

Ghandruk

Syauli Bazaar

Naya-Pul

Chapter Eight
Tour de Mont Blanc
France, Italy, Switzerland

Europe is known for valuing time together as a family, including engaging in many outdoor activities. With the Alps as a backyard there are exceptional opportunities to enjoy nature's playground. In the winter, of course, they ski and in the warmth of summer, they hike. The beauty and grandeur of the Alps is evident in every quaint town that lies at its feet. The magnificence increases tenfold when viewed from their shoulders. The Tour de Mont Blanc (TMB) is a circuit hike of the Mont Blanc Massif. Covering 170 km / 106 miles, it can be completed in 7 to 10 days. Despite only reaching a high point of 2,665m / 8,743' at the Col des Fours in France and Fenetre d'Arpette in Switzerland, the moderate altitude is deceiving. In lieu of extreme elevation there is an objectionable gain and loss of altitude almost every day. In total, the circuit climbs and descends almost 10 km / 6.2 miles.

You can begin the TMB in many towns and hike in either direction, although counter-clockwise is more popular. Be prepared to face hordes of hikers everywhere as many seek to circumnavigate Mont Blanc. Tenting is not easy in the alpine zone as appropriate areas to camp are rare. The huts pack guests in like sardines. People not reserving space in advance find themselves sleeping on the floor in the kitchen, hallway or any available flat surface. Hut cuisine is expensive, but good by trail standards. Still, it pales in comparison to the famous haute cuisine of the region. You can pack your food with you, but it would be a sin to miss experiencing some of the local tastes along the way. It doesn't get any fresher than buying the product right where it was made, from the gentle folk who made it! Speaking French while useful and appreciated by the locals is not necessary. This hike is accessible and scenic during the entire summer season but if you plan your hike to coincide with the peak of the wildflowers in July, you won't be sorry.

Fundamentals

Days Trekking: 10-12 days	**Approximate Elevation Change:** 1,658m / 5,440'
Distance: 167 km / 104 miles	**Price Range Independent:** Highly variable depending on where you stay and what you eat. You can easily do it for less than $100 per day.
Max Elevation: 2,665m / 8,743'	**Price Range Outfitter:** $1,750 - $4,000
Starting Elevation: 1,007m / 3,304'	**Challenge Level:** Moderate

When to Go

If you like good weather, the season is fairly short with the best weather from July to mid September. While there is always a risk of snowfall, it is far less during this time frame. Also, if you go too early, you risk deep snow on the passes.

Access / Local Information

There are many places to start the circuit. We flew into Geneva and took a bus to Les Houches, but you could just as easily start from Chamonix.

Difficulty

The trek is moderately difficult, but given that you only need to carry a few days' supply of food and no need for a tent, your pack can be relatively light. Unlike many other treks, there are multitudes of options for breaking the trek up into smaller segments if you need easier days. The ability to sleep at not just refugios, but hotels also makes it easier on your body.

Orientation

The Tour de Mont Blanc circumnavigates the Mount Blanc massif as well as some of the neighboring mountains as you walk through France, Italy and Switzerland.

On the Trail with Jeff

This trip was different than the previous Great Treks as my companion was no longer the "Mighty" Kirk or a friend, but instead my beautiful, new wife Jennifer. She is veteran of the trail, thru-hiking the Appalachian Trail and the International Appalachian Trail by herself. Both were far longer than the hikes we planned for the summer, although they were not at the altitude or with the massive elevation gains and losses of the Alps. While I used to joke about the "Nepali Flat," the many ups and downs along the trail, the Alps are also brutal in terms of daily gains and losses in elevation. In one day alone we would climb a vertical mile only to give it back the following day. In all, we gained and lost almost 9,450m / 31,000' without climbing much over 2,600m / 8,600'.

Our journey to trek the Alps was probably logistically the simplest of any of the Great Treks. In stark contrast to the long multi-day excursions with extensive layovers, this was a relatively quick red-eye from Philadelphia to Paris and then a connection to Geneva. We then were just a bus ride away from the start of the TMB. While there are many starting points to the TMB, we chose the small, quiet Swiss town of Les Houches. Nestled in a series of mountains we would soon be circumventing, it was easy to find our hostel. It was the cheapest place in town, but not "cheap" when compared to the third world standards I was accustomed. Compounding the issue was the exchange rate, which was not kind to the U.S. dollar. Where in the past we received large sums of bills at the exchange, we now received fewer Euros than dollars. So after dropping our luggage, we headed to a supermarket to try to reduce our expenses. We purchased dinner, breakfast and lunch for the next day for both of us for about $25. We are nothing if not frugal shoppers.

We cooked dinner at the hostel and then started the arduous task of sorting our gear, splitting supplies for both treks (as we planned to complete the Haute Route directly after the TMB) and lightening our load. "Light," of course, is relative when carrying all of your own stuff and having a ridiculous amount of camera gear with no six-foot tall friend to share the load. Decisions became tough. I hated to leave my laptop behind, so I took it without the battery. I am guessing that luxury only cost me about two pounds. We also decided to create a third pile of equipment we wouldn't use on either trek. The water filter, tent, stove, pots, etc. were all put into this pile as we were "roughing" it in the refugios along the way. This meant buying food at each stop, but greatly lightened the weight on the back, the chores each day and of course many Euros from our wallet. We did take two emergency meals that could be reconstituted with water. We hoped we wouldn't need them.

Day 1 - Les Houches - Bionnassy - Les Contamines

I woke up at 6:00 am ready to start. The sun cracked over the mountains, highlighting the tips. The day looked clear and relatively warm so we quickly packed up the room, went down for a fast breakfast, stored our extra luggage and then hit the road. We hiked through town to where we were supposed to pick up the trail. We saw the tram that many people take to avoid the beginning incline, but this seemed like cheating. In hindsight it would have been better to take the tram and walk the alternate route that was longer, but supposedly more scenic.

Unfortunately, like in many towns along the way, the directions were confusing. Although the path we were on would have merged with the TMB, nothing was marked. The lack of signs was definitely a foreshadowing of things to come. So we pulled out our trusty guidebook, for the first but not the last time, and it directed us to the proper start. We turned off the road and onto a trail and got slapped. The trail climbed steeply. From the very first step we struggled. The relentless incline upward gave us no hint it would ease. Apparently, the Swiss never heard of switchbacks. While I know that neither of us were in our best shape, our wedding, house repairs and illness had taken their toll, but this felt obnoxious. It was demoralizing how poorly I felt, but still we plodded along. After a little over two hours we reached the small town at the pass of Col de Vosa, but more importantly, we found a friendly restaurant open that was more than happy to charge us 3 Euros ($4.50) to split a very tiny refreshing bottle of apricot nectar. Small and expensive was a popular combination on this trip. The restaurant was situated by a train station shuttling the less adventurous visitors up and down.

As we pushed on, we got the answer to one of our many questions. Did we time the trip properly to observe the wildflower fest offered by the trail? As the palette of colors displayed alongside the path indicated, our timing was perfect. We marched on with new confidence, knowing most of the ascent was behind us. Sadly, the down proved punishing in a whole different manner. The descent was steep enough that our focus was at our feet instead of the breathtaking wildflowers blanketing the meadows. The trail was literally carved out of the flowers with flora covered walls rising on either side of the trail. While the flowers in Patagonia stretched farther, there was little variation. Here there were whites, purples, yellows, blues, not to mention the variegated ones. Passing one small village after another, the flowers helped distract us from the pain emanating from our legs. We stopped for our packed lunch of bread and savory French cheese. The nice thing about carrying cheese for lunch is you can blame the heat for your reason to stop early in the day. After all, we could not let such savory cheese melt.

Just as the elevation gain department mellowed out we were presented with the continued challenge of confusing and contradicting directional markers. This is where having a wife who speaks fluent French came in handy. Good thing I didn't leave her home on this trip! She was great. A few words in French, spoken with a perfect Parisian accent and just about everyone

was friendly to her. Well, that's not quite true. There was a curmudgeony old man who barked out his window at the other trekkers who thoughtlessly decided his lawn was a good resting place. I do have to admit it looked comfy, but we marched on without committing the same transgression.

A kilometer down the road we were faced with another sign pointing in a different direction to the TMB and our destination, Les Contamines. We backtracked and met up with more disoriented trekkers. There were lots of us aimlessly milling about. They spoke Spanish, with some broken French. We spoke English, French and my sprinkling of third-grade level Spanish. Together we spoke in Frenspanglish, a unique mixture of the three languages and determined the right way to go. About 30 meters past where we were confused we found the needed sign. For some strange reason the signs always seemed to be just past where you required them.

We entered the forest and walked comfortably until an unexpected last rise sapped our remaining strength. When we arrived in Les Contamines complications began. The inexpensive nearby hostel was full. Walking to the next cheapest lodging meant a long trek out of town, clearly unacceptable. So we compromised our budget on the first night, gave in and stayed in an inexpensive hotel. It was quite a sacrifice. After a sweaty day on the trail we had to endure hot showers, a real bed, a clean private room and our dinner and breakfast cooked for us. Adding insult to injury, our room had a great view of a renaissance-like church surrounded by chalets that one would expect from an Alpine village. OK, it wasn't bad at all. We resupplied, took a nap and had a magnificent meal – potato soup, salad, beef manicotti, a cheese course and a sweet dessert of chocolate covered cream filled pastries. I have to admit, this did beat Raman noodles and a PowerBar. After dinner we went to bed, yes, a nice, warm, clean bed. We could get used to this.

Day 2 - Les Contamines - Col de la Croix Du Bonhomme - Les Chapieux

We set the alarm for 6:00 am hoping to get an early start. Waking over an hour before the alarm, I sat on the balcony and read in the early dawn light. The moon was still shining full, mountains draping the landscape, I was in heaven. Jennifer got up at 6:00 am and we quickly packed up and waited for a 7:00 am breakfast call. Everyone was still sound asleep. Breakfast was light and quick, putting us on the trail an hour later. Boys and girls at home, do you remember *Mr. Robert's Neighborhood* or at least *Eddie Murphy's Mr. Robinson's Neighborhood*? Do you remember the word of the day? Well today my word of the day was "GRADUAL." It has such a pleasant sound. If you go gradually up or gradually down, life is good. With the exception of a pleasant start to our hike, the makers of the TMB trail knew nothing about the word gradual. The TMB seemed to go insanely steep as we climbed and dropped with such intensity that our quads felt like they were going to snap. In Nepal you primarily go in one direction with lots of smaller ups and downs to give your legs a break. Here in the Alps, there is none of that! There was nothing to give your weary legs a rest.

As we started our hike, we bumped into our often lost Spanish friends. They were very animated, speaking far quicker than I could comprehend. I got them to slow down and simplify what they were saying. They finally resorted to drawing with their sticks in the ground to communicate with us. Then it was all clear, they were asking us to mark the trail for them. Talk about the blind leading the blind. After a brief gradual beginning, the path stretched straight up. "Slap," yesterday's word of the day returned. We slowly climbed, taking lots of breathing breaks. Eventually we rewarded ourselves with a "snack" break next to a understated, dimly lit waterfall that was pleasantly framed in mossy rocks. This put us well behind the pack, even our Spanish friends.

Overall the trail was marked much better than the previous day. Still, our progress was slow. We continued to crawl up 1,400 vertical meters / 4,500', breaking every hour for a snack, drink, lunch, any excuse would do as we climbed. As we approached 1,160 vertical meters / 3,800' the view was spectacular with snow covered peaks all around us. We stopped for lunch and my vegetarian, I mean flexitarian wife, decided to try some of the local sausage I bought in town the night before. It certainly beat the over-processed mass marketed sausage found in the U.S.

After the peak it was all downhill. Again, a brutal downhill. Shortly we reached the Refuge de la Croix, where to our chagrin we found out that everyone else was calling it a day. It sounded tempting, but with bad weather in the forecast we pressed on and continued down. Of course, the word gradual never appeared, just down, down and more down. At one point the snow-covered trail dropped, too steep to walk, so we sat on our butts and took a free ride sliding all the way. Eventually, we got close to where the town should be, but there was no town. We checked the guidebook and it appeared as if we were in the proper place. Our illusion was shattered when we approached what should have been the last sign pointing to town. Instead of leading the way, it pointed directly into a fenced off area. We continued on the trail for a minute, but saw an X constructed from the trail marker. Hmmmf, we were not in the mood. So, after scratching our tired heads for a bit, we decided the trail behind the fence was correct and crossed it. Finally, joy, great joy! A meadow, with a soft switchbacks cutting through it.

We reached the town only to find the hostel we thought we booked no longer was open and the gite, a dormitory style hostel, that was there did not have our reservation. Having no idea where our reservation was made, Jennifer was able to talk our way into an already very crowded scene. The chaos of 20+ trekkers trying to get organized was maddening. I didn't care. I looked like death with my shoulder screaming as if someone had stuck an ice pick in it. It turned out that my backpack was assembled incorrectly from the manufacturer and the load lifters weren't laying correctly. It hurt bad enough that I couldn't lift anything with my right hand. I couldn't remember when taking my clothes off hurt so intensely.

The shower felt good and once cleaned up we joined two Frenchmen for dinner. They apparently arrived late as well, although it was their first day. You could tell, because they were clean and tidy. Dinner started well, a nice vegetable soup followed by

cheese and potatoes. However, while very tasty looking chicken was brought to the other tables, we were served some kind of knarly sausage. Apparently, that was the price of coming late without a reservation. Jennifer, did I tell you how much I love her, was able to sweet talk us into getting a helping of couscous to round out our plate. As dessert arrived, the folly of dinner was soon forgotten. A custard fruit tart made everything better. With a full belly we went to sleep on the top of bunk beds.

Day 3 - Les Chapieux - Col de la Seigne - Refugio Elisabetta

The next day was much better. Although the walk started on a road, the scenery was great. A glacial-melt fed river to our right led the way along the gradual slope. Taking lots of photo breaks slowed us down, but it was fun chasing the small furry marmots around the countryside. After realizing my predicted word of the day worked, I decided on a new word of the day for tomorrow, "ice cream." OK, that's two words, but two glorious words.

The road led to a trail that wound slowly up the mountains. We did manage to reach the first refugio in what we thought was good time. That is, until a guy jogging the trail zipped up to us. Barely carrying anything but energy gels and fluids, he sprang past and was quickly out of sight. He was doing the entire loop in seven days. I realize there's a physical challenge, but rushing like that definitely has a cost. How could you see, let alone enjoy, all the trail has to offer?

We took a break at the refugio and then cruised on up the trail. It was mostly a climb, but we progressed fairly quickly. The grade was far more reasonable and, with the fix I applied to my pack, I was feeling much better. It was the first time on the trip I was feeling like the old me. As we approached the highest elevation of the day, the Italian Alps loomed large in front of us. A layered tapestry of mountains, one could now clearly see the allure of the Alps. While I have seen much higher, bolder and more majestic mountains, the weaving of one mountain after another provided a texture I had never witnessed. We took in one more long photo break and then headed down.

While the GPS got confused in the valley, it seemed like the book was equally off by its estimation of the location of the Refugio Elisabetta. This time it was off by both distance and altitude. Still the trail was kind and the views outstanding, so we ambled along comfortably. However, when we reached the refugio - or shall I say when we reached the base of the path leading up to the refugio - we discovered that the book left out a little detail. The short, but painfully steep climb up to it.

The facade of the building was the nicest of any refugio so far. The bunk-style dormitory had eight people sleeping in a row and stacked three rows high. The narrow mattresses were connected with no room what-so-ever. As shocking as it was, we were the first to arrive, so we took the lower bunks far in the corner, hoping they wouldn't fill up. We were glad that we were not there during high season in a few weeks.

The refugio was equipped with an interesting coin operated shower. One coin per customer and a coin equaled twenty liters of hot water, regardless of how long your shower took. Now twenty liters may sound a lot until you visualize that's less than

five gallons of water. It proved to be enough, at least enough to wipe off your stench. I could get used to trekking while clean. Given the proximity of the sleeping quarters, I hoped everyone took advantage of the luxury.

Our solitude did not last long. The place was soon packed by a horde of trekkers. Group after group arrived until over sixty people were staying in the crowded rooms. It was quite a spectacle. At dinner, a friendly French guy named Jim invited me to shoot Mount Blanc in the good light. In the name of international diplomacy, how could I refuse? So, just as dinner ended we left with two other trekkers and headed back up the trail. Mount Blanc was indeed bathed in beautiful late day light. Jim commented, "The Italian side is ugly, unlike the beautiful snowy French side." Yes, there is national pride everywhere. I must say, while I did agree with him, it was the contrast of the two sides that made Mount Blanc look striking. I also learned a new term, "Bushshit." Apparently, the entire world, except a few left in America, knew what to think of the former president's verbiage.

When I returned Jennifer did not look pleased. The rambunctious Spanish group was trying her patience. Apparently as she tried to sleep, they yapped away. Nevertheless, when they decided it was time to rest they "shhhhed" everyone else. Oddly, I felt I was one of the quiet ones on this trip. Language barriers made it difficult for me to converse with many people.

Not ready to sleep, I took the e-book reader out and read for a while in the common area of the refugio. Upon returning to the bunk room, I was greeted with a chorus of snores. It was earth shaking. One gentleman's snoring, at least I hope it was a guy, was without a doubt the loudest snorer I ever heard. He was not alone though, others answered his call as if they were having an animated conversation. Beer, trekking and sharing a room is not the best of combinations. That is unless you've imbibed as much as they had. It was easy to forgive though, as they really were wonderfully charming, kindhearted people and we had ear plugs!

Day 4 - Refugio Elisabetta - Courmayeur

We awoke at 6:00 am for a 6:15 breakfast. It was unusually warm out, especially given the higher altitude. A fog had rolled down the valley, giving our refugio a very secluded, mystical feeling. We hit the road by 7:00 am along a dead flat valley guarded by a series of mountains whose reflections lit up the pools of water alongside the trail. Of course, flat and gradual did not last long and we were soon climbing another 450 vertical meters / 1,475'. We took it in two stages. I was feeling much better with my shoulder healing and my legs gaining strength. We had one harrowing stream crossing, a quick stop for

water and then reached our high point for the day.

Too bad the fog had not lifted and the clouds obstructed the peaks. While it was an awesome site, the photographer in me yearned for better light. I saw firsthand why so many of the guidebook photos were less than ideal. Getting good light in the Alps was not easy. What was lacking in the mountainside view was more than made up for in wildflowers. While not the large fields we saw earlier, the sheer variation of flowers was captivating. One yellow flower looked like a tulip. Another looked like a miniature iris.

After a nice break we headed down and I mean DOWN! Over 1,500m / 4,920' straight down. That's close to a mile for you reading in the States. We made good time and hit the Rifugio Maison Vielle for a lunch break. Just to play with my already challenged language skills, they now spelled refugo, rifugio. We sat down in lounge-like chairs, feet up, and engulfed tasty sandwiches. I had a ham

and cheese, while Jennifer stuck to a straight cheese sandwich. The bread was amazing and it cost a lot less than the previous day's stale, sorry excuse for a sandwich. We decided to order another and to my surprise my flexitarian wife opted for the prosciutto and cheese. The trail was turning her into quite the carnivore. Now if you remember my word of the day, "ice cream," I was a bit off. I should have said gelato as that is actually one word and the refugio had some. Stale and freezer burnt as it was, it still slid down just fine. Eventually our little bit of paradise came to an end as the clouds starting to roll in prompting us out of our seats.

As we strolled out of the refugio, commenting on it's idyllic location, we were shocked to see just a few hundred meters away the trail morph into a hideous jeep road with an insane incline. Aside from the obvious repulsiveness it was also downright dangerous. The road was ripped up, full of loose rock, and we struggled not to slip. We wound down toward the town of Dolme, which, true to form, didn't have clear trail markers once within its borders. The guidebook came to our rescue, helping us navigate through the picturesque old village.

After passing through the town, Courmayeur was next, as was our hotel. The hotels for the money were a better bargain than the refugios, but part of this was due to the remote location of the refugio. Our hotel was nothing special, but it was clean and quiet. A private room is quite a treat after sharing a room with 24. Since our room had a balcony, we decided to bring dinner back. We purchased a bottle of wine, pizza and focaccia. We also made a trip to the supermarket where we bought cheese, olives, snacks and grapefruit juice to accompany dinner. In addition, we bought toasted bagel-like bread (there are no real bagels outside of NY), brie and more olives for lunch. Wait, weren't we supposed to be trekking? My plans to drop any weight on this trip were rapidly dissolving.

Day 5 - Courmayeur - Rifugio Bonatti

By now, I lost track of what day it was and that's always a great feeling. Breakfast was served late, 7:30 am, but in addition to the normal toast, jam and hot cocoa (yes, I am still a kid) they had Cocoa Krispies and Cocoa Puffs. Charged on a sugar high, we hit the road and once again quickly got lost. Apparently the "trail" went through a section of road that was under construction. We blew right past it and took a nice tour around the town until we found our way back onto the path.

Today's slice of the TMB started with 800m / 2,625' straight up and then proceeded over rolling hills. We were definitely feeling much better. This was partially due to the gentle switchback nature of the trail, the heavily-wooded cover protecting us from the sun and our recuperative afternoon. Along the way we met two women from England, Jane and Ann. They com-

plimented us on how fast we were moving. This made both Jennifer and I feel better. Hanging at the back of the pack was not our norm. They told us they were shut out of the Refugio Elisabetta. So apparently, even in low season, you really needed to book ahead each day. Of course, based on our experience they might have been the lucky ones.

We stopped for a long lunch. Even with the large group from the night before heading up, there was plenty of space for us to relax. While eating all of our goodies and chatting with Jane and Ann, suddenly there was an intruder! Jane's cell phone rang. A lot of the joy of these trips is the disconnection from home. A few minutes later she pulled out her iPod to look up a phone number. Ha, and people call me a tech head.

The afternoon's walk started straight up, and while it looked as if the path rose for many hundreds of meters, the main TMB path veered off and leveled out. The weather remained fine, although the scattered clouds detracted from the mountain view. If the sky was clear, taking the higher alternate route promised to provide a more spectacular view. However, we took the main trail which was draped with flowers on both sides and flanked on our right by one mountain after another; all this while strolling on a relatively flat path. As we wound around, at first all we saw was the flag of the refugio perched atop the rolling hillside. While we could have forged ahead and saved half a day, why hurry? As we approached Rifugio Bonatti we were breathless, not from the altitude or the exertion, but from view up to the refugio and it's tightly packed wildflowers heading down to the base of the river and mountains that towered above it.

I had another quick twenty liter shower, with kids in the stalls next to me singing off key in what I think was Italian. Who knows, it could have been their shrieks as their shower ran out of hot water. One great perk of this refugio was its drying room. A small room with a space heater can be quite a blessing on a trek. We took advantage, washing a bunch of clothes and then hung them for a quick dry.

Dinner was fabulous: pasta salad, soup, carrot salad, mashed potatoes and an unidentifiable bean patty. Dessert of a fruit tart that tasted like a homintoshin, a Jewish delicacy served during Purim, rounded out the meal. As we headed to sleep it was just the four of us in a huge room. Two other smart people got the idea and joined us in quiet slumber. Apparently they had reached their limit of their noisy group as well.

Day 6 - Rifugio Bonatti - Grand Col Ferret - La Fouly

Today was hump day. We passed the halfway mark. My knee was a little sore, but beyond that, I was feeling strong. This may have been partially due to breakfast. In addition to the usual toast, hot cocoa and such, we also had fruit. Granted it was canned, but fruit of any kind is a luxury on a trek. We said goodbye to Ann and Jane and hit the trail. As we wound down we passed staggering numbers of wildflowers. We made good time and quickly reached our first rest stop. After a quick break we started working our long way up to the Italy/Switzerland border. As we rose, the mountains stood before us with their ever shrinking glaciers hanging off their faces.

Upon our arrival at the refugio about halfway up, we grabbed a quick sandwich and drink and then pressed on for the Col. We were following a large group of Americans who were traveling extremely light. Jealous of their lack of load, we wondered if they were day hikers. Upon reaching the top, we were surprised at the true enormity of the group. There were over forty people milling about who were on a guided tour of the Alps that took seven days, lots of bus transfers and guides to help carry their belongings. Everything was arranged so they just had to walk. They were very curious and amazed that we were a group of two and unsupervised.

The goals of trekkers in the Alps are far more heterogeneous than other treks. In contrast, in Nepal if you were on the Everest Base Camp trail you were most likely headed to or from Base Camp. In Patagonia's Torres del Paine, you were most likely walking one of the two main options. Here in the Alps people day hike, some hike sections of the TMB, others hike with guides and support crews, or they thru-hike like us. It's a wonderful blend, allowing the trail to be preserved better than if it were used only for purists. It also allows many people who couldn't otherwise appreciate the Alpine beauty to experience its grandeur.

After a nice rest and snack we headed down into what looked like worrisome clouds. Luckily the clouds cleared revealing rich, green mountains crowned with pillowy white snow. Countless stringy waterfalls worked their way down as the snow and ice melted. Not too far along the trail we stopped at a dairy farm that looked more appropriate as a set in a post-apocalyptic *Mad Max* film than in the Swiss Alps. Importantly, my wife sniffed out fresh pressed apple juice and piquant cheese hidden in the dark pit of a building that they called a shop. Quite a difference from what was considered a treat on a Nepalese trail, a Snickers bar.

We pushed on, winding down and hoping the town was nearby. As we finally approached the town of La Foley, there was a crane dredging the river. Instead of watching where I was going, I started watching the crane. This didn't last long, because quite quickly I was flat on my ass having slipped in the mud. To be accurate, I landed on my elbow and thigh, but quickly rolled to my butt. While my ego was bruised and I was a complete muddy mess, the camera was safe and it appeared my wounds were not life, nor trek, threatening.

We walked into town in search of our hotel. The town looked more like an old western town than something I was expecting to see in route. Were we somehow magically transported to Hollywood's back lot? We found our hotel and its very cramped bunk room. Luckily there were only two other guests sharing the quarters, so it was fine.

I finally got Internet access. It was as slow as in Nepal and a lot more expensive. Who would have thought 21st Century Europe was so technologically challenged? For dinner they served barley soup, chicken on rice and dessert, but my appetite was in overdrive and even the generous portions weren't enough.

Day 7 - La Fouly - Champex

I woke to the Beast of Arrrghh. Arrgh being how my leg felt. It was as if Rocky had used it instead of meat for a sparring partner. I was lucky this was supposed to be the easiest day of the tour, 15 kilometers / 9.3 miles and only 500m / 1,650' up and down. We got on the trail a little later than usual, but with only a 4 ½ hour walk we saw no reason to rush. Aside from my upper thigh screaming all mighty hell on each and every step, the walk was quite pleasant. This was probably the worst trekking injury I've incurred and exactly why I do not mountain climb. A mistake like mine on a climb results in death. Let me make it clear, I have no desire to die.

The hike strolled down, in an early morning fog, through one tiny village after another. These villages looked utopian with diminutive houses appearing as if they hadn't changed in 100 years, small gardens and most importantly, very obvious trail markers. As we wound through the valley the sky cleared, revealing one of the strangest mountains I've ever seen. It was as if someone took a meat slicer to the side of the mountain. An immense flat slab of stone was pancaked to its side.

We got over the halfway point and then the pleasantries ended. We had a steep 500 meter climb on a trail that was graded reasonably well. Along the way we kept being told we were crazy, actually cuckoo. Over and over again we were mocked by an invisible friend, the bird that inspired the cuckoo clock. The trail wound up the forest, occasionally popping out the side of a cliff. One area actually had waist high chains, but they didn't seem necessary without any snow on the ground. Perhaps they were needed in poor conditions.

About halfway up the remaining climb we found Shrek and Fiona's house. Its entrance was a door built into the side of the mountain which was completely surrounded by stone. We couldn't tell how old it was or when it was last used. There was a chimney on the side next to a really long, high ladder that went straight up the rock face. I wanted to climb it, but my far more sensible wife deterred me. Perhaps she didn't want to have to lift me off my ass two days in a row.

We then made our final push into Champex. The city was a charming town centered around a crystal clear, pale lime green lake whose hues varied greatly as the clouds rolled by. Not long after noticing the lake our attention was drawn to a creperie. This was no longer the TMB, but the "Tour of Food." The town had prices in Swiss Francs, which were fairly reasonable, but if you paid in Euros many places ripped you off on the exchange rate. We would anticipate this if we paid in U.S. dollars, but I expected more uniformity with Euros. Ironically, we had Francs earlier and exchanged them because no one would take them. Sometimes you just can't win.

Dinner consisted of salad and stringy, gooey cheese fondue. This included a raid on the supermarket beforehand for olives and cranberry juice. Yes, we are weird, we know that, but for a town this size the facilities were surprisingly poor. The supermarket was half empty and we couldn't even resupply our dwindling quantity of pain killers in any form, not even aspirin. We headed to bed early, because a place in town had a breakfast buffet that started at 6:30 am. We planned to hit it hard.

Day 8 - Champex - Alp Bovine - Col de la Forclaz

I started the day with a splash. A splash that went right down my back. Just as we were departing the hotel, my hose popped off my water bag and soaked my butt. With the air temperature at 10° C / 50° F, it was not a refreshing feeling. Our foresight in using all water proof bags for the gear within our packs kept pretty much everything inside dry. I was distracted from the dampness of my clothing by breakfast. There was bread, yogurt, cheese, fruit and hot cocoa.

We hit the trail by 7:30 am, expecting the day to be moderately challenging. For the first hour or so we gradually descended through a forest, but with no sun shining on us, it was a bit chilly. One cool aspect of the trail was the not-so-random clumps of wildflowers. Whenever there was a hole in the canopy for the sun to shine through, the wildflowers capitalized on the light source and erupted.

Most of the climb wasn't very dramatic offering few views. As we progressed along the trail Jennifer was fidgeting with her underwear. Turns out she put them on backward. Not shy, at least when no one is around, she popped her boots off and did the switcheroo. The trail was reminiscent of the Appalachian Trail and was very rocky. A few stream crossings broke up the trail and as we approached our maximum elevation for the day, it flattened out into a gigantic meadow strewn with wildflowers galore and the view of distant mountains rising above them. We wound around to a small dormitory for a drink and snack before charging up the last fifty meters of climbing we had on tap for the day.

As we descended to the Hotel Forclaz we were amazed how early it was. We heard roar after roar of motorcycles whizzing by below and feared our peaceful trip would take a turn for the worse. Unfortunately, there were no other alternatives unless we wanted to walk a double hike. We arrived at the hotel before 1:00 pm, our earliest arrival yet. It wasn't as bad as it seemed, but it was a peculiar place. We saw the motorcyclists, who were sunning themselves on a grassy hill. It seemed like most people here came for the view via mood-breaking internal combustion. We were the first thru-hikers to arrive and they wouldn't check us in until 2:00 pm. So we rested for a bit alongside the bikers until they let us officially enter.

Day 9 - Col de la Forclaz - Col de Balme - Tre-Le-Champ

We got up, packed up, and were ready to blow town after a quick breakfast. However, at 6:55 am we found the door to the eating area locked. They insisted we wait until exactly 7:00 am. This was without a doubt the least friendly place of the trip. We later found out from another hiker that they were one of the only places that required a deposit to hold a reservation. This wouldn't be a big deal, but they wouldn't put it on credit card. I paid for the room and asked if he could call ahead so we could book the next place. He told me he was too busy and couldn't be bothered. He already tried the night before and that was all the effort he was willing to put forth. He said I could try from the pay phone. The hotel was the only place to charge us for the calls made to book ahead. He said they would probably speak English. I explained my wife was fluent in French (he would only speak to her in English, again the only person to do this), he was like, "Oh, yeah." So you get the idea, we weren't very pleased with the Hotel Forclaz.

The plan was to break often and snack a little each time, but once my stubborn wife got rolling there was no stopping her. We wound up a well-shaded, with a significant switchback trail. It was early and it was already feeling quite warm. With all I was carrying I was sweating bullets. Twice I suggested we break. Jennifer wanted to march on, she claimed to be cold! It wasn't very cold in my world!

We passed a few picnic tables and benches. It was one of the first times we saw so many on a trail. Maybe someone was giving us a hint to rest. About halfway up we passed another table. This time Jennifer agreed to stop. So did the friendly French guys who we shared the room with at the Hotel Forclaz.

Once we started again, we exited the forest and looked up through the clearing. Deceptively close, at the top of the hill was a place to buy refreshments. To our dismay, it took us a good hour to reach it. Along the way my GPS batteries died. I got 45 hours out of one set of lithium batteries. Not the "up to seven times longer" they claim, but twice as long as my rechargeables and a good 15 hours longer than alkalines. Lithium batteries are a lot lighter, and while they are expensive for some purposes they are great for the GPS on long treks and recyclable. We grabbed a drink at the top and received a continuation of unfriendly service. It seems like we hit the rude corner of the tour. Not looking to dawdle we got rolling with our French friends and a third guy we were leap-frogging along the way. He led us off the TMB along a side trail. We commented it didn't look right, but he kept insisting "this is the trail!" I am sure you can tell how this one ended up, and I do mean up. Straight up the wrong trail, adding untold distance to our trek. The view at the top was nice, but pretty similar to the one from the day before.

We all marched down, a bit frustrated, and headed for Tre-Le-Champ. If indeed the boorish man from the hotel was correct, and they were fully booked, we would have another 3 ½ hour climb straight uphill once we got there. Two hours later we reached Tre-Le-Champ and strolled up to our hopeful lodging. Jennifer asked if they had room. The expression on the woman's face did not look like we would be ending our hike at Tre-Le-Champ. She took us around the auberge to show us the attic, saying it was the only space. Victory! While only about 3 feet high, we didn't care. After all, one does sleep horizontally. We ate the rest of our lunch and added a fresh salad from the auberge. During our meal, my knee swelled. Not good! We then attempted to reserve the next night's lodging, it was booked as well. This was really becoming a problem! There was still one more place to try and the woman in charge of the auberge was very sweet. She did get us a place, but it was closer than we would have liked. This meant tomorrow we would have an easy day to recover, and frankly we needed one.

Dinner was great. Apparently we hopped back on the Tour de Food. It consisted of salad, beef stew, mashed polenta, a cheese course and dessert. We sat next to a lovely German couple who traveled the world for fun, work and volunteering. We chatted about many things, including politics. It's amazing how consistent the political views are on the trail. There were no Bush lovers here. Another common discussion is why do Americans not understand the concept of conservation. After dinner, we went to our private little attic and slept wonderfully.

Day 10 - Tre-Le-Champ to Le Brevent

Since the day was going to be a short one, we planned to hike an alternative route which would take us by a scenic lake. The day, like so many, started with a climb. Fortunately, my knee wasn't too bad. Today was different though, because after we traversed a series of switchbacks up 500m / 1,640' or so, we had to climb a series of vertigo-inducing metal ladders, which the book described as endless. We took our time getting to the ladders, not wanting to be tired as we climbed. We sat and took in the view just before starting our assault. They really weren't horrible, considering how flimsy similar setups were on other treks. The only real issue was the weight of our packs pulling our bodies away from the ladder. We took one ladder at a time until we got through all eleven of them. We appeared to be done, except perhaps a small climb uphill, which turned into a series of false summits as we wound around and around. There were two more small ladders and some additional climbing, but we reached the top without any incident and, of course, took a nice break.

Sadly, ominous clouds loomed over the horizon, so we decided to head for the refuge, note the change from refugio, and drop off our packs. If the weather cleared we'd double back and head for the lake. Shortly down the trail from there a baby goat appeared. Oddly, it wasn't spooked by us at all. Separating from Jennifer, I followed it around and it led me literally down the goat path where I met up with Papa goat. He also didn't seem to mind my presence. After taking a few photos - I know, odd for me - I caught up with Jennifer. The refuge, which seemed so close, just kept getting farther away. I was walking with both cameras in my hands and no poles. I started to regret the decision not to repack the backup camera. As we approached the refuge, Jennifer suddenly went down. She hit her head and her shin. I couldn't tell how badly. Helping her up, at first I thought it was more of an ego bruise than a physical problem. However, as she hobbled to the refuge it appeared that she took quite a hit. She progressed very slowly and got to the refuge, nauseous and dizzy. Against my advice she took a nap to try and sleep it off. I was very concerned and not sure what to do. My wife can be quite stubborn about these things.

Day 11 - Back to Les Houches

One would hope that the last day out of the circuit would be an easy one. The guidebook's preview made the day look reasonable. However, the Tour de Mont Blanc would still have a few surprises for us. Shaking off her mild concussion, at first we strolled along making good time, thinking, ahhh, how comfortable this hiking thing can be. Soon a rock scramble appeared, then a few hours later the trail turned into a snow-covered quarry of large scattered stones. The snow was slick and mostly untraversed. We toiled along, but knowing we were closing in on completing the circuit, it was easy to push ahead. At the end of the scramble was the peak where a tram could take us up and therefore also down. Tempting as it might have been, after eleven days we refueled a bit and proceeded. It was our last big descent and we figured it was clear sailing. There was a refuge halfway down, so we stopped for a bite to eat. As we did, we got buzzed by a glider. It was pretty wild to be that close to a plane soaring at eye level with no motor. Heading out of the refuge we figured it would be our last push. However, after dropping quite a few vertical feet, I realized I left my water bladder on the table and had to run back to get it. I must say, without a pack on I felt like I was flying like the glider. Ahhh, how I missed having a porter. I vowed that my pack would definitely

be lighter for the Haute Route, which we planned to start a few days later. We made it down fine, pigged out, and slept at the hostel in which we started!

Epilogue

Oddly, the most civilized of the Great Treks so far turned out to be the most hazardous to date. Perhaps we were just drunk on good food and soft beds. It's easy to let your guard down when you are walking in and out of such quaint European towns. The TMB is not for the thrifty, but with many options when in town, a wide range of economic levels can be met.

For those fit and just breaking into trekking this is an excellent trek with which to get started. Never more than a few days from a major town, it's easy to pack light, much lighter than we did, and restock your supplies along the way. For those uncomfortable with culinary adventures, there's no worry about eating snakes, bugs or mystery meats on this trek. Only gastronomic delights abound on and off the trail.

More so than any of the other circuit treks, the TMB is not about the destination, just the journey. Sure that's a cliche, but the TMB is more of a collection of subtle delights than any specific highlight.

It's also very easy to hike just a section of the trail and break up your journey into a few rewarding trips.

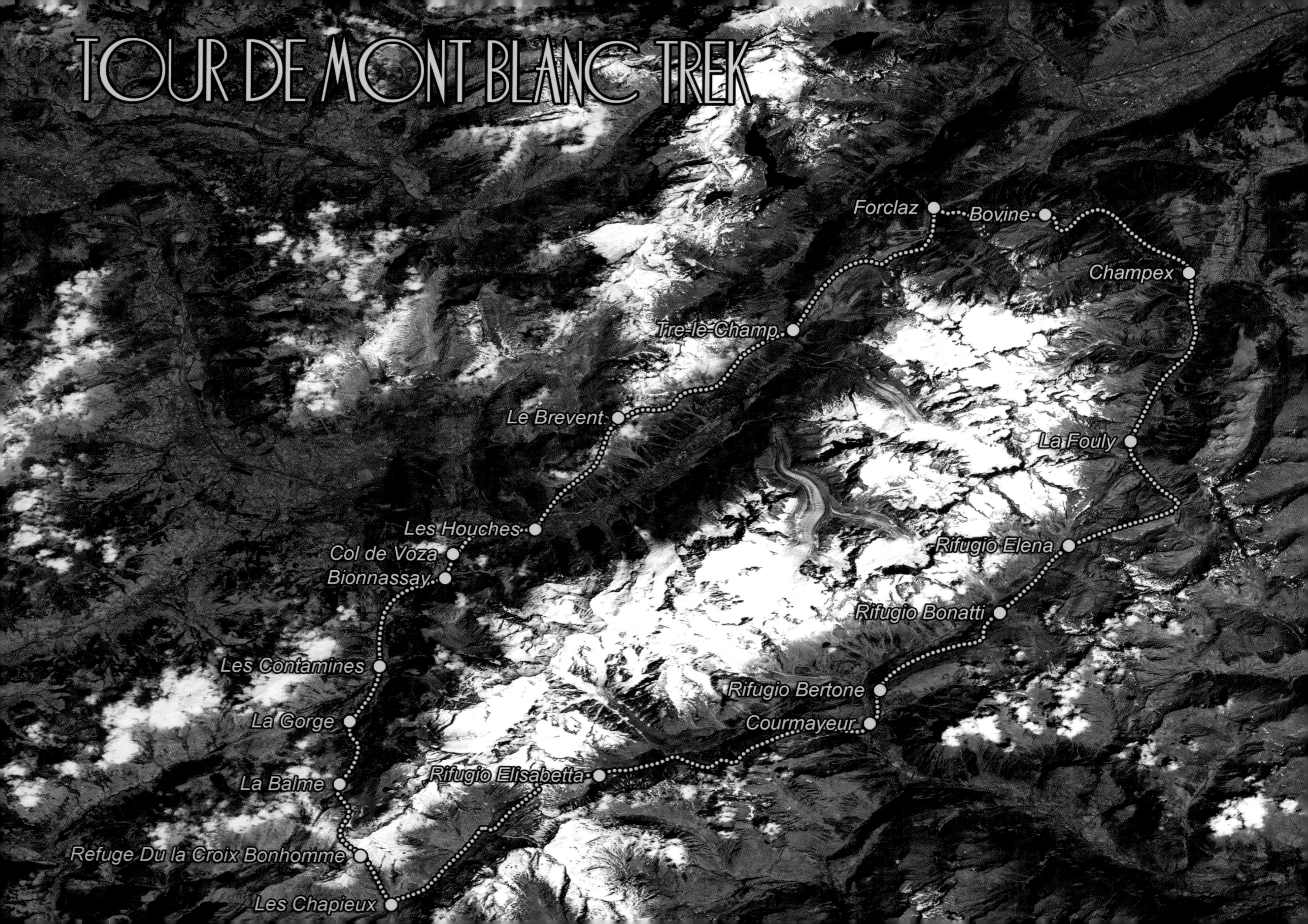

TOUR DE MONT BLANC TREK

Champex
Bovine
Forclaz
La Fouly
Rifugio Elena
Rifugio Bonatti
Rifugio Bertone
Courmayeur
Tre-le-Champ
Le Brevent
Rifugio Elisabetta
Les Houches
Col de Voza
Bionnassay
Les Contamines
La Gorge
La Balme
Refuge Du la Croix Bonhomme
Les Chapieux

Chapter Nine
Haute Route
France, Switzerland

Haute Route, in French, literally means "high route." While there are many high walks now dubbed an Haute Route, the original is the Alpine path connecting Chamonix, France to Zermatt, Switzerland. Passing ten of the twelve loftiest peaks in the Alps, it is no surprise that it is skied extensively during the winter and well-hiked during the summer. Most hikers choose to travel from Chamonix to Zermatt for a dramatic finish at the base of the majestic Matterhorn, but you can go in either direction. Shorter options are plentiful, ranging from very accessible day hikes to multi-day excursions.

As you hike by meadows filled with abundant wildflowers, shimmering tarns and glaciers, you climb up ten alpine passes known as cols. You will be humbled by the scale of the valleys spilling in front of you. Similar to other treks in the Alps, it is crowded without many usable campsites and reservations for the gites & auberges (huts) are recommended. Planning your trek requires great flexibility due to the ever-changing mountain weather and you are sure to encounter inclement weather. There is a choice to take a higher route requiring some technical skill and crampons. We traveled the lower level option that does not require crossing glaciers that can collapse rendering the trail impassable. While the lower route does have the risk of rock slides, avalanche areas are well marked. Traveling through two French speaking countries, it is helpful if you can speak a little French and any effort is appreciated. At huts enough English is spoken to get by, but in some of the very small, rural mountain communities only French is understood. Whatever your language skills, you are sure to take in unrivaled views as you travel through the birthplace of European mountaineering in the 1900's.

Fundamentals

Days Trekking: 12-14 days	**Approximate Elevation Change:** 1,965m , 6,447'
Distance: 184 km / 114 miles	**Price Range Independent:** Like the Tour de Mont Blanc it is highly variable depending on where you stay and what you eat. You can easily do it for less than $100 per day.
Max Elevation: 2,965m / 9,728'	**Price Range Outfitter:** $2,250 - $3,500
Starting Elevation: 1,000m / 3,281'	**Challenge Level:** Moderate

When to Go

Like the Tour de Mont Blanc, the season is short. Therefore, do not leave before mid July and plan to be off trail by mid September. If you leave too early, you run the risk of not making it over the high passes. Note that the days get shorter the longer you wait. It's a balance between less snow and amount of daylight.

Access / Local Information

Fly into Geneva and then take a bus to Chamonix where you start the trek. However, given the point-to-point nature of the Haute Route, if you want to have something other than what's left in your pack when you complete the trek, you'll need to arrange the shipping of your belongings to Zermatt. Another option is to do what we did and hop on a roundtrip train leaving our luggage at a hostel in Zermatt. A final choice is to fly into Zermatt and then take the train to Chamonix.

Difficulty

Weather changes quickly in the high Alps and it is easy to underestimate the effort required to complete this trek. While not climbing above 3,000m / 10,000' in altitude, going through three high passes in one day can be a challenge.

Orientation

A point-to-point trek from Chamonix, France to Zermatt, Switzerland, the Haute Route traverses along the northwest section of the Pennine Alps.

On the Trail with Jeff

Day 1 - Chamonix to Trient

After a few days break from concluding the Tour de Mont Blanc (TMB) in July, I embarked alone for the start of the Haute Route. With all my travels this was the first time I backpacked without a companion. Given the toll of the TMB and Jennifer's concussion, we agreed it was best for her to take an extra two days off, since the first day was practically a repeat of the TMB in the opposite direction along a slightly different trail. In addition, the second day's walk was one of the hardest of the trail and had the potential for a lot of snow. Jennifer planned to take a bus and meet me in Champex, a stop along the TMB, where we would journey together to Zermatt.

I left Jennifer at the train station in Chamonix, saddened that we were separating, but with a lighter load. She took a lot of my weight until we met again. The plan was for me to walk the first two days in one so that we could have more time in Zermatt when we finished. The directions from the book were pretty clear, although there were two places I got very confused just getting out of Chamonix. I really missed not having Jennifer to ask for help. Once I got out of town the trail was gorgeous. No big mountain views, just a soft -hmmm soft- trail that meandered through the forest with moss-covered rocks, a clear glacial stream, song birds chirping and a near complete absence of people. It was the perfect start after the noisy, body-beating trail of the TMB.

I thought I was making good time, but the time estimates in the book and the trail weren't jiving, so I just plowed ahead. I got to the first town, Argentiere. I stopped for a quick drink and then headed to Le Tour. The trail continued to be quite pleasant and shaded most of the way. Once I got to Le Tour I saw hordes of people entering the trams to climb up to the col. It's certainly the more civilized way to go. Instead, I hit the trail and was mocked by the repeated shadows of the tram carrying the less adventurous to the top. The end of the tram line marked the halfway point of my climb. So I stopped and had a little lunch; leftover sausage and day old bread. I then trekked up to Col de Baume, the stop along the TMB where we lost our way. I was wiser now, or so I thought. I studied the massive array of signs carefully and followed the one marked to Trient. It was a gentle trail, but after about 10 minutes I saw another signpost. This one pointed to Trient in the opposite direction. Apparently there were multiple ways to get to Trient and I was on the long trail. Back I went and down the trail we had walked up to get to the col on the TMB.

As I entered Leputy, the town before Trient, I was blown away by the wildflowers. They seemed to have expanded since we last walked through. I met another couple as I walked from Leputy to Trient and they were totally lost looking for the campground. I can't imagine the added effort camping would add to this trip. Sometimes it's worth spending the extra money for facilities.

Shortly after I arrived in Trient, a postcard quaint town with an old church at the center. Almost no one was around. I got an eerie feeling I had stepped into a B-grade horror movie where they eat lone travelers. I walked around this tiny town for half an hour unable to locate the dormitory. I was totally frustrated. One woman gave me directions in French, which only helped a little. There was even a map of the town and a picture of the dorm. It was of no help. I know, I suck! Eventually I found it by chance. It was hidden behind another building and was the very last one in town. The dorm room was huge, although it filled up as the day grew long and people started to limp in from crossing the Fenetre d'Arpette. It was the pass I would be climbing the following day. The painful strides and wobbly movements reminded me of the day-after-amble of first-time marathoners. It wasn't pretty. One woman declared, "I am caput!" and then dropped into her bed. Heeding the warning of the difficulty, I called it an early night.

Day 2 - Trient – Fenetre d' Arpette – Champex - Le Chable

When I awoke the entire room was still fast asleep. I was lucky to wake at the right time as previously I relied on Jennifer's watch. After a quick breakfast I headed out the door by 6:45 am. Luckily, I had no problem finding the trail. It was the clearest description yet. I walked in almost total solitude with no one out the door before me. Given my light load, I was making fast progress. If I was lucky I could climb the 1,400m/ 4,600' in time to hit the pass as the early morning light illuminated the glacier. I was fortunate to climb while shaded by the mountain and with a moisture wicking breeze keeping me dry.

As I rose, the glacier was increasingly lit up by the sun. I hoped to see the extravagant view of the ice falls close up as highlighted in the guidebooks. However, as I climbed up the path, the glacier pulled farther and farther away from me. It turns out the "classic" shot was no more. Another victim of global warming, the glacier was in rapid retreat to the point that it no longer resembled old photographs. Don't get me wrong, it's still spectacular. It was just diminished from my grand expectations.

As I continued one guy came cruising down the mountain. A runner, training for something, flew passed me. When he did, he patted me on the back. See, even without French I could communicate. I continued in what became a boulder field, amazed at the nimble dexterity of the runner who had traversed it so gracefully. Luckily, it was marked clearly and I made steady progress to the pass. When I reached it I was the only one there, a reward for my early start. I plopped down for a bit for a break and took in the solitary view. While the glacier behind me was beautiful, I felt the emerging valley beneath me was much more majestic. It had great contrast between the scree, sharply, rising peaks and valley floor.

After 15 minutes or so the first hiker from the other valley reached the top, so I left to let him enjoy the fruit of his labors without disturbance. As I started my descent the scree was a death trap. It was loose and incredibly steep. The book warned about this, but I was surprised at just how unstable it was underfoot. This continued for the first 100m / 330' of the decent. While the next 150m / 490' were slightly better, it was also difficult to maintain solid footing. This made it hard to enjoy the ever improving view of the valley that was opening in front of me.

While descending the wildflowers were phenomenal in their individual splendor, their variety and their numbers. Perhaps they should call this "La Route Fleur." Looking back over my shoulder, I was treated to huge stone guardians on either side of the pass I crossed. Finally, as I approached Champex to meet Jennifer, the once perfectly marked trail got confusing. I prayed I wasn't on the wrong trail as I saw another one below with lots of people walking on it. I had faith, continued and lucked out that the two trails met at the foot of the town.

I walked through town to find her hotel. I was happy to discover it was the first one and her backpack was in the lobby. Then I noticed the note, "Went to lunch." Where's the faith? I wandered through town, peering into one outdoor restaurant after another, until my sweetie saw me and came running with a big grin on her face. We ate a very over-priced, horrific pizza. Really, 32 kilometers / 20 miles from Italy you would think they could do better. Jennifer and I headed out for my second double in two days.

The trail was supposed to take us through "Working Switzerland." While the book tried to make it sound appealing, it could only be enjoyable to an urban planner or a person in need of an easy day. With the added mileage I had already walked and now the full weight of my pack on my back, I saw little appeal. We crossed lots of roads and kept second-guessing ourselves as to the proper direction. The peak of our dismay was when we came upon a dirt bike track, motorcycles roaring, dirt kicking into the air. This was our non-picturesque introduction to Le Chable, the town we were to spend the night.

We hobbled to our hotel and then went to a pub for dinner. They had Guinness on tap, so I excitedly ordered one expecting to soon forget the day's woes. The waitress came by and dashed my hopes announcing the tap was having trouble. I was totally dejected, I do so love my Guinness. She brought another beer, which was OK. Then a few minutes later she came by with a dark foaming glass, filled with a cascade of bubbles, which could only belong to one thing. The waitress stated that she saw my disappointment and milked the tap to get one out for me. All praise our determined waitress! She even let us borrow her computer to check on the U.S.Olympic Trials results. Sadly, they were not posted yet. This, of course, is what happens when the creator of *www.racewalk.com* doesn't go to the Trials, but goes hiking instead.

Day 3 - Le Chable - Cabine du Mont Fort

We got up at 5:45 am and hoped to roll out the door quickly to beat the poor, late day weather forecast. Having to climb a vertical mile / 1,600m, we definitely wanted to beat the precipitation. As we got organized, Jennifer noticed that she did not have her rain jacket. Quite an essential piece of equipment considering it was already raining. Our hearts sank. As she realized that she left it in the bar the night before, fear came over us. The bar didn't open until 6 pm. Even our hotel wasn't officially open yet, so Jennifer waited like an expectant puppy at our hotel door for someone to arrive. Since there was little I could do to improve the situation, I selfishly went back to sleep. I know, I am a good husband. At 8:00 am Jennifer came back with a smile and a jacket. The women from the hotel called the owner of the bar. He was kind enough to retrieve it.

The early morning rain had now stopped, so we hoped this was all for the best and hit the trail. Again, we quickly got confused trying to navigate our way out of the village. Once beyond the town limits, our directional challenges did not improve. To make matters worse, evil, ominous-looking clouds appeared, as did a cold, wet, miserable rain. About a quarter of the way up we found shelter, a locked up cabin that fortunately had a small covered stoop. Two other Haute routers, Nacho and his girlfriend, were already there waiting out the storm. We plopped down next to them, just as the rain stopped. I toweled off a bit, snacked, switched shirts and we marched forward.

At the halfway point we reached a warm, dry restaurant. Some trekkers were pulling out, as the restaurant was too expensive for them. It was $13 for a bowl of soup, but it was an excellent bowl of soup and did I mention the restaurant was warm and dry? Needless to say we stopped. After refueling, I changed quickly into my rain pants and headed out the door. I picked up my pack and looked down the trail. We were totally fogged in and Jennifer instantly disappeared into the white mist. I called out to her and was surprised to hear her voice reply from just a few feet away. We were indeed in a complete white out.

We climbed a trail that was a series of agonizing switchbacks. Now, if we could see the views it probably would not have been so bad. However, we saw just clouds. Eventually in the distance we could see a cabin. Hopefully it was our cabin. As we approached, it played peek-a-boo, coming in and out of view. Each time we saw it, the cabin appeared closer and closer. When we were almost there, the clouds parted and the cabin shined like a beacon. True to form, once we arrived the clouds and rain returned. Safely inside the warm cabin, we didn't mind quite as much.

Day 4 - Cabine du Mont Fort - Cabine de Prafleuri

Bad weather in the mountains can turn a hard day into a seemingly never-ending, torture session. We had to climb three passes, the first was at 2,600m / 8,530'. So, we got up early hoping to get over some, if not all the passes, before the rain hit. The skies looked very undecided. As we rounded a corner of the path, the fog slithered up the valley and closed in upon us. The mountains should have been amazing, but we only caught brief glimpses peeking out from behind a blanket of clouds. Not far from the start, our hopes of a dry ascent were thrashed as the rain started. When we reached the first pass I wanted to stop to get a drink, a bite to eat and to put on my waterproof pants. Jennifer wanted to keep going. I was a bit upset that she did not want stop for me. We had a little spat, which is not good high in the mountains with inclement weather bearing down on you. What I didn't realize was she only wore a thin waterproof shell for a jacket with her zippers open to vent the sweat from the climb. Neither of us realized she was in the beginning stages of hypothermia. This was with two 2,900m / 9,510' passes left to climb.

Conditions worsened. Sleet and hail pounded us while the trail turned into a boulder highway. I needed to change my pants and add a layer, but I was afraid to stop with Jennifer freezing up. Luckily, the wind wasn't too bad. As we approached the second pass, three hikers from Wales (John, John, and Winn) joined us, having taken the shortcut from the cabin. It was somehow comforting to suffer together with others in our predicament. As we approached the second pass I heard frantic gasps for air as Jennifer went into a full blown asthma attack. Could things get worse? After a hit from her inhaler, we made it over the pass and looked straight down into a slick, wet, steep, snow-covered descent. I wondered how the hell we would get down and over yet another pass. The navigation along the snow-filled trail turned out to be more intimidating than difficult, but the weather was worsening. Jennifer was now incoherent and mumbling as she walked. I just barked at her, kindly of course, to

keep her moving. It's one thing to have a trekker in trouble, it's quite a different matter when it's your wife and your mother-in-law may kill you if you let anything happen to her.

The beautiful lakes I looked forward to photographing had an enormous towering glacier above them. However, they were in clouds and we were in no condition to stop for a photo. When we reached the lakes, the small stream we were meant to cross was a roaring river. While we were able to traverse a makeshift crossing downstream, the three Welsh guys tried the direct route. One appeared not to have waterproof boots and was trying the old and ineffective method of placing plastic bags over his boots. Of course, our so called water proof boots weren't giving us much protection.

We started up to the third col and things were getting worse. My core temp felt like it was dropping fast and Jennifer's Raynaud's syndrome was fiercely flaring up, cutting off the circulation to her hands. We stopped, I popped my gloves off and got her hand warmers out while quickly throwing my fleece on under my jacket. My hands were like ice blocks and I couldn't find Jennifer's fleece buried in her pack. Needing to keep moving, we pushed on without getting it. I threw my gloves back on and with the added layer, I warmed up quickly. Unfortunately, Jennifer was still suffering. Halfway to the col, instead of the trail rising toward it, we had another intimidating drop and this one lived up to its threatening look. All I heard from Jennifer were despairing moans. "Keep moving," I'd shout until we finally got over the col.

When the weather broke a little we paused so I could get Jennifer another layer. It was then that I realized the thinness of her jacket. No wonder she was in the "mumbles, stumbles, and fumbles" as she would later call it. I called it stage two hypothermia! It was still 45 minutes to the cabin with a nice steep climb, but I knew we had passed the serious danger and would make it without any permanent damage to my new bride.

We arrived to the cabin with boots, socks, pants and packs all soaked and added our stuff to a heap of equipment hanging to dry. Joining the chaos of trekkers who had converged on the cabin from many different routes, we warmed up quickly with a bowl of soup and a sandwich before sacking out for a bit. Of course, now that we were inside and dry the sun broke through. A guided British group strolled in short one person who had altitude problems. They had already lost one to a broken ankle. How did the poem *Ten Little Indians* go? As the sun looked like it would stay out for a while, people started migrating their clothes outside. It was a seemingly good idea; that is if you discount the dog playfully running off with people's socks and the donkey snacking on a shirt or two.

Cabine de Prafleuri was the most penny-pinching place I have ever stayed. I've heard of paying for electricity to charge your devices, but they had a coin-operated machine for the light to a room that slept twenty people. On top of this, at breakfast when we reached for a second piece of rather cheap, mass produced cheese, they barked, "only one piece per person."

Day 5 - Cabine de Prafleuri - Arolla

The day started out great, leaving "Cheapskate Cabin" by 7:30 am. We marched out of the valley on an icy pre-dawn slope that made our footing questionable. We carefully ascended and when we reached the first rise I realized I screwed up and didn't pick up our sandwiches for lunch. Jennifer took the news well. Since we were the first on the trail and a large group was tracking behind, we didn't turn back. Our early start paid off when we walked into a undisturbed herd of big horns. We quietly approached and they barely seemed to notice our presence. One barked orders to the others, but they all seemed content to hang out and nosh on the grass. After passing the herd, we came upon a self-service cabin. It was exactly the kind of place we needed the day before to shelter ourselves from the storm.

We ambled the most relaxing few miles of our Alpine trek following the length of a five kilometer / three mile lake that was created by Europe's tallest dam. At the mouth of Lac de Dix, it is nearly one thousand feet high and taller than Egypt's largest pyramid. Alongside the trail inquisitive marmots popped up and down like a game of "Whack a Mole." The views of the mountain glaciers and valley were exactly what we had missed the day before. We had a quick snack on the far end of the lake and then we started up a 600m / 1,970' ascent to the col. At first it wasn't too difficult, but after a short while we were climbing up a steep stretch of scree. It was quite challenging. As we climbed we completely lost the trail and it got scarier with each step. With nowhere else to go but up we climbed toward what looked like solid ground. We climbed about 100m / 330' and then realized we were headed to a dead end. Our friend Nacho and his girlfriend, who sadly followed in our footsteps, appeared about 50m / 165' below us. He signaled to go the other way, but his path didn't look much better than ours. Simultaneously, we saw the real path far below us which unfortunately was headed in the opposite direction.

This was bad. As hard as it was to get up, it would be dangerous to get down. I've traversed crazy descents before, but this was by far the most hazardous. Worrying about our safety, I stored my camera in my pack, a true sign of fear, and remembered my Jedi Knight training. Obi Won guided me down one step at a time. I skooched my butt on the ground, building a pile of scree between my legs to slow my progress. I came to a dead stop after every foot of descent to make sure I didn't accelerate. Jennifer followed behind me with equal caution. This worked great from my perspective, although it tore a hole right through the seat of my pants. It also didn't work so well for the hikers below us as our mini avalanches rained down upon them.

After what seemed like hours, and probably was only 30 minutes or so, we reached the trail and safety. My pants were the only casualty, which were a complete loss. Poor Nacho and his girlfriend were still way above us, hoping to find an alternate high route. I emptied a ton of stones and dirt from my boots and counted our blessings that we didn't have bigger issues.

We regrouped and actually followed the tail of one of the guided groups. While there are many negatives to hiking with a large group, there are indeed positives. Knowing where you are going was one of the biggest advantages. They were exceptionally kind and one girl gave us some cheese and bread. Remember, the day started with my leaving our lunch at the cabin. We trailed the group all the way up to the col. The path up was steep, but this time well marked. We proceeded slowly, fatigued by our detour. The col was much farther than we expected, but was indeed worth it when we got there. The col itself was quite small, but with a spectacular view. A German family was there who had hiked from the other direction. It seems like any day hiker could reach the cols easily since they were carrying little to no weight. It wasn't just the hike that made it tough. Instead it was the toll of the day-after-day abusive weight on our backs that made each climb much more difficult. The trip down was incredibly pleasant by comparison. The trail was steep at first, but then mellowed and provided ever improving views of the mountains and glaciers. We kept hoping the town would appear over the next rise, but there were many disappointments as the trail continued onward. Finally, we dropped out of the forest into a quaint reasonably-sized town. There was one small obstacle, an electric fence. It's a good thing Jennifer knew French or I wouldn't have known which part of the gate was safe to touch. We had a little trouble finding our hotel, but when we did we scored big. We had a the whole place to ourselves for only $40 a night.

Day 6 - Arolla - Lac Bleu - Les Hauderes - La Sage

Today was supposed to be an easy recovery day and we were determined to make sure it was. We planned to breakfast where we had dinner as they served delicious looking omelets. Sadly, when we arrived we found out they don't cook breakfast. Instead of the tasty omelets they offered overpriced cereal and fruit. We opted for the supermarket and then hit the trail.

We were headed to Lac Bleu, but there were two possible paths. One was low and easy and one higher and harder. We debated which to take, because Jennifer's injuries were amassing. Her arm was sore from the fall on the TMB, the site of her ankle surgery was acting up, and her Achilles was hurting. In the end she said that we should go up the higher path, but this was more because I wanted to go than she felt like it was the better choice. This turned out to be a bad decision because, although

the trail was not physically challenging, it was treacherous underfoot. The trail did have nice views, including many great were the wildflowers, plenty of new IDK's (I Don't Know what it is).

We reached the lake without incident and it truly lived up to its name as it was crystal clear and blue. Beyond it we traversed a trail through three villages taking our time and stopping for a snack and then lunch. We arrived in La Sage early, relaxed and not sweaty at all. We got a little ice cream at one of the hotels and lucked out. They let us use their Internet for free. We were especially fortunate as they were the only Internet access in town.

We bought a bunch of snacks and gorged on olives, cheese, crackers, cookies and the leftover wine I carried in my SIGG bottle. We dined on our balcony looking over this small Alpine village with two giant mountains watching over us. The best part was some kind, generous soul left sunburn cream for communal use. It was actually more of a moisturizing cream which we turned into a massage cream. There are advantages to hiking with your wife.

Day 7 - La Sage - Cabane de Moiry - Barrage de Moiry

This day was supposed to be a 10 kilometer / 6.2 mile hike, but with a lot of altitude gain and loss. The weather was perfect with crisp cool air easing our 1,600m / 1 mile ascent. We were climbing at a good pace, following the trail until it vanished into a field of wildflowers. We saw where we needed to go, but couldn't find a way to get there. You could just hear that Pepperridge Farm guy saying, "You can't get thar from here." With nowhere else to go, we walked through a field, waist deep in flowers.

Once we got back on the trail we headed toward a grassy meadow and once again the trail disappeared. This was right after we passed one of the guidebook's "unmistakable landmarks." We were frustrated and didn't want to repeat our scree fiasco. So instead of chancing it, we followed a jeep road up and to the next set of buildings. Fortunately, that turned out to be the right decision and we were back on track. From the higher vantage point we could see the trail we were supposed to take, but it literally materialized in the middle of the meadow. The start of it was completely overgrown.

Knowing we were no longer lost we took a small break by a tiny pond reflecting the mountains around us. Although it was tiny it had relatively large fish darting about. As we sat a large white furry Yeti ran by. As my father-in-law Ken gave me strict instructions to protect his daughter, I didn't break out the camera until the danger was gone. Therefore, the only evidence we

122

have are the photographs of the tracks of the stealthy, geographically misplaced creature. We pushed on for the col and when we reached it, we had it to ourselves for an early lunch.

We cruised down an equally steep slope and reached the end of a large man-made lake. From there we had to climb another 500m / 1,640' up to Cabane de Moiry on the edge of a giant ice fall. It looked impressive from a distance and we hoped as we reached the cabin we would be in for a striking display. As we climbed the views didn't improve. Actually I felt they got worse.

As we got close to the top we heard the warning horn of explosives. We thought they were trying to prevent avalanches, but when we reached the cabin the horns were for construction. Actually it was for destruction. The cabin was in disarray, construction vehicles were hard at work and the stench of explosives were in the air. When we inquired about Jennifer's reserved vegetarian meal their response was "pick around the meat." We had some overpriced, horrid soup. Subsequently, we inquired where the bathrooms were. They were outside in the middle of the construction zone. To get there you had to traverse unstable steps that were barely held together and situated hanging over the edge of a cliff. This was not the mountain escape we envisioned. We both looked at each other and simultaneously decided to leave. This meant walking back down the 500m / 1,640' decent and then a few kilometers to the next lodging at the far end of the lake. The staff was surprised and mocked us for wanting to leave. Call me strange, but with a choice of hanging around a construction site or hiking along a peaceful lake, I'll take the lake. So, we walked down and headed to the restaurant and barrage (refugio) of Lake Moiry. From a culinary perspective we totally made the right choice. The restaurant served as close to gourmet food as we had since coming to Europe. We started with a fresh mixed salad. It was followed with a delectable beef and polenta dish and finished off with a delicate melon puree.

Day 8 - Barrage de Moiry - Col de Sorebois - Zinal

Again the weather was supposed to change for the worse, so we got a bagged breakfast the night before, ate early, and headed onto the trail by 7:30 am. We had only a single 550m / 1,800' climb right at the start of the day. At the very least we hoped to achieve the col before the rain started. We climbed with a beautiful view of the lake while shaded from the sun. We took our time, making steady progress. Again, almost no one was around. We seemed to be the only early risers, which we didn't mind. We got to the col by ourselves and had a quick snack while keeping an eye on the sky and the dark, worsening clouds that were crawling in our direction.

As we headed down we entered a ski slope. It was weird to have the trail marred by ski lifts, but it makes sense since we were traveling though prime ski destinations. As we descended we passed more and more people heading up into the bad weather. Most of them were day hikers. It wouldn't have been a day I would pick to climb into the open and inclement weather. As we got farther down our path was blocked by three very lazy, lounging cows. They didn't seem to want to move for us. I half expected the little French guy from Monty Python to pop out and taunt us. After Jennifer played with the cows for a bit and was covered in cow snot we headed into the forest. The path was steep, but not too treacherous. Although fairly dark, both sides of the path were covered with huge pink and white wild flowers as high as our shoulders. Just before we left the forest and entered town it started to sprinkle. It seemed like we timed things perfectly. We reached town, a real town, complete with a supermarket, hotels, showers and the Internet. Voilà, my favorite French word, which means, "there it is." Oh, and voilà, crepes, too!

While the rain subsided for a bit, it came on strong later. The problem was the next two days contained high passes with lots of rain predicted. I was so relieved when Jennifer brought up the idea of letting me walk on alone and meeting me in two days in St. Nicklaus. In addition to her injuries (ankle, Achilles, and arm) an old knee injury was acting up. I was very proud of her. If we went over the passes together, not only could she develop problems, but the slower pace in bad weather could cause me issues as well. She clearly wanted to walk, but was being smart and incredibly unselfish. There was a bright aspect to the new plan. Originally Jennifer was going to walk out on a low valley trail as I took the high route. By Jennifer getting more rest, we could slow down and walk the high route together.

Day 9 - Zinal - Gruben

As we went to bed the storms came, big booming thunderous storms. The kind of storms that make your dog yelp. I was not looking forward to walking alone in the rain and cold. Still, I slept well and got up to a surprisingly hearty breakfast of yogurt, meat, cheese, juice and fruit. Too bad I was gearing up to walk in the cold rain or I would have feasted. I ate a bit, said goodbye to Jennifer, and hit the trail in the cold, but relatively light rain.

The trail was great and the rain stopped after a few minutes. To top it off, the usually confusing directions of the book were crystal clear. By forty minutes I was overheating and pulled off my jacket, counting my blessings. If I could do any part of the trail without rain I would consider myself lucky. As I rose, I actually saw glimpses of our goal, the Matterhorn. Maybe today would work out OK. Of course, then Jennifer would be disappointed she didn't come.

I hummed along, literally, as my Walkman™ was on, and then came to the part of the trail that was described as a "grassy slope drained by a stream and is faint in places!" I called it a bog; a big, wet, mushy bog. The fog was so thick that Luke Skywalker could see more through his blast helmet. I aimed for what looked like reasonable ground and luckily found the way markers. They were not as sufficient as the guidebook stated. The woman in the store yesterday said, "Sometimes the rocks move." A lot of rocks must have moved.

I made it to a landmark, a cabin with a cross. For my reward it started to rain. My boots already felt like bags of water on my feet, how much worse could it get? I was a few hundred meters from the col, so I ate half a Snickers bar and pushed up. The rain wasn't horrible. I stayed focused, watching the trail through the pea soup. The GPS told me I was close and then, voilà, there it was, the sign for the col.

Now it was all downhill. On the other side of the col the trail was blocked by snow, but after some careful maneuvering I was descending comfortably. As I flew down, following the guidebook's directions, I passed a sign that said 55 minutes to Zinal. Disaster then struck. I followed the way markers to the single most treacherous trail I have ever traversed. It reminded me of the trails in the jungle of Burma, but I didn't have a machete or, more importantly anyone with me to notice if I fell. With the overgrowth nearly pushing me over the edge of the soaking wet trail I continued on even though it was less than a foot wide. I didn't know what to do as the trail markers were clearly visible. The guidebook described the trail as overgrown, so I hesitantly forged ahead. I had to cross a large stream that was not mentioned in the book. I thought that maybe with all the rain a stream formed that was normally insignificant. With the path continuing to climb, I was disheartened. I checked the GPS and it said I had gained about 100m / 330', when it should have been descending. Still the markers pointed me forward. The book left off short climbs before, so I continued. My fear was if something went wrong and I slipped now, no one would be behind me. I saw another trail heading down. So I scoped it out and it lead nowhere. One of the blessings and curses of Alpine hiking was the seemingly endless number of trails. I decided to backtrack and retreat. Once on the road again I found the right trail twenty meters from where I turned off. What the hell! I scooted down it and got to the outskirts of town. After about 20 minutes I was home free. That is if you excuse the electrified fences in the way; notice the plural.

It stopped raining and the sun appeared. The hotel had a wood burning stove to dry my boots and something I never expected, an outdoor ping-pong table. A wonderful group of Swiss hikers adopted me for the night. They were hiking for the weekend; what a weekend to pick. They reenforced how it is the journey and the camaraderie as opposed to the destination. We played ping-pong for a while, ate dinner and then they taught me a game that translated in English to "The Dice."

Day 10 - Gruben – St. Nicklaus – Gasenried

I got on the trail by 7:40 am after a quick hello and goodbye to a second group of British hikers. It was rainy, but not too bad. The directions out of town were great and the trail itself was solid. I made excellent time. The rain slowed to where the sky was sweating on me more than actually raining. I was content, given the forecast. There was absolutely nothing to see as the fog blocked everything. It was sad because the views were supposed to be spectacular. It was so bad, I placed my camera in my pack in disgust.

The ascent to 2,900m / 9,500' went really well. I climbed to the col in two hours and twenty minutes, forty minutes ahead of schedule. I tried to move quickly as I knew if I were late to meet Jennifer she would worry. At the top of the col it was bitterly cold and windy enough to almost blow me over. So I headed straight down. The path below was also sure-footed and I was making good time. Soon hikers coming from the other valley started passing me. They were quite happy to hear that where they were going, where I came from, was clear of snow. About a half an hour from the town of Jungu I sort of saw a herd of big horns. They were very close to me, but in the fog they more or less disappeared. One got up on its hind legs as it looked out over the cliff. Ahh, to have had my camera with my long lens, but it was with Jennifer so I could save weight. I took out the camera with the lens I had, but in the twenty seconds it took to get in hand, the fog rolled over the big horn and it disappeared.

As I descended I was supposed to look for a sign post. I found one, but it didn't have the option for Jungu, or Jungen as the book spelled it. Instead, it had Juntal. Was this yet another synonym for the town? I thought so and followed the trail, which had the familiar red and white markers. As I progressed I watched the GPS and map paint two entirely different pictures from what I expected. I couldn't see more than 15 feet ahead of me and after walking for ten or fifteen minutes, I got that sinking déjà vu feeling. I decided this wasn't the trail and doubled back headed down the unmarked trail. Lo and behold, a few minutes later I came upon the correct sign. Later, I would find out my Welsh friends made the same mistake, but they didn't turn around. They went all the way to Juntal and then walked a longer route to Jungu.

I reached Jungu shortly after retracing my steps. While it was quaint, it was not "the loveliest Alp hamlet between Chamonix and Zermatt" as the book hyped it to be. Ideally, it would have been a good place to stop for the night and then walk from there to St. Nicklaus to Gasenried the next day. Having lost a lot of time I headed down to St. Nicklaus where I was to meet Jennifer. It was a far drop, but contained switchbacks most of the way down.

Jennifer was waiting for me with lunch. She's a good wife that Jennifer! After a quick bite, we headed to Gasenried together. Most people were opting to stay in St. Nicklaus and take a bus to Gasenried in the morning. We figured we would walk now and get an early start on the next day's journey. The trip started well until we reached the part of the trail that should have cut across a road, but the road was demolished. We wound around and found the trail again only to completely lose it shortly after. We ended up thirty minutes east of Gasenried and had to double back. We eventually found our hotel, but it was completely deserted with the keys in all the doors. After a bit of searching, we found the caretaker and he showed us to our room. It's was more than a bit eerie. We were the only people staying in the hotel and it was one of only two hotels in town. Eerie turned to awesome when we noticed they had a large fireplace stocked with wood. We asked and they let us start a fire. Warmth, romantic lighting and most importantly, boot drying made the night quite enjoyable.

Day 11 - Gasenried – Europa Hut

The weather was supposed to improve. From the view outside the window of the hotel, conditions, didn't appear much better. We had a feast for breakfast. It was the first buffet to include fresh eggs. The plan for the day was to head past the Europa Hut and continue on to Taschalp, a cabin three hours farther. That would give us another half day in Zermatt to work on our other photo project, *One Dress, One Woman, One World*. The problem was with the fog bowl outside we wouldn't see squat along the way. We called Europa Hut to see if we could change our reservation and they said they were booked other than emergency space. So we were in for a long and unrewarding day.

Due to yesterday's mishap finding Gasenried, we knew the exact way to the trail. We started on a frustrating note, the times on the sign were different than the book. "Who do we believe," I asked? We climbed steeply and were quickly rewarded with a herd of Chamoix crossing above us. They floated effortlessly up the rocky slope with such grace that I was jealous. Shortly after we came across another conflicting sign. One pointed to Grat, a way point with a good view, and the other pointed to the hut. Since there was no view we followed the more direct route out. As we turned on the trail we walked into a herd of friendly goats who were very interested in any food Jennifer might offer them.

After working our way around the herd, we approached the statue of St. Bernard. Who knew the lovable liquor-toting dog's name was based upon a real person? After a quick photo stop with the Saint, we headed up and around to the "Boulder Highway." We would stay on this for some time, intermittently crossing dangerous avalanche zones where we had to move quickly. When we hit the first avalanche zone I sent Jennifer ahead and followed five minutes behind for safety. As I was crossing, my GPS popped off my belt and fell into the dark abyss between the boulders. I exclaimed loudly, "Fuck!" and then quickly realized Jennifer would think I fell and yelled back that I was "OK." Unfortunately, Jennifer only heard the curse and then silence. I heard nothing of the ten or so calls Jennifer made to me, until finally I heard a frantic scream to see if I was OK. I yelled back that I was, and pulled out my head lamp to see if I could find the GPS. The light disappeared into the black hole. I accessed my options, which were few. The boulders weren't going to get out of the way and decided I had to leave it. Where is Fred Flintstone when you need him! I begrudgingly said goodbye to my trusty friend, which had all the unbacked up data for every step of the Haute Route on it. Of all my trips I felt this data was among the most valuable. The elevations and distances in the book were dead wrong. They had a complete lack of granularity that affected one's ability to determine their location.

With my data gone and no view to speak of, I focused on the ground. The wildflowers, while diminutive in comparison to those at lower elevations, were fascinating on a tiny scale. The colors produced by a prism were no grander than the wild assortment at our feet. Finally, the sky started to clear and we saw slight patches of blue emerging. We turned the corner to a wobbly suspension bridge. While wide enough, it bounced in the wind and tilted to one side. The walkway was constructed with plywood flooring that seemed way too thin for my combined body and pack weight of 240 pounds. Once safely across, it wasn't much farther until we reached the Europa Hut. The woman in charge agreed to squeeze us in, as long as we slept on a mattress on the floor. While we could have gone on, it didn't make sense to waste some of the best and most iconic views, so we decided to stay the night.

Day 12 - Europa Hut - Zermatt

On our last night on the trek, I was determined to get at least one night shot. Fortunately, the weather cooperated and I got up around 3:00 am for a quick one hour exposure of the mountains and glacier overshadowing our cabin. Once the clouds finally cleared, the view during the day was equally impressive. It seemed our delayed exit of the trail would pay dividends. The trail out, while still having too many boulders for our tired legs, was much easier than the previous day's. There were rolling changes in elevation, but no more 1,600 meter / 1 mile climbs. Instead, we were treated to ever improving views of the Matterhorn, more and more wildflowers, and a sea of blue butterflies. We stopped for a bowl of soup at the halfway point, enjoyed great views and then pushed on to the finish.

There were multiple ways to complete the trail. One way was to take the tram down. Not an option for us, it would be too anticlimactic. Another choice was to wind through every little village along the way. This was the guidebooks "proper" way to finish. After all, each village was a "can't miss opportunity" to experience the "best" of something. A third option was to take a direct trail to Zermatt. We contemplated our decision while having a noontime drink. We ordered a bottle of juice and received the tiniest bottle imaginable for $4.50. Typically, any place we stopped and used the bathroom we bought at least a bottle of juice. This was never an issue before, however, when I came out of the bathroom I was greeted by the waiter informing me, rather rudely, that I needed to buy a second bottle as I had used the bathroom as well. This made our decision easy to skip the rest of the wonderful hospitality and take the more direct route. Zermatt, crowded as ever, never looked so good as when we emerged from the forest and headed to our hotel.

Epilogue

In many regards the Haute Route is the Tour de Mont Blanc (TMB) on steroids. While the first two days of the Haute Route overlap part of the TMB, it is on the more challenging terrain than the TMB. This is a foreshadowing of the Haute Route in general. With three high passes over 10,000 feet the weather is far less predictable and the consequences of mistakes more extreme. As a reward you gain the breathtaking destination of the Matterhorn, dramatic views from countless cols, and an impressive wildflower display.

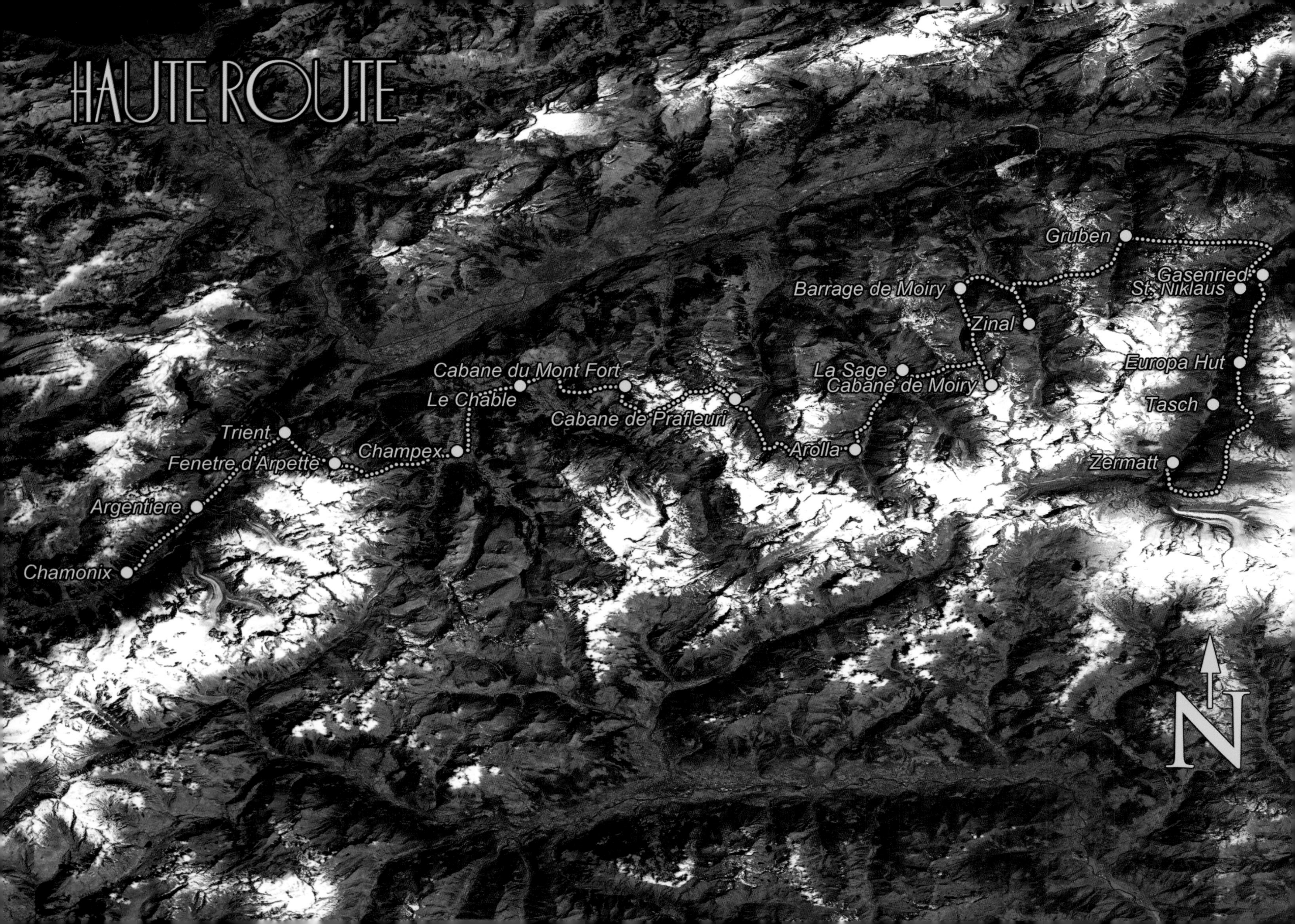

HAUTE ROUTE

N

Gasenried
St. Niklaus
Europa Hut
Täsch
Zermatt
Gruben
Zinal
Barrage de Moiry
Cabane de Moiry
La Sage
Arolla
Cabane de Prafleuri
Cabane du Mont Fort
Le Châble
Champex
Trient
Fenetre d'Arpette
Argentière
Chamonix

Chapter Ten
The Grand Canyon
U.S.A.

The American Southwest is an amazing geological wonder. Fascinating rock formations, Anasazi ruins, vast deserts and great rivers. The greatest is the magnificent Colorado: winding its way from the high Rockies of its namesake state through Utah and Arizona, ultimately, emptying into the Sea of Cortez. In truth, very little water makes it that far, as much of it is now diverted and dammed to quench the thirst of the great suburban desert metropolises of Los Angeles, Las Vegas and Phoenix. However, this hasn't stopped the river from making itself known as the great creator of one of the world's true natural wonders.

In northern Arizona the Colorado River makes its way through, in fact it cuts through, the granite uplift of northern Arizona, forming the ninety-mile long by one-mile wide Grand Canyon. This cut is nothing short of spectacular. Although, there are many other canyons and gorges in the world, and having seen numerous contenders, we can assure you there is nothing comparable to the breadth, depth, character and color of the Grand Canyon. Indeed, there is nothing like it in the world!

Although it took three million years to form this ultimate hiker's destination, the good news is you can hike the heart of it in as few as three days. In a lifetime one could hardly complete exploration of all the side canyons, nooks and crannies. However, you can get an excellent taste of what the American Southwest and the Grand Canyon have to offer. Hiking the canyon rim-to-rim-to-rim provides you the widest and deepest experience. The benefit, of course, is that you experience the geology of both rims, the inner canyon and the river itself.

There are several variations to this hike. There are multiple trail options on the South Rim, so you don't completely retrace your footsteps and you don't have to organize a shuttle as is necessary if you went just rim-to-rim. Our recommendation is to start at the South Rim and descend via the South Kaibab Trail. You can stay at Phantom Ranch Campground or Lodge upon your descent. Then head up toward the North Rim via the North Kaibab Trail staying the night at Cottonwood Campgrounds. In the morning you can leave your camp set up and day hike, without the added weight of your pack, to the North Rim. You can then return to sleep at Cottonwood before heading back up on the Bright Angel Trail the next day.

Fundamentals

Days Trekking: 3 - 6 days		Approximate Elevation Change: South Kaibab Trail 1,481m / 4,860' elevation change North Kaibab Trail 1,475m / 5,790' elevation change Bright Angel Trail 1,359m / 4,460' elevation change
Distance: 92km / 57mi roundtrip		Price Range Independent: $300 - $700
Max Elevation: 2,513m / 8,240' North Rim		Price Range Outfitter: $1,200 - $3,500
Starting Elevation: 2,214m / 7,260' South Kaibab Trailhead		Challenge Level: Moderate-Difficult

When to Go

The ideal Canyon seasons are late spring and late fall. Winter brings snow on the rims, especially the North Rim. Summer is unbearably hot. Carrying an overnight backpack is not recommended at this time. This is especially true in the inner canyon where the lower elevation and canyon walls make it an oven and nearly unsuitable for anything but early morning or late day hikes.

Guided vs. Independent Treks

There are many options hiking independently. Permits are available through the National Park Service starting the first day of the month, one year in advance for any day that month. The prime trails and campgrounds fill up quickly so get your reservation in early.

There are many guided options. You can ride the famous mule train down the canyon, and more importantly, ride back up. For those who plan way ahead, you can stay in comfort at Phantom Ranch Lodge at the bottom.

You can also mix and match, hiking independently and staying in comfort at the Phantom Ranch. Another option is to go budget and stay in their bunkhouses. You can also get meals at the Phantom Ranch to avoid carrying excessive weight up and down. Finally, you could use the mule train to porter your gear up/down or both, thus traveling with a large daypack.

Access / Local Information

For accessing the South Rim, Phoenix is your best bet. The South Rim Village is a four-hour drive from Phoenix. Flagstaff is much smaller and closer, only a two-hour drive, but has a more limited flight selection. It is an eight-hour drive from LA. The North Rim is easily accessed from Las Vegas, Nevada in a five-hour drive.

Difficulty

The central corridor trails in the Grand Canyon are well maintained, but still steep. Water presents the chief difficulty. There are few water sources and hiking in the heat and sun of the canyon can quickly dehydrate the most fit hiker. Therefore, hikers must carry a lot of water (3-4 liters minimum) and the weight that goes along with it.

Alternative/Additional Treks

There are many hiking alternatives in the Grand Canyon. It is easy to get off the beaten path. However, for rim-to-rim hikes this is only possible in the central corridor because it is the only place where there are bridges. It is possible to go just rim-to-river in several other places.

On the Trail with Jeff

Trekking rim-to-rim-to-rim in the Grand Canyon requires good timing and proper preparation. Mid-September was far from ideal as temperatures at the bottom of the canyon might reach 38° C / 100° F during the day. A dry heat maybe, but with 50 or more pounds on your back, it is far from pleasant. The problem is if you wait until much later in the season it can get quite cold at the rim. Given my school schedule, this was going to be my best opportunity for the trek. I'd visited the Canyon twice before; once totally unprepared. I defied the Park Service's warning and flew down to the river and back up in a day. Without a pack, and on the Bright Angel Trail that had plenty of water, I was able to round trip it in five hours. My second trip was as an overnight and one of my first times back packing. To say things went wrong was an understatement. I hoped not to have a repeat performance.

My third experience at the Grand Canyon was with my *Great Treks* partner Kirk, his girlfriend Kristy and my former student Ben. We had planned a five-day, four-night itinerary that started out like a Seinfeld episode. We called our hotel just before 9 pm to get more accurate directions and were rudely told if we didn't get there in a few minutes they wouldn't hold our reservation. To top it off they were going to keep our fee. This led to a frenzied search for a new hotel on Ben's poor excuse of a smart phone. As Murphy's Law would dictate, we hit unexpected traffic from Phoenix to Williams, AZ. Fortunately, the kind people at the Travelodge were willing to accept us when we finally arrived at 11 pm.

We repacked quickly, realizing as we did that we didn't bring everything we wanted. Given the time crunch, we would just have to make do with what we remembered. We managed four hours of sleep and then rushed out the door to the canyon. Ben and I arrived just in time to make the 6 am shuttle to the trail head to meet Kirk and Kristy at the shuttle stop. It was odd to arrive and not even peek 100 yards away at the giant hole in the ground, but we were focused on getting on the trail before the heat of the day engulfed us. At the rim it was actually cold enough that I put on my sweat shirt. It felt weird to be adding layers as we worried about the heat.

Walking Down, Way Down

Once at the trail head, we loaded up with water, took a quick picture and were on our way. At first the four of us stayed together as a group, stopping at the many views along the way. Looking out, we could see millions of years of history locked within the sedimentary rocks. It was a giant laboratory for a third grade science class. One benefit of hiking down into a canyon as opposed to other hikes is the amazing vistas appear immediately and continue during most of the hike. Stopping for a rest is always a pleasure as there is so much to absorb.

While walking down South Kaibab is steep and takes its toll on your knees and legs, it isn't particularly strenuous. However, it is important to note, there is no water, so you must pack enough to keep well-hydrated as the midday sun shines down upon you. On my previous trip we were advised to hike up South Kaibab. I strongly recommend you do not. Estimating the proper amount of water needed to hike all the way up is not easy given the conditions. As we descended I saw the many spots we attempted to shelter ourselves from the sun on the way up during my last ill-fated trek. I hoped this trip would not be as harrowing.

One great aspect of hiking in the park is the trails are amazingly wide and the easiest to follow of any of the Great Treks I walked so far. In addition, the construction of the path was absolutely topnotch. The park is a testament to our National Park Service (NPS).

With young Ben setting quick pace, he and I forged ahead. A couple of hours later, we traversed through a dark cave and descended to a bridge to cross the Colorado River. Shortly after, we arrived at a fork in the road between the Phantom Ranch and the campgrounds. We asked someone how far it was to the campground and they said 10-20 minutes. We didn't know they should have said 10-20 yards. For whatever reason, it seems the Minister of Disinformation had a strong foothold in the canyon. More often than not, people on this trail seemed to provide very inaccurate information. So, instead of grabbing a campsite, we waited for Kirk and Kristy to arrive. After eating half of our lunch, two umbrella-carrying figures appeared on the trail. Ahhh, the Mighty Kirk was wise and brought much needed shelter from the sun. We headed to the campsites, only to find them one minute down the trail. The campsites were great with plenty of room for two tents, a large picnic table, poles to hang our packs, food storage boxes to protect our precious edibles, even a bathroom with running water and flush toilets. Most importantly, there was a cool fresh stream to soak our tired bodies.

Kirk found a temporary tattoo of a T-bone steak. We put it on my arm and it was the closest to steak I was getting for the trip. Truth be told, you could buy a steak dinner at the Phantom Ranch for over $40, but when we were planning our trek that seemed excessive and a little bit like cheating. Now that we were down in the canyon and hungry, it seemed much more palatable, especially since they had beer to complement it.

We "cooked" the bags of dehydrated food we brought to make life easy. This was a departure from our norm, but seemed sensible given our plans. The first night's dinner was pad thai, and I have to say, it was surprisingly good. Sadly, it would be the only good bagged meal of the trip. We hung out with a few campers in another site and after years of trying I actually got someone on the oldest trick in the book. I succeeded duping a nice woman from Chicago after she heard something scurrying around in the brush. "What's that?" she inquired. I volunteered, "It's a Dickfer." "What's a Dickfer?" she asked. I said, "To pee with." Yes, third grade humor still amuses me.

To our surprise it was a skunk. It provided quite the split within the campsite. All the men were eager to spy on it. All the women wanted nothing to do with it and not too keen on the fact that we were shining our light on the nervous little critter. Unfortunately, I didn't have my camera. After that we decided to call it a night and from our own campsite we took in nature's nightly show. The stars and the Milky Way were out in full force with a new moon above. As we went to sleep, I peered out the tent windows at the stars and dozed off pleasantly.

Quest for the Perfect Campsite

We got up at 5:30 am and headed out quickly to beat the heat and hopefully be the first to arrive at the next campsite. We were warned that only one or two of the campsites provided any modicum of shade and we were highly motivated to be one of the lucky groups. As usual, hitting the trail early provided lots of benefits. The temperature was cool as the sun was hidden behind the horizon. More importantly, the deer were still out and prancing around nearby.

Overall the trail was flat, with just a few short steep sections to traverse. It wasn't long before we had made our way down most of the trail and had to decide if we wanted to visit Ribbon Falls. Yearning for the better campsite, we justified to ourselves that we could go back without our packs and see it after staking our claim to a choice spot. This, of course, underestimates the inertia that develops once you reach camp.

As we walked, Ben confidently and perhaps a bit naively declared, "If tomorrow is no worse than the steepness of today, we'll be in great shape." While he meant only the small steep sections, I feared he underestimated the difficulty of a continual steep trail as compared to 50 or 100 meters of ascent. We continued along and shortly succeeded in our goal, arriving at a completely empty campsite. We carefully estimated the path of the sun and shade provided in each campsite before making our selection. We would be camping in the middle of the canyon for two nights, so it was a relatively important decision, at least as far as our comfort was concerned.

While my body was holding up well, Ben's less seasoned feet had developed blisters. Again, there was a cool, clean stream to relax in, but given Ben's issues we didn't wade too long. The last thing we needed was an infected foot. Having made great

time, we had plenty of idle time to read and feed our growing hunger. We ate two lunches by the time our companions arrived. Kristy was a bit weathered from the trip. With less hiking experience than us, she wasn't sure she could complete the rim-to-rim-to-rim journey. Content to let Kirk go up and down the North Rim with Ben and myself, a debate ensued. What was the best option for Kirk to pursue. I felt bad for him. He wanted to go, but also wanted to be a good boyfriend.

We were warned to hang our packs and store our food in the metal boxes provided. As the sun went down we experienced firsthand why there was so much concern. Mice were everywhere! Not timid little creatures quivering in the shadows, but bold ones, with sharp, pointy teeth. While I've seen aggressive mice before, they usually wouldn't challenge the bottom of a boot or hiking pole. Scurrying over our boots and packs, these mice weren't afraid of anything. If we kicked them away, they just climbed the tree and attacked from another direction. One even disrespected Ben's bag by pooping on it.

Rimming the Canyon

As we feared, Kirk decided not to go to the rim with us, but to stay back with Kristy. So, Ben and I forged on alone as I was stubborn and did not want to alter my original plans thereby reducing our trek to a rim-to-rim. We awoke at 5:15 am, hoping to beat the sun, but were slow in our departure. We hit the trail 35 minutes later and walked quickly, almost racing up in fear of the sun. The trail contained switchbacks with a relatively gentle slope. Our muscles ached, but nowhere as bad as it would have been with the weight of a full pack. We made good time, stopping to shoot some photos and talk to those coming down from the rim. When we got about a half an hour from the top, we stopped at a great outlook. The view coming up to the North Rim was quite different from the south side. Far more foliage littered the stone landscape painting a unique vista. For the first time we could see the sheer magnitude of the ascent. Worrying that we still had to climb and that the sun was getting higher, we didn't dawdle. Worst case, we figured if we couldn't see much from the trail head, we could circle back to the viewpoint on our way down and eat lunch there.

Cresting the top turned out to be anticlimactic as there was no view from the rim. There was just a sign and a big pile of boulders that the National Park Service was arranging with heavy machinery. Clearly they were building a tribute to Big Ben for completing his rim-to-rim endeavor. Realizing we were only halfway through our journey, damn my grandiose plans, we wanted to get as far along the trail as we could before the sun stopped us cold, well hot. So, we ate quickly and headed back down. It was odd seeing the leaves turning so early in the season, but we were that high up!

We made it back to the viewpoint in no time at all, stopping for another sandwich and the scenery. The views from the north, albeit slightly down from the rim, were far more spectacular than the South Rim. Given its lack of proximity to anything and the need to actually walk to it, the views were probably safe from dreaded progress. Although given the Skywalk built on the South Rim, who knows. Sun be damned, we spent some time soaking in the beauty before returning to camp. Once on the trail we scurried quickly, getting to the last water stop where we met three friendly guys, one rim-to-rim veteran and his two rookie friends. The veteran wanted to know if you get the same, "frog in your throat," each time you complete a hike like this. "Absolutely!" I confirmed.

As we walked down with the burden of climbing behind us, we were able to take in the unique splendor of the tree-lined landscape with huge stone outcroppings that stood as sentinels along a 915m / 3,000' castle wall of rock. While one might feel covering the same ground would be boring, you get a completely different view traversing it in the opposite direction. The trail was actually blasted out of the side of the cliff and if you looked closely you could still see the dynamite blasting holes.

We got about a third of the way down, when our fear of the sun was replaced with the fear of loud, clapping thunder. Heat would have been bad, but lightning would be far worse. Ominous, trip ruining, dark rain clouds were rolling in behind us. We dropped a gear and went from tourist mode into race mode, whizzing by our newly found friends, beating the rain, and making it to camp two hours earlier than we had planned in our most optimistic estimates.

We relaxed in camp, playing chess with a set of cards. Yes, we were desperate for a distraction, but computer geeks can makeshift anything in the name of entertainment. Fortunately, the rain completely missed us and we enjoyed the rest of the evening. As usual we went to bed early and it would have been an uneventful evening, but Ben blew such a fart, he woke himself up. That was a new one for me!

Climbing Back Out

The next day, Ben and I intentionally didn't rise early as we planned to divide the day into a morning and evening hike. Kirk and Kristy, on the other hand, had to march up to 2,440m / 8,000' and exit via the North Rim. Once there, they had no predetermined method for returning to the South Rim and would take their chances on how to get back to their car. Without the fear of sun, we lazily broke camp and headed for the previously missed Ribbon Falls. From a distance, it didn't look like much. As we approached, the trail disappeared. It was the one part of the path that wasn't obvious. Our first of many attempts to find the correct route ended in a scree-filled dead end. Our second attempt was less harrowing, but no more successful, as we circled back to the main trail. On our third attempt, we found a circuitous route over a precarious rock face to find the falls. Clearly this wasn't the right way either, but it was good enough to get us there.

To our surprise, the falls were simply breathtaking. This was actually not due to the physical beauty of the falls as much as the ecosystem created by the falls and towering cliffs. Moss, foliage and red rock made the contrasting view unforgettable. After the obligatory photo shoot, we headed to Phantom Ranch via what turned out to be the correct trail, a fairly flat downsloped path. The walk was pleasant and without too much sun. The only challenge was avoiding a snake rattling its poisonous warning.

Once at the ranch, we had to endure stories about other hikers' pending dinner, hmmm steak, as we ate a piece of sausage that only cost $1.50. A bargain on any hiking trip, but we longed for the more substantial meal. We rested for three hours as the heat of the day pounded down upon us. Sitting in the shade, reading and refueling our bodies, life was pretty good. I distracted myself for a while watching a brave deer climb up a rock face in search of food, chatted with a park ranger and then headed back onto the trail.

At first we thought we timed the sun perfectly as the tall canyon walls blocked the late afternoon heat from our backs. The problem was we vocalized our thoughts. Schmucks, I know! We paid the price for our hubris as the sun popped out to spoil our mood. Still, there wasn't any elevation gain as we traced the Colorado River's path for the next hour and a half until we came to the beach that marked the end of the Bright Angel Trail. It was then up, up, up as my Nepalese friend Padam would say. As we climbed, the sun was blocked by the top of the canyon. It was just enough to shield us from the heat. Neither of us chirped about it this time, though.

We got to a fairly deserted camp at 5:15 pm and we were pretty much done. Lots of campers' belongings were scattered around, but there weren't any people. We set up quickly and as I headed to the toilets I saw the greatest sunset through the trees. Apparently, we didn't time our arrival well. One of the best sunset views of the canyon was a scant mile and a half from camp. Given our late arrival there just wasn't enough time to make it there before the sun went down. Not to mention we had no energy left in our bodies. Instead, we prepped and ate dinner in a dead, empty camp. People started trailing in after nature's show was complete, but we were already closing up shop for the night.

The Final Push

We left at the crack of dawn, barely able to see the trail in front of us. Traveling back over ground I've seen twice before, we were all business. Honestly, although it wasn't that hard of a hike, the previous four days' efforts had taken their toll as we trudged up. I kept wondering how Kirk and Kristy were doing. If all went well, we agreed to meet for breakfast. However, I gave the chances of our meeting up about the same as catching a bass in the Schuylkill River. For those of you unfamiliar with the polluted river in Philadelphia, that's about one in a million.

As we climbed, my thoughts focused more on a hot fresh breakfast than the trail. Eventually, we started meeting the day trippers heading down who were a bit surprised to hear how far we had travelled. I am sure our smell removed any doubt from their minds. Our trip paled in comparison to the courage of a few brave souls escorting a large group of Boy Scouts for an overnight affair. Now that's brave!

We made it back to the rim in a few hours and it looked even more impressive now that we could gaze across it and say, we've finished a rim-to-rim-to-rim. We didn't waste much time, though, as we made good on our promise to ourselves and headed

for sustenance. Sadly, Kirk and Kristy were nowhere to be seen and they didn't carry a cell phone. Later we found out they were fine, just a few hours behind us.

Epilogue

Finishing the Grand Canyon was a wonderful experience, but it won't be my last trip to the Grand Canyon. Someday soon I'll head back with my wife, as she would have enjoyed it as much as I did. Fortunately, the last of the Great Treks was planned for her spring break. Ben was a great partner, but completing the treks with my life partner is much more rewarding as the experience can be shared and remembered the rest of our lives.

Kirk's Corner - Less is More, Alternate Choices

As Jeff, his friend Ben, my girlfriend Kristy and I were walking through the "normal" flat pine forests of Northern Arizona, we could make out a clearing through the trees ahead. We knew what it was. It was the reason we were here. Just as the forest ended, a jaw dropping sight manifested before us. Almost out of nowhere, the world's largest canyon literally just fell away. Although I had seen it before, it still took my breath away. I stood frozen in awe with tingles down my spine. An interesting thing about the canyon is the subtly of the approach. It surprises you like no other wonder of the world. One minute you could be walking or driving along with no idea you were within 150 feet of one of the largest geographical features on planet earth.

We had come to hike the Grand Canyon, rim-to-rim and back again. Combining four schedules limited our timeline, resulting in substantial hiking distance and elevation changes, each and every day of our trek. It was September, still considered one of the dangerously hot months for hikes to the inner canyon. The temperatures are scorching and water is scarce or non-existent along some trails.

Kristy and I arrived the day before our hike. Our goal was to relax and enjoy an evening at the Canyon Rim. We had a lot of packing to do but we took a little time to walk along the canyon rim at sunset. We were not disappointed. As the sun set a double rainbow appeared over the canyon ending on the famous rock outcropping known as Zoroaster Temple. It was a great way to start our trip.

The first day we hiked down the South Kaibab Trail to Phantom Ranch. The sun was relentless. Our body temperatures rose as we labored along the steep trail. Safety in the shade was hard to come by. We huddled together under the smallest rock outcropping just to get a tiny amount of relief. Dehydrated and overheated we tumbled into Phantom Ranch Campground for our first night in the canyon. We soaked in the ice cold waters of Cottonwood Creek. Facing another grueling day in the morning, we tried to hit the sack early. The heat in the tent was oppressive and the cacophony of our fellow campers rummaging around the campsite could wake Sleeping Beauty. We hatched and executed a plan to sneak away from the official campground and go down to the banks of the great Colorado River. We looked around in the dark with only our flashlights as we tried to find a flat sandy bank away from the trail to layout our sleeping bags. As we settled in our eyes adjusted and the starlight beautifully illuminated the steep canyon walls. The rushing sounds of the mighty Colorado echoed around us. It turned out to be one of the all-time most superb nights of camping. In addition, it planted a seed of revolution.

After another torturous day battling the elements of the inner canyon, we finally realized there was another way. We didn't have to punish our bodies while hiking from dawn to dusk in the scorching heat for the next three days. Alternatively, we could take a rest day, which would include a day hike to Rainbow Falls two miles away, as rest is only relative. Then the following day we would continue to the North Rim and on the final day take a shuttle back to the South Rim to retrieve our car. Yes, indeed, there is little escape from internal combustion in today's modern world, even for hardened trekkers who prefer travel by foot.

I am usually a total team player, but, the more relaxed pace seemed like a much more enjoyable adventure. Jeff and Ben were fine with the split and we appreciated their flexibility. We were essentially two self-contained units traveling together so there was no problem dividing the group. It really meant only one night without camping together and our different paces on the trail meant we would hardly hike together anyway.

It turned out our trip to Ribbon Falls was the perfect day for a short hike and a little respite from the midday heat of the canyon. There were a number of hikers there when we arrived at about 11 am, but by 1 pm we had the whole waterfall to ourselves. We explored all the nooks and crannies of Ribbon Falls and photographed every possible angle. As the afternoon lengthened we ultimately laid down and fell asleep as the sound of the falling water echoed softly in the canyon. I can't imagine a more restful place than laying on those rocks. Late in the afternoon as the sun made its move toward the canyon rim, we rustled ourselves awake and headed back to camp. I can't say there was a spring in our step, but our bodies were grateful to have had a chance to recuperate in preparations for our final assault on the North Kaibab Trail the following day.

In contrast to our rest day, Jeff and Ben were battling their way to the North Rim and then back to Cottonwood Campground. The following day they would be going back down to the river and halfway back up the South Rim along the South Kaibab Trail. Finally, the boys had one more morning of hiking.

Our last day of hiking led us up to the North Rim, the very trail Jeff and Ben hiked the day before. It was a demanding trail, hugging the sheer red stone cliffs of Roaring Springs Canyon. We were somewhat refreshed by our rest day but still the heavy pack and beating sun took a toll on our strength.

We were relieved to finally arrive at the North Rim. We didn't have campground reservations, mandatory at this time of year, but it turned out they have a walk-in campground designed for hikers and bikers arriving on flexible schedules. We were able to camp at practically the very edge of the North Rim in one of the most amazing National Park campsites.

The following day we boarded the shuttle which took us the long way around the canyon bringing us back to our vehicle on the South Rim. The landscapes we passed were magnificent. It's a long way and at times I lamented not being on the trail with Jeff and Ben, but overall my body and mind were thankful for the slower pace of our modified route.

The old adage, less is more, was once again relearned. Sometimes a shorter, more leisurely trek can offer more relaxation, more beauty and more time to explore off the beaten path. When traveling and trekking, often times there is a rush to hike more in a limited amount of time. Sometimes pushing the limits is what needs to be done. Our world is one that prizes increased productivity and greater output. The flip side is that it is important to keep perspective. You may have a more pleasant experience if you take more time and go slowly. Don't try to do it all and you may find that you will maximize your enjoyment.

RIM TO RIM TO RIM – GRAND CANYON

North Rim

Cottonwood Campground

Ribbon Falls

Phantom Ranch / Campground

Bright Angel Trailhead

South Kaibab Trailhead

Chapter Eleven
Milford Trek
New Zealand

Much to the chagrin of the locals, people lump Australia and New Zealand together. However, those who have hiked the Milford Trek will tell you there is no comparison between the geographically close countries of the South Pacific. Frankly, there may be no comparison to any other place in the world. Where else can you walk through a lush, green forest denser than you can ever imagine and gaze at multitudes of waterfalls covering sheer granite cliffs peeking above the canopy. Strange birds, great facilities and humorous hut masters round out your experience trekking through one of the world's most amazing old growth forests.

Once used as a trail to collect pounamu (greenstone/jade) by the indigenous Polynesian tribe Maori, it's been a trekking destination since the late 1800's when Donald Sutherland and Quintin Mackinnon cut trails to allow tourists access to a remote wonderland. Back then it was a treacherous journey, but now Milford Trek is the easiest of the ten Great Treks, with wide level trails and an infrastructure second to none. Supervised by New Zealand's Department of Conservation, they meticulously oversee every aspect of your experience. However, be aware, rain is measured in meters per month and when it rains it pours. Trails flood as deep as your waist and you must be prepared. If conditions get too bad, fear not, the DOC will helicopter you from peril at no additional cost.

Fundamentals

Days Trekking: 4 days	**Approximate Elevation Change:** 869m / 2,872'
Distance: 53.5 km, 33.25 miles	**Price Range Independent:** $200 + food
Max Elevation: 1,069m / 3,528'	**Price Range Outfitter:** $1,500
Starting Elevation: 200m / 656'	**Challenge Level:** Easy, under good weather conditions

When to Go

The main trekking season is from late October to late April. However, some people choose to trek off season when the DOC huts are not necessarily staffed. If you go off season you will also have to contend with an increased risk of avalanches and slips.

The Milford Trek is very popular. you must book your trip well in advance, unless you get lucky due to a cancellation. The reservations start in July and it is best to book when permits first become available.

Guided vs. Independent Treks

There are two options for trekking Milford. You can walk independently and take advantage of the DOC huts (open and staffed in high season only), but you must be self-sufficient with your food and equipment needs. The huts provide a bunk to sleep on (you need only your sleeping bag), flush toilets and cooking stoves. They are staffed by wonderfully knowledgeable, helpful and witty staff. It is by far the best, most organized and competent system I have seen in the world. For more information on booking an independent trek visit *www.doc.govt.nz*.

In contrast, you can participate in a guided walk with far more luxurious huts which provide bedrooms as well as bunk-style lodging, hot showers and very comfortable common areas. Because gourmet meals are prepared daily, walkers need only carry their personal clothing and equipment. There's even beer and wine for purchase, if you want to wind down after your hike. This is a wonderful way for you to break into trekking, especially if you may need more guidance and supervision. While significantly more expensive than independent walking, the fees help subsidize the costs of maintaining this enchanted land. For more information visit *www.ultimatehikes.co.nz*.

Access / Local Information

The main access city is Te Anau, which is a small town that can meet all of your last minute preparatory needs. You can either drive or take a bus to Te Anau from the much larger city of Queenstown, which is a short flight from Christchurch or Auckland. If you are already in New Zealand you can also take a bus or drive from Christchurch.

Queenstown offers a lot more shopping and activities for adrenaline junkies including bungee jumping, zip lining, paragliding and more. Be aware that both towns exist primarily around tourism and it is expensive to buy quality equipment. Therefore, it is best to have all your equipment purchased in advance and use the towns to purchase food for your treks.

Difficulty

Milford Trek is considered an easy trek, but easy must come with the qualification that it is easy during reasonable weather, which is rare. The trek is 53.5km / 33.25 miles, climbs less than 1,000m / 3,300' and starts close to sea level. The trail itself is incredibly groomed, meticulously maintained and constructed with ladders and boardwalks where precarious footing existed in the past. The challenge, however, is the weather. It is rare to get four days without rain. On the Milford Trek rain isn't just a nuisance, it can be dangerous. In colder weather it can lead to hypothermia and when it rains hard the river levels rise quickly submerging the trail. They warn that you should be prepared to wade through knee deep water, but often people wade waist deep. In addition, people are periodically helicoptered past a section of trail.

Orientation

Milford Trek, the heart of Fiordland, is located in the south west corner of New Zealand.

Alternative/Additional Treks

There is much debate over which of the walks on New Zealand's South Island is the crown jewel. Milford is the reigning champ on most lists with the Routeburn Trek posing a reasonable challenge. In addition, some locals rate the Kepler Trek on par with the latter duo. While anyone's rating is subjective, based upon the weather conditions at the time they trek, I can say without a doubt that Milford Trek has the best view ten meters in front of you. Regardless of the weather, meandering through the dense forest of Milford provides a better close-up view than either Routeburn, Kepler or any of the other ten Great Treks. It also has the easiest trail to traverse in terms of footing, with Kepler a close second. Both treks are like walking on a garden path most of the time.

If instead you are looking for grander, higher views of mountains and valleys the decision becomes more challenging. We trekked Routeburn with better weather than either of the other two walks and therefore, we had a better opportunity to see all that was offered under the best of conditions. It's hard to say if the short, sub-alpine stretch of Milford would have compared. The answer is clear, though. You should walk both Milford and Routeburn, as long as you can handle the slightly more rugged trail on Routeburn. Given the amount of time it takes to get to any of these treks and their relatively short durations, why not do both? If you have time, add Kepler which has longer stretches of sub-alpine zones than the other two walks. However, although I was treated to a glorious sunrise at the Luxmore Hut on the Kepler Trail, in my opinion overall, the trek is not as grand as Milford and Routeburn. A final option is, if you have extra time, to head north for the Abel Tasmin or Tonga River Crossing treks as well.

On the Trail with Jeff

My last of the ten Great Treks was supposed to be the easiest one. Categorized as an easy four-day walk, the hardest part of the trek should have been getting to the trailhead. Coming from America, tickets were not cheap and the four flights we took were long and draining. Still, after a quick recharge in the adrenaline-junkie city of Queenstown, my wife and I were ready to complete my seven year journey to walk the world's best treks. Recognizing there is some debate over the best trek in New Zealand, my plan was to knock off Milford and then come back to complete the Routeburn and Kepler treks in succession and decide for myself.

The expectation of a straightforward experience dissipated quickly once on the bus to Te Anau, the small, but well-equipped access town for the Milford Trek. As the bus whipped us around the twisting Fiordland roads with the agility of a sports car, my stomach went south fast. Having travelled the world and eaten many varieties of food, I was about to lose my lunch due to motion sickness. It was a bit humbling. Breathing deeply, I occasionally peered up to observe the stunning ranch-laden landscape filled with sheep, cattle and even deer corralled in expansive pens. We even got our first glimpse of the sun. We should have cherished it though, as the weather forecast upon our arrival was rain, rain and more rain.

Severe Weather Forecast

I got up the next morning eager to complete my quest, regardless of the weather, when Jennifer began the day by asking, "How mad would you be if I said I didn't want to do it?" I am sure she was flashing back to her cold, wet slogging as she thru-hiked the entire 2,200 mile Appalachian Trail. I wasn't about to entertain the thought and declared simply, "We are going!" We checked, in vain, the weather forecast one last time with the "chippy" DOC staffer who said with a smile, "You'll get a true Fiordland experience!" as she showed us the weather forecast. "Severe weather warning," severe by Fiordland standards was not what I was hoping for. Their definition of getting very wet was a bit more extreme than my own. I guess I had kidded myself into thinking we would just get lucky. It is not uncommon for walkers to be helicoptered over flooded areas and wade waist deep on the trails.

Our trek started with a short bus ride to Te Anau Downs, where we picked up a boat to carry us to the start of the trek. Dave, our sarcastic boat captain, felt compelled to retell story after story of floods on the trail. "Don't avoid the puddles," he jested, "it won't matter," and then paused before adding "Got waterproof boots?" in inquiry and then answered his own question, "Good for you. Won't matter a bit, though, you're getting wet anyway." He then exclaimed, "Look at the dolphins on the left!" Everyone got up to look at the non-existent, fresh water dolphins. Were his warnings a sober dose of reality or the ever present, playful Kiwi sense of humor? It was hard to tell, but probably a bit of both.

When the boat stopped at Glade Wharf, we were required to wash the bottoms of our boots before entering the trail. They were quite serious about protecting the environment from invasive species, in this case a pesky form of algae known as "rock snot." Upon entering the trail we were overwhelmed with the intensity of the lush, green, monochromatic forest. Very wet trees enveloped in lichen reached up from a moss-plastered carpet that covers the rocks, the ground and many of the trees. Multitudes of chest-high ferns flanked us on all sides, with just as many puddles covering the trail. It was easy to understand why this area is affectionately known as "God Zone."

Almost immediately we passed the Glade House where guided groups stay. In addition to being supervised along the trail, their huts were luxurious, hotel-like accommodations complete with showers, meals and alcoholic beverages. However, there is a big difference between lodging facilities for independent or freedom walkers. We wouldn't have such luxuries.

Our first thirty minutes along the trail were spent in awe while we danced between the rain drops and around the puddles. However, soon Captain Dave's ominous predictions materialized and we walked on the trail with the lower portion of our boots completely submerged. As we progressed, sections of the impeccably well-groomed trail were closed and impassable. The detours were short, muddy swings around areas of the trail that slid or washed away. There were two side trips, one to a beech tree, which I didn't take. The other was to a boardwalk over a wetland bog that was blanketed with a combination of red, orange, yellow and green moss at the base of a huge valley. Too bad we could barely see the mountains around us. On a good day the view would be stupendous. Shortly after the bog, we passed a sign for a swimming hole. Who needs a hole when you can just swim on the trail?

We made it to the huts in an hour, much quicker than the trail signs predicted. This was the pattern on all of the Fiordland treks, as the time estimates were very generous. The huts were impressive, solidly built structures with plenty of bunks for tired trekkers. There were separate sleeping and eating/living areas with a wood burning stove to warm chilled bodies and dry soaked gear.

We arrived at the hut first. We quickly switched into dry clothes and hung out our wet gear, ostensibly to dry overnight. We relaxed for the afternoon and were soon introduced to our odd ostrich-legged hut master Ross, who entered the room and with a quick flip of his wrist tossed a bag of dead stoats (ferret like rodents that have devastated the bird population of southern New Zealand) on the table. The Kiwi sense of humor continued as Ross joked about the pending storm. "We've only had a meter and a half (five feet) of rain this month. It's only water. It doesn't go any farther than your skin." Had he not heard of hypothermia? Behind all the jokes was the serious possibility of being evacuated by helicopter. A heavy storm the week before led to one group being lifted from the trail. While helicopter evacuations are included as part of the price for your permit, it would be terribly disappointing to travel so far and not be able to complete an "easy trek." Sadly, evacs often occur more than once a month.

Ross' tone struck a more serious chord when we discussed the dangers of the trail. Most injuries occur going downhill, "So if you want to enjoy a view, STOP!" Given the propensity for bad weather, this was good advice. Apparently on average only one in four days had any reasonable amount of blue sky. In addition, he briefed us on fire safety and the threat of having your gear carried away by the clever but pesky Kea parrot. One of the smartest birds in the world, Keas watch, learn and steal everything on the ground. You must put your belongings up on hooks or lines or they'll take your shoes away and pull the feathers out of your sleeping bag. They are "the clowns of the mountain." We were urged not feed them, or "they just get bolder and more cheeky." The lecture continued, "Female birds banded on the left, men on the right, because after all men are always right." Detailing the name of every bird, he continued on like the rain, endlessly. Apparently other trekkers were warned by the DOC staff to be prepared for the rain, the cold and Ross' speech. Finally, he finished with his many life-like bird calls and progressed to discuss the flora. Everyone fidgeted in their seats, but happily, he wrapped up his talk and we headed off to bed.

I slept well, which was surprising given that the guy next to me cut a forest down with his snores. "How do you stand it?" I asked his son Hayson, but only got laughs for an answer. The worst part was everyone else thought it was me! When we woke there wasn't any rain, so we quickly got ready and hit the trail at 8:00 am, just after daylight. This trail began with a fertile green world even more lush and grand than before. We marched through ferns almost as high as your head, while songs of countless birds rang in our ears. In contrast to other treks, we saw a diversity and volume of bird life which included paradise duck, blue duck, rifleman, South Island Tomtit, South Island Robin, and Tui. Traditionally, birds were the main wildlife in New Zealand. The only indigenous mammals were two forms of bats. All other mammals were artificially introduced by man. We continued along the path with the Clinton River bordering the right side of the trail. It was spectacularly clear, slightly green in hue and laced with well-rounded stones on its bed. Littered along the ground were amazing fungal growths that looked like they belonged more in a coral reef than a forest. Given our progress and the less threatening weather, we took the detour to a hidden lake and were rewarded with a sighting of a pair of endangered blue duck.

Our progress was great and we briefly stopped at a shelter called the Bus Stop for lunch to recharge before our ascent up to the Mintaro Hut. Once we started climbing, I faded fast. In addition to my pack weighing far too much for my current fitness level, I was also probably a little dehydrated. While I certainly knew better, in my defense with all the water around you just don't want to drink. With about two kilometers to go, the trail rose steeply, and my energy plunged. This coincided with the rains starting. Luckily, it didn't get too bad, but it was just enough to sap the last bit of joy from the day.

Waterfalls gushed uncontrollably out of every crevice of landscape. Unfortunately, given the gray sky it wasn't picturesque. Covered by a giant fog bowl we arrived at the hut after five hours, an hour faster than scheduled. Not taking heaps of photographs did wonders for our walking schedule. Once again, we arrived first, which was especially important as only two rooms were limited to eight beds, the other room was large and probably quite noisy. On the wall was the weather forecast, it was a crudely drawn stick figure of a person under water with a snorkel. Given the con-

ditions, this was not particularly funny to us and certainly not very inspiring! Compounding our apprehension were posters on the wall explaining every cloud type. We did not take it as a good sign.

Peering out the window, we saw a speck of blue in the sky. However, it must have been lonely as it quickly disappeared. Over dinner a strange polluting smell pervaded the room. Ah, the scent of melting plastic. A young German guy, Johannas, hung what used to be his jacket too close to the wood burning stove. When the hut master came for his talk, he continued with the Kiwi sense of humor. "As you reach the top of the pass, you'll want to pop your jumper off, add another layer, and then put your jacket back on; that is, if you have one." Johannes didn't find this particularly funny. Then like all hut talks, he turned to the perils. Apparently the shelters at the top of the pass were closed for construction. He cracked, "so just carry on." Next came the flood warnings, "if the water is pumping, it will be knee deep!" If it got bad enough, they would helicopter us to the next hut. Either way though, we would have to walk over the high pass before getting a lift. That didn't seem particularly fair, but we hoped we wouldn't need the assistance.

After the talk we went to sleep to get an early start as usual. About thirty minutes later we heard a huge cheer erupt. Apparently, during the previous evening two guys drank whiskey until they passed out. The cheers were for their late arrival. Hopefully they wouldn't anger the demons of the local legends with their disrespect for the trail. There certainly were plenty of alleged demons with which to be concerned; some whose hearts still beat below the lake, some inhabiting the rocks and some inhabiting our hearts.

Downpour from Above and Below

The demons answered by dropping buckets of water all night long and it was still raining when we woke. So much rain was deluging down that water was pouring out of the rain barrel even though we were actively using plenty of water to cook, clean and flush. It was an "Australian's dream," declared one trekker. This was obviously before the floods in Queenstown. The ranger popped his head in to tell us the trail was passable and to head out. "The worst of the rain will arrive at 4 pm," was all we had to hear to get moving fast. This was a awful day to get terrible weather. It would block any chance of a good view and there were definitely very exposed areas with which to be concerned.

As we walked we saw mammoth sheer faces of granite with waterfalls streaming down. The trail was a reasonably steady grade and for the time being fairly sheltered. As we approached the Mackinnon Pass, the trail opened up and we were totally exposed. We saw the memorial to Mackinnon, one of the early establishers of the Milford Trek. Not liking the sky, wind, or rain, we said a quick hello and pushed forward. As we approached the pass, the winds picked up to a wicked frenzy. It took twenty minutes to reach the huts. With the wind at full-force, there was no mercy as the hut was locked. The wind thrashed us and our cheap ponchos around like a kite in a hurricane. We tried to regroup and get our ponchos under the backpacks, but it was an exercise in futility. Just as we tucked one section under, the wind whipped it back out. Finally, we helped each other get situated enough to move on, cursing into the wind.

Our mood had turned quite somber as we both flashed back to our ill-fated high Alpine crossing during the Haute Route. Unsure how long the trail was dangerously exposed we moved as fast as safety would allow us, wanting to avoid another bout with hypothermia as well as the late day floods. We turned the corner and hail lashed our faces. They had warned us about many of the conditions, but gale force winds and hail were not in the briefing. "This was supposed to be an easy walk," I kept thinking.

Amazingly, while I stood at 180+ pounds and had a heavy pack on my back, I struggled to keep my feet planted. How would my wife who was barely more than half my weight fare? My answer came from an electrifying screech, as my wife was blown over the ledge and left hanging by one hand. There was a somber silence as I pulled her back to safety. Later she told me she never looked down. My wife is indeed smart! I pondered back to the Gardner Pass on the Torres del Paine Trek and realized this must have been the equivalent of the winds that we luckily missed. As we continued, there was an unspoken fear of what else to expect.

Almost every inch of landscape was covered in a waterfall, but their beauty was not enough to lift our spirits. I felt Jennifer had dropped her sense of humor over the cliff and it would take getting warm and dry before it returned. Let's face it, this was not fun. Finally, 20 to 30 minutes later we got out of the worst of the exposed area. The next challenge was crossing all the waterfalls we had observed. This included walking straight down one. As I lead the way, I heard another screech as Jennifer's feet submerged and the icy water encroached into her boots. I praised my mighty knee-high alpine gaiters as they held the flood at bay.

Once through the worst of the falls we came upon the most elaborately-constructed series of ladders and boardwalks I have ever seen. What a contrast to Burma where we hiked over the edge of precarious cliffs composed solely of tree roots and climbed logs with wedges cut into them for steps. The welcome structures on the Milford trek helped us drop altitude quickly.

Our next challenge was crossing one rapidly rising stream after another. The mighty Milford Trek was determined to breech my boots and soak my feet. Fortunately, my trusty Asolo's were holding strong. We forged on and even noticed a couple of Weka wood hens along the trail. We stopped at the turnoff for Southerland Falls. However, given the pending, dooming rain and the sheer number of waterfalls we already saw and felt, we took a five-minute break in a shelter before heading to the hut. To overdose on even more waterfalls, I felt it was like gorging on too many Buddha statues in Thailand. Eventually, you just don't want to see any more. At this point all sorts of analogies clogged my mind to take my focus away from the rain. Trekking is like drinking, when you've had too much, you swear you will never do it again, but somehow you are always lured to repeat your transgression.

As we marched, the river on our left was rising and rising fast. The tributaries, if you can use that word, were the most ferocious waterways I'd ever seen. As we progressed, the older bridges on the side of the trail were underwater. Little by little, areas of the main trail started to succumb to the flood, until finally the entire trail was submerged. The race was now on; could I make it with dry feet? It wasn't much to cling to, but it was all I had.

Just as I had thoughts of making it, there it was: an evil demon wall of water stood in our path. On one side of the trail was the river, on the other side was the wall of the mountain. The only way to proceed was straight ahead along the flooded path. Blocking it was a jet stream of water shooting across at a 45 degree angle, making it impossible to cross. Jennifer went first. "Screech!" The icy cold water hit her hard. I stared into the freezing shower and hoped my race walking skills would help get me through without too much damage. One, two, three, Go! A quick, chilly splash went down my back, but I made it with dry boots. At this point, Jennifer had totally given up and was stomping through the trail without regard for her personal wetness level and she certainly didn't want to hear that I was still dry.

"Woo-Hoo," shouted my wife. My spirits lifted, but in false hope. It was just another bridge and by the time we made it to the hut, I was calf deep in water. Amazingly my boot/gaiter combination was holding firm against water's intrusion. Johannes beat us to the hut. Everyone else trailed in later. Each person reported deeper and deeper water. Knee, thigh, waist deep water was conveyed without much joy.

As we sat drying out, the son of the snorer, Hayson, came in and we pleaded with him not to sleep in our room. He laughed and busted us, "I saw you mouth 'shit' last night when we came in your room." Then he promised that they would move. We felt bad, but really wanted sleep. Somehow, they stayed and only the silent sleepers moved out. I suppose they knew what was best for them. While our sleeping issues were important to us, a bigger riff was brewing in camp. Apparently, one of the two late arrivals from the night before was injured and asked his friend to carry most of his gear. Instead of waiting for his savior, he took the opportunity of the lightened load to walk ahead and wait warm and dry in the hut. When the Aussie finally arrived it didn't take a rocket scientist to realize that he was not pleased.

Where's the Easter Bunny?

We went to bed early, but I awoke at 3:00 am to a brightly lit room. I ran to the window and saw a clear, glorious sky outside. The moon was shining down upon us and I took some of my first interesting photographs of the trip. I went back to bed, with a calm feeling that we would finally have a good day of hiking.

On our final day we left at 7:00 am, with perfect weather. While we had our first clear views of the mountains, the waterfalls were dramatically diminished from the previous day. The water level changes quickly since it basically just drops straight down without much storage capacity. We continued along the trail and saw the Mackay Falls and Bell Rock. Unfortunately, the spray of the waterfall was cold and wet. Given that we had experienced enough of the cold and wet, we moved on quickly.

In the rush, somehow I lost my lens cap. Although I retraced my steps, I didn't find it. Begrudgingly, we headed out with my fear mounting that I couldn't replace it before the next hike.

The last milestone of the trail was a shelter where we were supposed to wait, since the end of the trail was infested with sand flies. It was bone-chilling cold, so instead of sitting in discomfort, I headed back for a cool shot of a diminutive waterfall. When I returned, Jennifer was shivering and ready to roll. So we pushed on stopping at the first open area in the sun and relaxed with the warmth of our old friend beaming down upon us. As we sat, a day hiker came by hiding Easter eggs. "Are they edible?" we asked, "How many did you hide?" We briefly debated searching for them and eating them as they wouldn't survive long enough to be discovered by his family. On a positive note, we tested the local, natural insect repellent and found that it worked well on the sand flies. As we walked the final section of trail, I wanted to savor the end of a seven year journey. However, Jennifer clearly was ready to be done. Fittingly, the end of the walk was much how I imagined the entire walk should have been, a nice and relaxing stroll through enchanted woods. When we reached the final destination, there were two rooms to wait for the boat. One room was for guided walkers and the other for the independent walkers. This seemed really unnecessary. While I understand the guided walkers pay more, the constant reminder of the separation was very trying. I decided to walk out to the dock to relax and when I returned there was quite a bit of excitement in our waiting room. One kind fellow found my lens cap!

After the hike, I was incredibly sore. Glad to be done, I had a constant reminder with every step that I was out of shape and had just walked for four days with too much weight on my back. I decided to go for a deep tissue massage and prepare for our next hike on the Routeburn Trek. After a very painful hour and a half, I got up from the massage and read the following passage on the wall.

"You cannot stay on the summit forever. You have to come down again. So why bother to go in the first place? Because that which is below does not know what is above, but what is above knows what is below. One climbs, one sees. One descends, one sees no longer, but one has seen. There is an art to conducting oneself in the lower regions by the memory of what one saw higher up. When one can no longer see, one can at least still know." -- Rene Daumal

The timing was perfect. It nicely summed up my seven year journey in words I could never have articulated and it explained my desire to continue on to the next mountain wherever that may be.

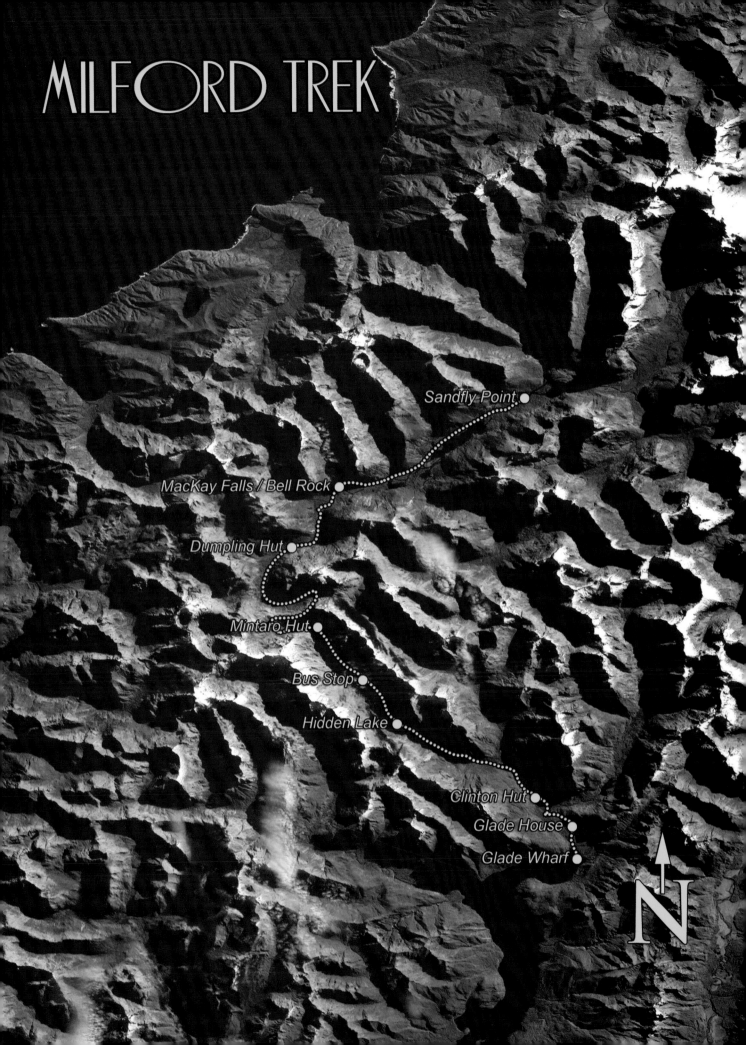

MILFORD TREK

Sandfly Point

MacKay Falls / Bell Rock

Dumpling Hut

Mintaro Hut

Bus Stop

Hidden Lake

Clinton Hut

Glade House

Glade Wharf

N

Appendix A - Equipment

Deciding what to bring on your trek can lead even the most veteran trekkers scratching their heads. The desire to be well equipped versus the pain of carrying too much weight is a debate that rages before any trek. Granted if the trek has porters, the decision to add a few items to your stash becomes easier, but ultimately, we all wish to take more than is required. There exists a exorbitant choice of equipment that can be carried and worn during a trek. We purposely do not make specific recommendations on products as the state-of-the-art changes rapidly. Instead, here is a helpful list of essential items for any trek, as well as many suggestions for additional items that enhance your trekking experience. Many decisions must be made on a trek by trek basis taking into consideration the season, your fitness level, needs and ability to haul everything from beginning to end. You must always remember that what you pack in, you must pack out, or at least eat along the way. So don't take more than you need. There is rarely a place to responsibly discard unwanted items once your trek begins.

Altimeter - If you don't carry a GPS, or even if you do, you can get a watch that measures your altitude, barometric pressure and temperature. While not cheap, they don't add much weight and are a great asset. Some even have GPS functionality.

Backpack/Day Pack - A properly fitting backpack is imperative for carrying your gear. If porters are carrying most of your stuff, this may be replaced with a daypack. A backpack needs to be large enough to easily hold your gear, stable enough to feel comfortable on your back and accessible enough to get your personal items out quickly during a hike. While some are made to be waterproof, we prefer traditional packs with dry bags inside. Whichever pack you decide on, don't obsess solely on the weight to capacity ratio. Choose a pack that distributes the load well and make sure you try it out with a full load before initiating your trek. Also, pay attention to how accessible water is from the pack. Can you easily reach the side pockets where the water bottles should be stored? Does it have a special sack to store a water bag with easy access to it's hose?

Bandana - Bandanas have many uses from being worn on your head, keeping the sweat out of your eyes, to being utilized as a knee brace, tourniquet, sun shade, snot rag, etc. I even bought one on the Everest Base Camp Trek that doubled as a map.

Boots, Hiking - While I've seen a few insane people out hiking in flip flops, a pair of good sturdy waterproof hiking boots is a must. They should have adequate ankle support and must be thoroughly broken in before you begin your trek. Breaking in time varies depending upon its stiffness. We recommend wearing them at least five times for an hour or more. In addition, wear your boots for a two-hour hike on varied terrain. When purchasing your boots always try them on at the end of day, as your feet swell. What fits comfortably early in the day, may not by evening's calling. Also, make sure you walk up and down an incline to test the fit on the toe box and heel cup.

Camera - I could write chapters on the appropriate camera equipment to capture your experience. Unfortunately, there is an evil tradeoff between the quality of your equipment and the weight of it in your pack. I carry two DSLR bodies and numerous lenses, a tripod, lens cloths, plenty of camera memory, a remote camera release, a flash or flashes, etc. The key is to get the lightest of whatever equipment will do the job. Thus I use a carbon fiber tripod and have a lighter, lower-quality camera as my backup.

Camp Shoes - No matter how much you want to reduce weight and no matter how comfortable you believe your boots feel before the trek, once you've hiked in your boots day after day, you'll want something more comfortable to wear in camp. Since you won't be walking with a pack, or for any considerable distance in your camp shoes, I recommend going as light as possible. Recently I've started wearing aqua socks as a camp shoe. A slip on neoprene shoe, they are light, compact and can double as a shower shoe or can be slipped on when you need to cross a river. Other water shoes may make a reasonable option as well.

Clothing, Layered - Weather on treks tends to be unpredictable. Your best defense is to layer your clothing and almost never bring cotton. Synthetics and wool are superior in almost all conditions except perhaps desert climates. Having many layers allows you to add or remove layers depending upon how warm or cold it may be. Minimally, you may have a single Techwick t-shirt and then as it gets colder you may have an undershirt, long sleeve shirt, fleece jacket, down jacket and / or rain jacket.

Convertible Pants - It's rare that a multi-day hike doesn't require some form of pants. Often temperatures vary greatly at different points on the trail. So, unless the trek is entirely alpine, convertible pants are a great way to save space. By unzipping the lower portion of the pant legs, your pants become a pair of shorts. It's best to bring more than one pair, just in case you go butt-sliding down the side of a mountain. Of course, the mighty duct tape can help out in such situations.

Dry Bags - If rain or river crossings are a possibility, then keeping your equipment dry is a challenge. While you can get a waterproof backpack, a better way is to use a pack cover and either a bag liner or a series of dry bags. We prefer the latter as they also help organize your pack's contents. Many companies now make extremely light weight dry bags in varying sizes.

Duct Tape - No legitimate trekker is without a small roll of this all mighty cure-all. Incredibly versatile, it can be used to patch a tent, backpack or even the seat of your pants. It's even found its way onto my camera for a quick field repair.

Electrolyte Powder - I usually bring enough electrolyte powder to make two liters a day of fluid. This helps ensure I don't over hydrate with water and adds a bit of flavor to water that sometimes has a less than ideal taste. It also is a good source of simple carbohydrates to help keep your blood sugar up while trekking. Which product you choose is a matter of personal preference. Just make sure you try it out on some practice walks before you hit the trail so you know your stomach tolerates it well.

First Aid Kit - Don't rely on other people to have emergency medical supplies. Every trekker or at least one person per group should carry some first aid supplies which minimally include: band aids, antiseptic, ace bandage, antihistamine and alcohol wipes.

Flashlight - When the lights go out, you'll need some way to see in the dark. A head-mounted flashlight is best, as you don't want to carry a flashlight in your hand to head to the bathroom or to read in bed. We found out the hard way that it pays to have a strong light. Trying to save on weight, my wife and I brought two Petzel emergency head lamps, powered only by a tiny lithium battery. While they did save on weight and were fine for reading in bed, when a unknown wild animal stalked our camp on the Continental Divide Trail, neither of our head lamps were strong enough to see what it was. Unfortunately, while Kirk had a traditional head lamp, the batteries weren't strong enough to light anything but the animals hungry eyes. So, always make sure your batteries are charged and you have an ample supply for the entire duration of your trip. I always keep at least one spare pair as it is all too easy to fall asleep with your light on, draining the majority of your batteries in a single night.

Gaiters - While it is tempting to leave them home and save weight, a pair of knee-high gaiters have saved me more than once. What's the point of having expensive waterproof boots, if snow or water invades them from the top. Investing in a pair of gaiters keeps your feet warm and dry.

Gloves - If you are hiking in warm weather a pair of gloves won't be necessary. However, for cold weather hikes, a pair of mittens, not gloves, are best to keep your fingers warm when you hike. For mildly cold temperature, and for when you need to operate a camera or filter your water, a pair of thin gloves or glove liners are great.

GPS - Although not usually essential, a GPS can greatly enhance your trek. In addition to tracking your progress along a map, they usually include an altimeter to allow you to gauge your progress along an ascent or descent. Be careful on your selection of a GPS since battery life varies greatly. The model I use gets 40 or more hours from two lithium AA batteries. This usually means I can have it on while I walk an entire two-week trek, only changing the batteries once.

Hand/Foot Warmers - On cold treks consider bringing a few hand and foot warmers for the really cold days. You probably won't need them every day, so don't overstock as weight adds up quickly. However, having a set for your summit day often makes it far more enjoyable.

Hat - Whether to block the sun or keep you warm, a hat is vital for almost every trek. Sometimes you'll need one to provide shade, other times insulation. Often you'll need it for both!

Insect Repellent - Nature almost always attracts the bugs, at least for part of your trek. In many situations these insects won't just annoy you, but they will carry disease. Therefore, a good insect repellent is vital. Usually the most effective is some form of DEET™-based product. However, I am always concerned with using a strong chemical on my body, especially when hand washing is limited. I tend to buy a local natural repellent once I get to the trekking location. After all, the locals should know best. Often this works fine, but if it doesn't, I am not proud and I carry a DEET™-based product as a backup. A word of caution, though, you don't want your insect repellent to come into contact with the rest of your equipment. I always store it inside two Zip Lock™ bags.

Jacket, Water Resistant - Outside of a sheet of plastic, there aren't really any total waterproof jackets. Given enough rain, most water resistant jackets bleed through. Unfortunately, wearing a pure plastic sheet doesn't work either, because the heat generated internally results in enough sweat that you might as well have been rained on. A good water resistant jacket is the best you can do. We tend to like GORE-TEX™ products, which can be found in many brands.

Knife - While you don't need a knife like Crocodile Dundee, carrying a simple Swiss Army knife can be a life saver. Just don't forget to pack it in your checked luggage.

Lighter / Matches - Fire was a gift from Prometheus, let's not insult him and be caught without a way to start a fire in an emergency. You can bring either a lighter or waterproof matches to get one started if the need presents itself. One word of caution, these items should be kept in your checked luggage.

Maps - It always helps to know where you are going. Ideally, get a waterproof map, or laminate one yourself.

Medications - Obviously this is a personal matter and one best discussed with your physician. However, as modern medical attention is not likely to be convenient in the middle of a trek, it is best to carry some form of the following medications: anti-inflammatory/pain relief, anti-diarrheal, allergy, GI, and depending upon where you go, possibly anti-malarials.

Personal Hygiene - You're not going to come off the trail smelling like roses, so bring utilitarian personal hygiene supplies, but not things like deodorant (which can attract bugs). My list includes: a tiny toothbrush, toothpaste (which can be powdered) and dental floss.

Personal Location Beacon - While I have never used one, a personal location beacon is a good idea for any remote or solo trekking. The news is littered with stories of lost hikers, usually without a beacon. In an emergency it could be a life saver. Minimally, carry a safety whistle. Also, it is important that you leave a detailed itinerary with friends, family or the authorities.

Poles, Hiking - Walking with the assistance of hiking poles reduces the stress on your knees and body. While some people resist using them, we find them invaluable. A sturdy pair of poles can also be a life saver. We've both fallen on our butts numerous times while completing the Great Treks. Without hiking poles, we would have fallen many more times. Get a pair and avoid injury. They come in many varieties, including very light weight carbon fiber poles. Some have shock absorbers, although the combination of carbon fiber and shock absorbers didn't prove to be dependable. Try out a few varieties and select a pair that doesn't feel too heavy in your grip or wallet. Pay careful attention to how the poles adjust in size. You'll want a pair that has a sturdy lock, but one that is easy to open and close, because you'll adjust them more than you think. On the trail many elongate their poles on the way down and shorten them on the way up.

Shelter - If you are not sleeping in guest houses or refugios then you'll need a tent, tarp or bivy bag to sleep in at night. Tents come in many prices, shapes, weights and sizes. We tend to travel with a small two person tent. Make sure there is a compartment to shelter your belongings if you don't want to store everything in your tent at night. Be aware it's not just your food critters might snack on, so be prepared to hang everything not covered by your shelter.

Shoelaces - Take a spare pair of shoelaces or some nylon braided p-cord that can be cut into shoe lace size strands. You can rarely predict when a shoe lace will break, but you can always predict that when one breaks, you'll want a spare.

Sleeping Bag - There are two broad categories of sleeping bags: down and synthetic. They each have their advantages. A down bag is lighter and will generally keep you warmer, however, when they get wet, they take a long time to dry out. Also, while they remain damp they lose a lot of their insulation value. In contrast, a synthetic bag is much less expensive and dries out quickly when wet. When selecting a bag, also pay attention to the temperature rating. We own multiple sleeping bags and take the one most appropriate for the expected nighttime temperatures. If predicted temperatures range wildly, bringing a sleeping bag liner gives you added flexibility.

Sleeping Pad - If you are sleeping in a tent or on a hard floor, a lightweight sleeping pad makes the night a lot more comfortable. They come in two main options: a closed cell foam pad or a self-inflatable style. They vary greatly in price and weight, so do your research carefully. If you are planning to sleep in guest houses or refugios, you may choose to skip a pad. As always, the choice may come down to how much weight you want to carry.

Snacks - You'll want to supplement your meals with snacks. Care must be taken when selecting them. I always keep an eye on the caloric content as compared to the weight of the snack, trying to keep the calorie-per-ounce ratio as high as possible. It is also important to make sure your snack food can handle the trail conditions. Obviously, potato chips will not hold up well on the trail. In addition, some foods, like chocolate, won't survive a hotter climate. Other foods may become difficult to chew at colder temperatures. Choose wisely, as your snacks become a major luxury item on the trail. Also, vary what you bring. After 10 days even the best of snacks get boring. Finally, if you are traveling abroad, check the custom's policies on carrying food into the country or you may lose it at the airport.

Socks - Regardless of how long a trip's duration carry three pairs of socks. It's best to switch off each day so that the previous days' socks have a chance to dry out. However, sometimes a day is not enough, thus having a third pair is a good backup. Socks should be made of wool or a synthetic material. Make sure you wear socks of the appropriate thickness for your trek.

Sunglasses with Retaining Strap - Protecting your eyes from the harmful rays of the sun is especially important as you climb higher. In addition, the snow's reflection can be blinding. Therefore, a high quality pair of sunglasses is a must. I tend to favor glacier glasses that block out 90% of the light, but others prefer polarized lenses to shield their eyes.

Sunscreen - Most treks expose your skin to all sorts of torture. The sun is not your skin's friend, so protect it by applying sunscreen liberally and often. Minimally use a lotion with SPF 30, but remember it's not just the rating that matters, but that you repeatedly apply it multiple times per day. It is also a good to ensure your sunscreen has zinc oxide in the ingredient list.

Tops - Cotton kills. It's a simple motto to live by. Except possibly one shirt for camp, I bring moisture wicking shirts. I have many varieties depending on the weather I expect. I usually have short and long sleeve shirts with some that have a zipper in the front to regulate temperature. The exception to this is in desert or very arid climates.

Toilet Paper - Some treks provide toilets with toilet paper, others do not. Either way, you don't want to get caught in the middle of the trail without an emergency supply. You can buy specially rolled toilet paper that takes up less space or roll up a stash yourself. Of course, you could always use suitable leaves, if they exist. On second thought, take a roll. In either case, make sure you follow proper protocol by burying your waste at least six inches deep and away from a water source. Always check local regulations to be sure.

Towel - While not a necessity, a light hi tech towel is a nice luxury.

Underwear - Like socks, I like to have at least three pairs of underwear on a trek. On a longer trek I may add a fourth pair, but usually you can wash them out along the way after wearing them a few times. Recently I've switched to hi tech undergarments made with Techwick for their moisture wicking abilities. In addition, the hi tech garments tend to be lighter in weight.

Watch - While all too many days of trekking have started with a rooster call waking us up, it's essential to have a watch to ensure you get up on time as well as mark your progress during the day. Given the invasion of cell phones, many people have foregone a watch as a redundant item. However, as fewer people (hopefully) will carry a cell phone with them on their hike, one needs a way to know the time.

Water Filter - An absolute must on any trek is a reliable, safe water source. On some treks, you do not have to worry, but in most areas drinking untreated water runs the risk of many diseases. Make sure the filter you choose can cleanse the water of bacteria and protozoa including giardia and cryptosporidia, viruses, as well as chemicals and industrial pollutants. While you could treat water with Iodine, the taste and side effects are usually not desirable. Another reason to skip Iodine is that it will not remove pollutants. Instead, we almost always carry a filter and begin each day with the ritual of pumping water into our water bottles that we know is safe to drink. Be aware that filters need to be changed or cleaned periodically. Read the manufacturer's instructions to ensure it works properly.

Water Storage - Whether you choose to carry your water in bottles or a bag, you'll need adequate storage for a few liters of water at a time. I usually carry a bag with at least a four liter capacity, although admittingly I do not always fill it up. My preference is to carry two bottles, non-BPA, and a dromedary bag with a mouth piece. I place filtered water in the bag that I can drink while walking and combine an electrolyte powder with filtered water in the bottles. This strikes a nice balance so that I don't skunk up my bag with sugary drinks that are hard to clean out, while ensuring that I get enough electrolytes to prevent hypernatremia.

Wet Wipes / Hand Sanitizer - I am not one to obsess about cleanliness, after all a little dirt makes you stronger. However, on a trek I pay a little more attention to personal hygiene. Often on a trek a water source is scarce or not reliable, so instead I will cleanse my hands with a hand sanitizer before eating or after using the outhouse. A dropper of bleach can do the trick as well as serve as a backup for purifying water. In addition, wet wipes can substitute, albeit poorly, for a shower.

Appendix B ~ Training to Trek

The swoosh of a helicopter flying to the rescue may seem dramatic, however, if you are the person being picked up it is not only embarrassing, but can be highly expensive. All too often people embark on a trek without properly preparing for the mental, physical and emotional needs of their journey. Trekking up a mountain, down a canyon or just across the countryside is a joyous and rewarding experience; however, one must be prepared for the activity they are undertaking. Many trekkers are lured into the idea of journeying down the path by fabulous photos, stories or just boasting rights to say they completed the arduous task. Others may have good intentions, but have no idea what is physically required or how to prepare for it.

While predicting the exact nature of your fitness-related problems is impossible, by following the advice presented here the chances of physical difficulties are greatly reduced. Using my experience as an internationally recognized walking expert, all aspects of getting in the proper shape for your journey are explained. This includes how to warm up, cool down and a prescription of how to train in the months preceding your adventure.

Obligatory Disclaimer

Trekking is an athletic event and like any athletic endeavor it begins with a doctor's approval. It is important to inform your doctor of the conditions your trek entails. These include the number of days the trek comprises, the distance covered per day, the change in elevation per day, the extremes of temperature, as well as the highest altitude achieved. This gives your doctor at least some rough guidelines as to your exertion level, but bear in mind that not all doctors are knowledgeable to give fitness advice. Clearly, get advice from a doctor in the know.

Getting Fit or Fitter

Preparing for a trek follows the same principles as a runner or walker readying themselves for a long distance competition. The key difference is that you are not racing to a finish line, but instead enjoying the journey along the way. Forget the "No Pain No Gain" philosophy of the 80's. Instead supplement "Minimum Effort, Maximum Gain." We are not promoting laziness, just the opposite. By being smart, you maximize your training efforts and the return on your time investment.

Training is about adapting the body to stress so that it gets stronger and thus increasing its ability to handle more stress in the future. Toughening your body up to withstand the stress of your trek is the key. This is not done overnight. The more difficult the trek you plan to achieve, the longer it takes to prepare.

Trekkers need a balanced approach, strengthening the entire body, if they are to be successful and injury free during training and during the trek. Everybody has a weakest link, if broken, slows or possibly prematurely brings the trek to an end. It is important to strengthen your weak links as well as all the major muscle groups. In addition, a weak link may develop where you previously did not have an issue. Imagine being in great shape, but wearing ill-fitted boots and developing a severe blister. Unless you have an incredibly high pain threshold, that blister will slow you down and actually may cause other injuries since you then favor the blistered foot.

The key behind many successful training programs is the concept of "specificity of exercise." If an athlete wants to succeed, they must train in a manner similar to the activity in which they plan to participate. While cross training helps, a trekker's best method to train for a trek is to trek.

Unfortunately, that is far easier said than done. Few of us live near a trail similar to the one to be traversed during the trek. So, what do you do if you live in a city, or in the "flatlands," if your trek climbs high in altitude? Our ideal is probably unachievable for most. Further complicating matters is that you cannot simply simulate thin air or extreme weather easily. Still, there is a lot we can do to help. Here are some basic guidelines about training.

The Cardiovascular Workout

Whether for a workout or for the trek itself, how we prepare the body for the effort it is about to perform and recover from is the same. Indeed, many of us were taught incorrectly how to get ready for a workout. Stretching is not the first activity. Stretching a cold muscle accomplishes little and may lead to injuries. Stretching has its place, but it's later.

Instead, the first activity is to warm up the muscles and get blood flowing. This may be accomplished in many ways. One easy method is to just simply walk slowly before starting to trek with your pack or at a normal pace. Another approach is to perform a series of mild exercises that get blood flowing and increase your range of motion at the same time. Performing a few of these exercises in succession has a surprisingly significant impact upon the body. Once warmed up you can perform the cardiovascular workout.

After the workout, stretch the entire body. Each major muscle group needs attention. Your continued injury-free walking is greatly aided by re-elongating your muscles after a day's hard marching. If you have a few key areas that give you difficulty, once warmed up, it is sometimes helpful to add a few targeted stretches before you begin your workout. This does not, however, take the place of stretching afterwards.

Handling the Distance

Since the primary activity during trekking is walking, your best form of training is to go out and walk. Ideally, if you build up to walk comfortably under normal conditions you stand the best chance of success on your trek. The key to building up to this mileage is a gradual build up in daily and weekly mileage. While everyone starts at a different point, a good guiding principle is not to increase your weekly mileage by more than 10% per week.

Training for Changing Elevation

Flatland walking is not sufficient to prepare you for most treks. You need to condition your body for climbing and descending. If you are fortunate to live near a varied terrain, then you can walk your workouts on ideal training landscape. By walking at least one of your longer walks up and down a hilly trail, your training becomes far more effective. By mirroring the conditions of your trek you work both the muscles needed for walking down as well as up hills.

Since most of us do not have access to the perfect training grounds we must simulate them. One might think a stair climber is appropriate. However, it's far from ideal. A stair climber allows you to simulate walking up, but not down a hill. Most people don't realize that descending actually is more destructive to the body. This is for two reasons. First, there is more stress on the body as you go downhill, especially with weight in your pack. Second, as you descend the muscles elongate in what's called an eccentric contraction. These types of contractions break down the muscles more than the concentric contractions caused by walking uphill.

A better solution is to simulate your hill training by climbing up and down flights of stairs. Ideally, walk up a few flights and then back down a few, repeating the process a number of times. I typically start my training for a hard trek by climbing and descending about 20 flights of stairs. Then I gradually build up to about 100 flights. This number is highly subjective as flights vary in size and the amount of elevation you may climb in a day varies greatly. Once or twice a week I substitute my walking kilometers / miles for this type of stair exercise. Typically, I start without a pack on my back, but as the time for the trek nears, I wear the same pack I will during my trek and load it to the approximate weight it will be during the trek. I suggest you do the same.

When walking up and down steps try to vary which leg you lead with, as well as whether you take one or two steps in a stride. By changing your step you approximate real world conditions. You need to be accustomed to varied terrain. The more you simulate the conditions experienced on the trail the better prepared you will be.

Cardiovascular Training Schedule

This schedule has a five day a week format with three days of walking and two days of stair workouts. Note the longer days are on the weekend for convenience. Ideally, if your schedule permits moving one of the longer days to the middle of the week, do so. It provides your body recovery time from the other long walk of the week. Also, note that if you have time you can add an addition short day of walking to the schedule. However, even if time permits, I wouldn't recommend walking seven days per week. The body needs to recover.

Week	Sunday	Monday	Wednesday	Thursday	Saturday
1	4 mile walk	20 flights	4 mile walk	20 flights	4 mile walk
2	5 mile walk	24 flights	4 mile walk	24 flights	5 mile walk
3	6 mile walk	28 flights	4 mile walk	28 flights	6 mile walk
4	3 mile walk	10 flights	extra day off	10 flights	3 mile walk
5	7 mile walk	32 flights	5 mile walk	32 flights	7 mile walk
6	8 mile walk	36 flights	5 mile walk	36 flights	7 mile walk
7	9 mile walk	40 flights	5 mile walk	40 flights	8 mile walk
8	3 mile walk	10 flights	extra day off	10 flights	3 mile walk
9	10 mile walk	44 flights	6 mile walk	44 flights	8 mile walk
10	11 mile walk	48 flights	6 mile walk	48 flights	8 mile walk
11	12 mile walk	52 flights	6 mile walk	52 flights	9 mile walk

12	3 mile walk	10 flights	extra day off	10 flights	3 mile walk
13	13 mile walk	56 flights	7 mile walk	56 flights	9 mile walk
14	14 mile walk	60 flights	7 mile walk	60 flights	10 mile walk
15	15 mile walk	65 flights	7 mile walk	65 flights	10 mile walk
16	3 mile walk	10 flights	3 mile walk	10 flights	3 mile walk

Can you achieve success on your trek without walking that much? The answer is probably, yes. However, the less fit you are the less enjoyable the trek will be. Many trekkers feel like they are just hitting their stride on the last days of a trek. They are in shape to enjoy it just as it finishes. So, try to train for a trek instead. This way you'll be set to enjoy all the trek has to offer without struggling with the trail. I didn't always follow my own advice and I paid for it at the beginning of some treks.

Leave Time to Recover

After completing your training, allow your body a week to recover from your preparations. Plan to finish your training schedule with an easy week before your trek starts. Notice how Week 16 is an easy, not hard, week to finish the schedule. This enables your body to rebuild and refresh itself as well as giving you time to travel to your destination. During the week before your trek walk three or four times for no more than three miles.

Pacing

Trekking should be fun. The goal should never be to race to each destination. Aside from increasing the likelihood you won't make it, you'll miss many great sites and experiences along the way. Finding a comfortable pace is key. If you follow our training schedules, you should have discovered a comfortable pace in which you can walk for many hours while maintaining a pleasant conversation. To consistently walk faster than is comfortable decreases the likelihood of a successful trek.

Aside from the distress of the increase in exertion, there is a more important reason to take it easy. When you breathe hard, your heart rate rises. The higher your heart rate, the more carbohydrates your body burns. Accessible carbohydrates within the body are in short supply, why waste them? A better source of fuel for trekkers is the body's fat reserves and we would love to get rid of them. When the heart rate is lower, these are utilized as a greater percentage of your body's energy source and conserves the carbohydrates for the steep climbs.

Handling the Ups and Downs on the Trail

Treks are rarely flat. On the Everest Base Camp Trek our guide dubbed the less steep sections of the trail as "Nepali Flat." You see, there were no flat areas on the trail, just steep and less steep. The key to successful trekking is to not overtax yourself charging uphill. Your goal is to maintain your heart rate as much as possible. This usually means slowing down as you climb a steep grade and accelerating slightly on the downhills. However, it's not just about speed; it's about your stride.

When climbing a steep grade, imagine yourself like a bicycle rider. When climbing a hill, bikers switch gears into a mode that requires less effort. As trekkers we can accomplish the same by taking shorter, quick strides, reducing the effort per stride. By increasing your turnover, you make up for some, but not all of the loss of stride length.

Here's a simple test to illustrate the method's effectiveness. Try running up a few flights of steps as fast as you can. Do it once leaping over two steps per stride and then try it one step at a time. You certainly can get up the steps quicker taking two at a time (simulating longer strides) than one at a time (simulating shorter strides), but your breathing is more labored and your heart rate much higher when the longer strides are taken.

Going downhill the process reverses itself. Take longer strides, allowing the trail's grade to help you along. For an added bit of speed, lead with your hip. By swinging your hip forward with each stride, you extend your stride a few inches with each step and thus get added distance for almost no effort. Remember to use trekking poles to help absorb the stress of your body's weight as it strikes the ground with greater force on the downhills.

Break in Those Boots!

Ideally, wear the boots you plan to trek in for some portion of the training. I recommend at least one day a week early, and a few days a week in the last month of training. This gives you plenty of time to ensure the boots fit properly. Poor fitting boots lead to blisters and black toe nails. Both are devastating during a trek. Ill-fitted boots are the primary reason for black toe nails and can lead to the nail being lost. Keep in mind, boots have a mileage limit. It's impossible to give a universal number applicable to all boots and people. However, a few hundred miles is probably a good average. Therefore, if you train by my prescribed method and you wore your boots for every step of the 16-week program, you would probably require a new set of boots, which would also have to be broken in before taking them on the trail.

In addition to wearing your boots, you should wear your pack and fill it to the approximate weight of your trek. Again once a week early and a few times a week later should ensure that your pack fits properly and you are comfortable with the weight you plan to carry.

Cross Training

The activity of walking does not completely prepare you for the trek. By adding other forms of training, you certainly decrease the monotony of training and can strengthen your body in a few key areas to help prevent injuries.

Strength training is a great cross training activity and is recommended even if you walk the prescribed amount. Strength training is usually accomplished with a weight program. Lifting lighter weights in sets of 15 repetitions builds strength without bulk. A simple broad-based approach works. Perform 3 sets of 15 repetitions for the quadriceps, hamstrings, biceps, triceps, chest and shoulders. For those who are coordinated or under supervision, free weights are preferred for arm exercises over machines. When walking along a trail your body will not be sitting in a machine and guided through its paces. Free weights teach coordination as well as strengthening the ligaments, tendons and smaller muscle groups required to balance the weight in your hand.

Most people are imbalanced. One leg or arm is stronger than the other. Ideally, symmetry of strength and range of motion is desired. By performing all exercises one arm or leg at a time, you can work on closing the gap and, for best results, start with your weaker limb first. Only perform as many repetitions with the stronger limb as you perform with your weaker limb. This prevents the imbalance from growing.

Training the Core

When it comes to the trek, a strong abdomen and back goes a long way. Cursed by too much time strapped to a desk, many of us start a trek with back problems. These certainly do not go away with 40 or more pounds strapped to our back. The key is strengthening the stomach muscles as well as the surrounding muscle groups known as the core. There are thousands of exercises that strengthen your core. Here we demonstrate a few mainstream exercises and indicate whether it helps with posture issues related to leaning forward or backward. Keep in mind, the key to a truly strong core is to vary the exercises performed over time. Perform 3-4 core-strengthening exercises every other day for a month and then vary the exercises so that you build strength in a slightly different manner. Again performing a large number of repetitions in three sets is good practice.

BACK EXTENSION MACHINE EXERCISE

Motivation: For those with a healthy back, a back extension machine strengthens the lower back to hold you in a good upright posture and helps to correct leaning forward.

Steps: Since there are many different types of back extension machines, follow the instructions at your local gym. Please do not do this exercise if you have back problems. See Figures 13-1 and 13-2 for the intended motion.

Figure 13-1

Figure 13-2

Motivation: This exercise strengthens the lower back muscles as well as the glutes, upper hamstrings and to some degree the shoulders.

Steps:

A. Lying on your stomach, hold your arms and legs straight out as shown in Figure 13-3.
B. Simultaneously, exhale and raise your arms and legs five inches off the floor (Figure 13-4). Be sure to keep them straight.
C. Hold for 3 seconds.
D. Inhale as you lower your arms and legs.
E. Repeat 15 times.

Figure 13-3

Figure 13-4

 ALTERNATE ARM AND LEG EXERCISE

Motivation: This simple exercise doesn't require a gym or even weights. It strengthens the lower back muscles as well as the glutes, upper hamstrings and to some degree the shoulders and thus helps to correct forward lean.

Steps:

A. Lying on your stomach, hold your arms and legs straight out.
B. While exhaling, raise one arm and the opposite leg five inches from the floor (Figure 13-5). Be sure to keep them straight.
C. Inhale as you lower your limbs.
D. Exhale while raising the opposite arm and leg, keeping them straight (Figure 13-6).
E. Inhale while lowering your limbs.
F. Repeat, 2 sets of 10.

Figure 13-5

Figure 13-6

Motivation: This exercise helps correct leaning forward because, if your lats aren't strong enough, your torso is pulled forward by your abdominal muscles. This is especially true for people who have done a lot of abdominal work while neglecting their back.

Steps:

A. Sit in front of a lat machine.
B. Grab the bar with your palms facing away from you, and place your hands at end of the bar (Figure 13-7).
C. Pull the bar down in front of your body.
D. Lower the bar all the way down to past your chest (Figure 13-8).
E. Return the bar back to the top, stopping just before your arms completely straighten.
F. Keep control while raising and lowering the weight. Don't let the bar swing back excessively as you return to a starting position.
G. Perform 3 sets of 10 repetitions.

Figure 13-7

Figure 13-8

Motivation: If you already have strong pectoral muscles (located in your chest), a rowing machine balances by strengthening your rhomboids (located in your upper outer back, between your shoulder blades and your spine). Strengthening your rhomboids pulls you upright so that you don't lean forward.

Steps:

A. Sit on the seat of a rowing machine and grab the handles of the machine with straightened arms (Figure 13-9).
B. Pull back on the cable(s), keeping your back straight while exhaling (Figure 13-10).
C. Lower the weight, slowly straightening your arms while inhaling.
D. Repeat steps B and C 10-15 times for 3 sets.

Figure 13-9

Figure 13-10

Motivation: Another great exercise to correct forward lean without having to go to a gym is this exercise which works the back extensors.

Steps:
A. Lie on your back.
B. Place your feet on an exercise ball.
C. Place your hands at your side (Figure 13-11).
D. While exhaling, raise your butt from the floor and hold for 2 to 3 seconds (Figure 13-12).
E. While inhaling, slowly lower your butt back to the floor.
F. Repeat 2 sets of 15 repetitions.

Figure 13-11

Figure 13-12

Figure 13-13

Motivation: Tight pectoral muscles pull your shoulders into a forward, rounded posture, thus causing you to lean forward. This exercise loosens them.

Steps:
A. Stand in a doorway.
B. Place one arm against the doorway, holding your arm at an 80-degree angle with the side of your body. Bend your arm at your elbow at 90 degrees if necessary (Figure 13-13).
C. Lean forward, maintaining a vertical body alignment, until you feel the stretch across your pecs.
D. Hold for 30 seconds.
E. Repeat five times on each side.

161

Motivation: This stretch corrects leaning forward if your abdominals are tight. It stretches them into extension.

Steps:
A. Lie face down, extending your legs behind you with your feet together (Figure 13-14).
B. Place your hands on the side of your body, even with your shoulders.
C. Keeping your legs on the floor and feet flat, push your body up while exhaling (Figure 13-15).
D. Hold for five seconds.
E. Lower your body down while inhaling.
F. Repeat ten times.

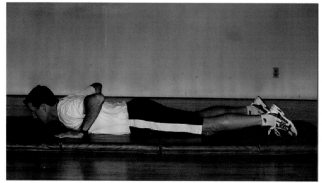
Figure 13-14

Figure 13-15

 STANDING BACK STRETCH

Motivation: This stretch corrects the problem of leaning forward due to tight abdominal and back muscles. It does so by stretching them into extension.

Steps:
A. Stand with your feet shoulder width apart.
B. Place your hands behind your back (Figure 13-16).
C. Lean backwards (Figure 13-17).
D. Hold for two seconds.
E. Slowly return to the upright posture.
F. Repeat ten times.

Figure 13-16

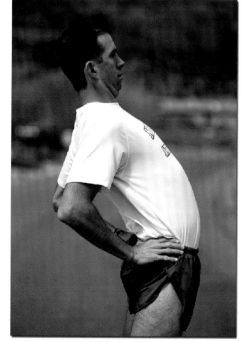
Figure 13-17

BALL RAISE EXERCISE

Motivation: This exercise strengthens the abdominals and shoulders, helping to prevent leaning backward.

Steps:
A. Hold an exercise ball in front of your body (Figure 13-18).
B. Exhale while you raise the ball to the height of your forehead, making sure to keep your back straight.
C. Continue to exhale as you hold the ball in place for 2-3 seconds.
D. Inhale while you slowly lower the ball to your waist.
E. Tighten your abdominals as you raise the ball.
F. Repeat 15 times.

Figure 13-18   *Figure 13-19*

TRADITIONAL STOMACH CRUNCHES

Motivation: This exercise is a very basic method of strengthening your abdominal muscles without overly stressing your back. Strong abdominal muscles help to prevent a backward lean.

Steps:
A. Start by lying down on a firm surface.
B. Bend your knees and bring both feet toward your buttocks, so your legs form a triangle with the ground (Figure 13-20).
C. Place your hands across your chest, and begin to curl upward by tucking your chin to your chest.
D. Slowly roll your upper body off the ground as much as eight inches, pressing your lower back to the ground as you curl (Figure 13-21).
E. Always exhale while curling your body upward.
F. Hold for three seconds.
G. Lower your body to its original position by reversing your movements and inhaling as your body lowers to the ground.
H. Repeat the exercise as many times as possible while maintaining good technique (up to a maximum of 100 crunches).

Figure 13-20   *Figure 13-21*

Figure 13-22

Motivation: This exercise allows you to get a more comfortable posture and remove your backward lean by stretching your upper back.

Steps:

A. Wrap your hands around a pole, standing far enough back that your arms are straight.
B. Lean backward, feeling the stretch through your upper back (Figure 13-22).
C. Hold for ten seconds.
D. Repeat three times.

BICYCLE EXERCISE

Motivation: This exercise puts a literal twist on the *Traditional Stomach Crunch* in that it adds a twisting motion to work a greater range of abdominal muscles.

Steps:

A. Start by lying down on a firm surface with your hands behind your head.
B. Touch your right elbow to your left knee, lifting your torso up slightly as you do (Figure 13-23).
C. Simultaneously lower your raised elbow and knee while raising the opposite knee and elbow (Figure 13-24).
D. Repeat the exercise 25 times.

Figure 13-23

Figure 13-24

Cooling Down with a Good Stretch

Always stretch when you have finished working out. When your muscles are tired they become tight bands that fight you when you walk and may lead to injuries. In contrast, when you loosen your muscles by stretching, you facilitate relaxed, efficient hiking; prevent injuries; and increase your range of motion. If that is not reason enough, stretch just because it feels good!

Be patient while stretching. Stretch each muscle for 20-30 seconds, 2 or 3 times with each leg. Make certain to use good technique, as improper form leads to stretching, and possibly overstretching, the wrong muscle group. Remember when stretching one limb at a time, symmetry is key. Always start with the least flexible limb, as human nature leads you to focus longer and more attentively on the first stretch. Otherwise, by repeatedly stretching the more flexible limb—as many people do—you increase any imbalances. Perform each of the following stretches after each workout. In addition, add a few of the core stretches if you are not performing the core workout immediately after the walking workout.

 TRADITIONAL HAMSTRING STRETCH

Motivation: This is an effective seated stretch of the hamstrings and an excellent post-training cool down.
Steps:
A. Sit down, placing one leg in front of you.
B. Bend your other leg with the sole of your foot facing toward your straight leg and the knee pointed out (Figure 13-25).
C. Keeping your back straight, lean forward from the hips, reaching towards your toes (Figure 13-26).
D. Ideally, you should reach past your toes, but remember not to overstretch or bounce while trying to touch them; just stay within your comfort zone.
E. Hold the stretch for 20-30 seconds and repeat 2-3 times with each leg.

Figure 13-25   *Figure 13-26*

 TRADITIONAL CALF STRETCH

Motivation: All of the climbing you will do can lead to tight calves, make sure you stretch them after walking or performing a step workout.

Steps:

A. Place both hands at shoulder height on a wall or pole in front of your body.
B. Keep your arms fairly straight and your lead leg bent under your body.
C. Place the heel of your rear leg 1½ to 2 feet behind your body.
D. Keeping your rear leg fairly straight but not locked in position, place the heel of this foot on the ground.
E. You should feel a stretch down the outer part of your rear-leg calf muscle. If you don't, try moving your rear foot back a little farther (remember to place your heel back on the ground after you move your foot back).
F. Throughout the stretch, your upper body should remain vertical and straight; do not bend forward.
G. Alternate legs when finished.

Figure 13-27

Motivation: The calf is not a single muscle; it comprises two muscles, both of which need stretching. The previous stretch worked the outer calf muscle. The *Bent Leg Calf Stretch* may not feel effective initially, but it utilizes an excellent position that stretches deep in the inner calf muscle. You can start this stretch as you finish the *Traditional Calf Stretch*.

Figure 13-28

Steps:

A. Place both hands, shoulder high, on a pole or wall in front of your body.
B. Keep your arms fairly straight with one leg slightly bent under your body.
C. Place the heel of your rear leg 1 to 1 ½ feet behind your body. Notice that this is about six inches in front of the placement for the *Traditional Calf Stretch*.
D. Keeping your rear leg fairly straight and in a stable position, place the heel of your rear foot on the ground.
E. Now, keeping your heel planted, bend the rear leg so that your knee drops a few inches closer to the ground. You should feel a deeper, but less pronounced stretch in your calf muscle.

While not as pronounced as the other stretches, this one definitely works on the targeted muscle.

STANDING SHIN STRETCH

Motivation: If you do not treat your shins kindly, you'll surely develop shin splints and know firsthand how this tiny little muscle can cause big problems. The *Standing Shin Stretch* is just one way to take care of it. However, be careful not to overdo it, otherwise the shin muscle will get back at you on your next walk.

Steps:

A. Balance yourself near a pole or wall and put your weight on the supporting leg (Figure 13-29).
B. Now touch the other foot to the ground, toe first and pull your rear foot forward just to the point where it is about to move forward (Figure 13-30).
C. Hold it there. You should feel the shin muscles elongate and loosen up.

Do not rest on your big toe as shown in Figure 13-31.

Figure 13-29

Figure 13-30

Figure 13-31

166

Appendix C - Resources

No one book can cover all the information required for a successful trip to the ten best treks in the world. A list of additional books and maps are provided to round out your education.

Beyond the Last Village: A Journey Of Discovery In Asia's Forbidden Wilderness, Alan Rabinowitz, Island Press, 2003
Chamonix to Zermatt: The Walker's Haute Route, Kev Reynolds, Circerone, 2007
Into Thin Air, John Krakauer, Anchor, 2009
Myanmar (Burma), Robert Reid, Lonely Planet, 2009
New Zealand, The Great Walks, Alexander Stewart, Trailblazer, 2004
The Man Who Walked Through Time: The Story of the First Trip Afoot Through the Grand Canyon, Colin Fletcher, Vintage, 1989
The Snow Leopard, Peter Matthiessen, Peguin Nature Classics, 1987
Trekking in East Africa, Mary Fitzpatrick, Lonely Planet, 2003
Trekking in the Nepal Himalaya, Bradley Mayhew, Lonely Planet, 2009
Trekking in the Central Andes, Rob Rachowiecki, Lonely Planet, 2009
Trekking in the Patagonian Andes, Carolyn McCarthy, Lonely Planet, 2009
Tour of Mont Blanc, Kev Reynolds, Circerone, 2007
Watching Wild Life East Africa, Matthew Firestone, Lonely Planet, 2009
Walking in the Alps, Helen Fairbairn, Lonely Planet, 2004

Appendix D - Trek by Trek Comparison

Trek	Country	Region	Type	Access City
Annapurna Circuit	Nepal	Himalaya	Circuit	Kathmandu
Annapurna Base Camp	Nepal	Himalaya	There and Back	Pokhra
Everest Base Camp	Nepal	Himalaya	There and Back	Kathmandu
Everest Base Camp w/ Kala Pattar	Nepal	Himalaya	There and Back	Kathmandu
Grand Canyon (Rim-to-Rim-to-Rim)	USA	Arizona	There and Back	Grand Canyon Village
Haute Route	France, Switzerland, Italy	Alps	Point to Point	Geneva/Varied
Inca Trail	Peru	Andes	Point to Point	Cusco
Kachin Tribal Village Trek	Myanmar/Burma	Kachin	There and Back	Putao
Kilimanjaro (Machame Route)	Tanzania	East Africa	There and Back	Arusha
Kilimanjaro (Marengu Route)	Tanzania	East Africa	There and Back	Arusha
Milford Trek	New Zealand	South Island	Point to Point	Queenstown
Torres del Paine Circuit	Chile	Patagonia	Circuit	Puerto Natales
Torres del Paine "W" variant	Chile	Patagonia	Point to Point	Puerto Natales
Tour de Mont Blanc	France, Switzerland, Italy	Alps	Circuit	Geneva/Varied

Trek	Starting Elevation			Highest Elevation		
	Starting Point	Meters	Feet	Highest Point	Meters	Feet
Annapurna Circuit	Besi Sahar	760	2,493	Thorung La	5,416	17,759
Annapurna Base Camp	Dhampus	1,770	5,807	ABC	4,130	13,550
Everest Base Camp	Lukla	2,850	9,400	EBC	5,300	17,500
Everest Base Camp w/ Kala Pattar	Lukla	2,850	9,400	Kala Pattar	5,500	18,200
Grand Canyon (Rim-to-Rim-to-Rim)	South Rim	2,111	6,926	Bright Angel (lowest)	750	2,461
Haute Route	Chamonix	1,000	3,281	Col de Prafleuri	2,965	9,728
Inca Trail	Qorihuayrachina	2,600	8,530	Dead Womans Pass	4,200	13,780
Kachin Tribal Village Trek	Upper Shangaung	457	1,499	Mt. Phon Khan Razi	3,635	11,923
Kilimanjaro (Machame Route)	Machame Gate	1,490	4,888	Kili Summit	5,895	19,340
Kilimanjaro (Marengu Route)	Marangu Gate	1,980	6,496	Kili Summit	5,895	19,340
Milford Trek	Te Anau	200	656	Mackinnon Pass	1,073	3,520
Torres del Paine Circuit	Laguna Armaga	45	150	John Garner Pass	1,220	4,000
Torres del Paine "W" variant	Laguna Armaga	45	150	Mirador Torres	305	1,001
Tour de Mont Blanc	Les Houches	1,007	3,304	Fenetre d' Arpette	2,665	8,743

Trek	Ave. Days	Min. Days	Distance		Elevation Change	
			Kilometers	Miles	Meters	Feet
Annapurna Circuit	20	17	248	154	4,656	15,276
Annapurna Base Camp	11	9	120	75	2,360	7,743
Everest Base Camp	12	10	101	63	2,450	8,100
Everest Base Camp w/ Kala Pattar	12	10	92	57	2,650	8,800
Grand Canyon (Rim-to-Rim-to-Rim)	5	3	39	24	(1,361)	(4,465)
Haute Route	14	4	184	114	1,965	6,447
Inca Trail	4	3	50	31	1,600	5,230
Kachin Tribal Village Trek	10	9	Unknown	Unknown	3,178	8,745
Kilimanjaro (Machame Route)	7	5	63	39	4,405	14,452
Kilimanjaro (Marengu Route)	5	4	66	41	3,915	12,844
Milford Trek	4	4	53.5	33	873	2,864
Torres del Paine Circuit	11	9	141	88	1,175	3,850
Torres del Paine "W" variant	6	4	69	43	260	851
Tour de Mont Blanc	11	10	167	104	1,657	5,440

Conclusion: Jeff Salvage

"Not all who wander are lost." JRR Tolkien

In 2003 I journeyed to Nepal on what seemed like "just another trip," a crazy, whimsical adventure that I expected to enjoy, but not change who I was. Personally, I had finally put the demons of not qualifying for the U.S. Olympic race walking team to rest and I was adapting to my non-competitive life. At the time I wasn't a photographer, environmentalist or writer. I had no trekking experience and didn't feel the "call of the wild." While I didn't know it, I was wandering.

I was on a journey without a purpose, but that journey defined who I am today. An intense person, I was ready to fill the void left from a lack of competition and evolve in a new direction. My first trip to Nepal served as the catalyst to this genesis. While I always enjoyed travelling and new experiences, combining travel with my passion for walking opened up countless untold worlds. The Everest Base Camp Trek showed me first hand nature's grandeur, while simultaneously physically challenging myself. It awakened a desire within me to see the greatest treks in the world. However, it was after completing my trek off the beaten track through the jungles of Burma that I knew I had much to learn about people and cultures. Growing up as a sheltered boy from Long Island, I knew little of the world outside the typical concrete suburbs of my neighborhood. I was raised with the idea that a wealth of materialism equals success. Trekking opened my eyes to other realities and greater possibilities. While I had small tastes of other cultures in the past, nothing dramatically altered my life path. The slow pace of ambling allowed for more interaction with fellow trekkers and locals than I experienced as an athlete. Qualifying for the Olympics would have been the pinnacle of my track career. However, I am far richer for slowing the pace down and changing course.

Upon returning from one of my trips a colleague proclaimed, "I see the mountains have touched you," and indeed they had. The simple pleasure of the remote Burmese villages taught me to slow down and notice the subtleties of the seasons. Now trees seem to bloom more colorfully, sunsets are richer and subtle smells of the seasons are more pronounced to me. The shock of seeing dramatically retreating glaciers in separate hemispheres ignited my environmentalism. I now grow vegetables in a garden that gets larger every year, power the house with solar energy and have cut my carbon footprint considerably. Each time I trek, as the miles fall under foot, civilization melts away; at least as much as is possible with all my digital equipment. The full impact of this transformation often doesn't hit me until I return home and start to rush and worry about insignificant day-to-day problems. This is a stark contrast to life on the trail. Getting back to basics helps put life in perspective when I return and it is something I remember when life throws obstacles in my path.

Most importantly, trekking is the primary connection that drew me to my wife Jennifer. We met online. While countless women claimed they liked to hike and are "outdoorsy," she wrote about trails I yearned to walk and some I didn't even know existed. Together we slogged through the Milford Trek to finish the Great Treks and complete my near decade quest. Now I do not wander alone on a trail, but we purposely wander together in search of new adventures and insight. Having only completed a few treks in the U.S., we plan to spend the next few summers hiking with our chocolate lab. I am certain the experience of sharing the trail and a crowded tent with our four legged family member will open new doors on our journeys in nature. Perhaps it is time to begin the sequel *Great Treks with Your Dog*, time will tell.

Conclusion: Kirk Markus

"You know to me a mountain is a Buddha. Think of the patience, hundreds of thousands of years just sittin'
there being perfectly silent and like praying for all living creatures in that silence. Just waiting for us to
stop all our frettin' and foolin'" - Japhy Ryder from Dharma Bums by Jack Kerouac

"So, are you done playing Marco Polo?" asked my grandpa upon my return from a several month journey to Asia. Grandpa didn't ask about my trek to the base of Mt. Everest or the views of the glacier covered Himalayas. He didn't even say, "I can't wait to see your pictures." It was puzzling as I was very excited to tell my grandfather about my journey. He was a microcosm of the twentieth century. With a keen memory and many life experiences, he was largely responsible for my wanderlust and passion for the mountains. Grandpa visited every national park in the contiguous forty-eight states. He took me on my first trip west of the Mississippi and through the Rocky Mountains. I distinctly remember overlooking a beautiful mountain valley in Colorado, vowing to return to hike into those forests and mountains; which I have. Despite all this inspiration, I don't think grandpa ever understood my desire to travel outside the country for extended periods without the safety of a formal job upon my return.

For me, however, playing Marco Polo is as much religion as lifestyle. Theoretically, it actually is quite simple; I love to travel! This passion consumes me so much so that it begs the eternal question, "How much is enough?" I haven't answered that question. Sometimes I don't try. Occasionally, after several months on the road and trail I am ready to come home. Even then it might only be a matter of days before I'm pouring over maps and visualizing the next big trip, next mountain range, next Great Trek.

One of my most well-travelled friends, Ruben (over 75 countries and counting) succinctly stated, "Traveling is about seeing all that you're not seeing." There are, of course, many interpretations to this anecdote. First, in the course of our daily lives we see very little of this great big world firsthand. There are very few ways to get as close to the simple village life than on the trail. Second, and perhaps more simply, the more you travel the more you want to travel. When you're on the road you are always experiencing so many incredible places. Instead of your list of destinations getting shorter, it actually gets longer.

Trekking for me goes hand-in-hand with traveling and my passion for mountains. The feeling of accomplishment at the summit of the peak or the pass is exhilarating. The sense of camaraderie with friends, trekkers and fellow travelers creates a special bond, as well as the hospitality of families in villages along the trail make these trips so much more rewarding. A pilgrimage to the wilderness rewards the soul. John Muir best expressed this feeling when he wrote, "On a swift flood we are all borne forward, and only when I am in the wilderness is this current invisible, where one day is a thousand years and a thousand years is one day."

When I am on the trail in remote foreign lands, the sights, sounds and smells of daily life in the developing world are very rich and stimulating, some more than others. I think back to my experience in Burma with its exotic, colorful markets, unique foods, fascinating history and Orwellian government. There is always much to experience and always something new and interesting around the next corner: unique shops, devout religious ceremonies, funerals, playing school children and wedding celebrations. These are all an integral part of small village life that the trekker often gets to see and be a part of firsthand. Time is needed to absorb these experiences.

In 1993-94 I quit my traditional job, one I'm sure my grandfather was proud I had, and spent a year traveling and trekking outside of the U.S., primarily Africa and Asia. This included my first Great Trek experience on the slopes and summit of Mt. Kilimanjaro. My experiences on that trek and during that year are reflected in the following passage I wrote several weeks after its conclusion:

"As I reflect back on my adventure, I've seen the struggle for survival on the plains of Africa, man and beast alike; civil war in Russia, the legacy of communism in China, tragic poverty on the world's two largest continents, many hungry faces, relics and reminders from the horrors of war, environmental disaster and the remnants of the Holocaust. But tragedy aside, "hope springs eternal." Hope for life and the future. The kindness and generosity of the people I met on the road was astounding. The human spirit perseveres through the most difficult times.

What legacy my trip will leave is uncertain. In some ways it seems like a vision, or just a distant memory, as if I was in a dream living a National Geographic Special. The people I have met, the wildlife and incredible landscapes have made a lasting impact. Although much contemplating was to be had, I'm not sure if I have any better understanding of why I "had" to make such a trip or what lessons or insights can be learned from traveling to the developing world. Perhaps these are too ambitious of questions to answer for a trip that is "only" one year. What I can say is this: Always be true to yourself, who you are and what you do."

While backpacking through Alaska a few years later I came upon a small cabin in Lake Clark National Park. My guide brought along a copy of *One Man's Wilderness*. It was the autobiography of Richard Proenneke who built the cabin with hand-tools, back in the 1960's before it was part of the national park. He lived there on and off for the better part of the next twenty years. When he was not there he left the following note on his door for the handful of souls who might happen to pass by:

"You didn't find a padlock on my door for I feel that a cabin in the wilderness should be open to those who need shelter. My charge for the use of it is reasonable, I think, although some no doubt will be unable to afford what I ask, and that is - take care of it as if you had carved it with hand tools as I did. If when you leave your conscience is clear then you have paid the full amount."

That is something for all of us to at least consider "philosophically" in our daily lives.

Perhaps the ultimate answer to the ultimate question is that traveling and trekking is a quest to understand and know the human spirit in all its wonderful differences and, more importantly, in all its wonderful similarities.

As I write these final words, I have just returned from a trip to Guatemala. Safe at home, "back to normal." Home to the fretting and fooling world of 24-hour cable news, anytime-anywhere world wide web, automatic garage-doors, weekly trash pickups, plentiful ATMs and eternal hot water. This world seems indifferent to my return, as if it were on autopilot and I am not needed to tend to the machine. It's not too surprising. It's a big world, one that leaves me pouring over my maps, dreaming of my next great trek, my next Marco Polo journey.

About the Authors

Jeff Salvage

Jeff Salvage pursues his interests—trekking, photography, race walking, writing and computer technology—with a focus and intensity that can only be described as passionate. An internationally recognized walking expert, Salvage is The Arthritis Society of Canada's National Trekking Trainer, cofounder of *www.greattreks.com*, as well as founder of *www.racewalk.com*. He's written seven race walking books and a set of DVDs that are recognized world-wide as the most comprehensive, professional educational material available. Several of these are used to train the coaches of the world's largest marathon training program, the Leukemia Society's Team in Training program. Along with two-time Olympian Tim Seaman he cofounded *Race Walking Clinics of Excellence,* providing an unparalleled opportunity for the sport. In addition, many of his trekking and race walking articles appeared in *Walk! Magazine* and *Active.com*.

Complementing his writing achievements are his skills as a professional photographer. His sports photographs have appeared in *Sports Illustrated*, *ESPN Magazine* and countless newspapers across the U.S. His most recent publication, *One Dress One Woman, One World*, is a coffee table book documenting his and his wife's travels with her wedding dress. Following its release it has gained much attention by local, national and world-wide media.

Off trail, Salvage teaches computer science at Drexel University while pursuing numerous creative projects.

Kirk Markus

From a suit in the halls of corporate America to a paintbrush at McMurdo Station in Antarctica, Kirk wears many hats, clothes and colors. However, he is most comfortable out on the trail in the remote wilderness. Over the years Kirk has led many friends on their inaugural backpacking and trekking trips at home in the Rockies and across the globe and, so far, all have lived to tell the tale. Kirk is a seasoned wanderer, having trekked and traveled to over fifty countries and all seven continents. The seeds were literally planted at a very young age. When Kirk was attempting to prepare the garden, with spade in hand, his mother looked out the window and asked, "Kirk, what are you doing?" Kirk replied, "Mommy, I'm turning the world over!" When not traveling Kirk shares time between Chicago and Colorado.

Other Publications by Walking Promotions

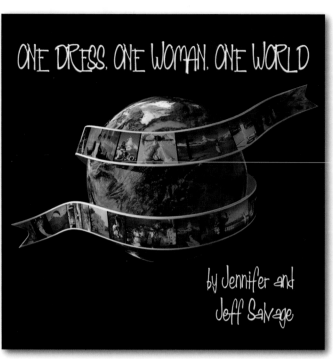

If you enjoyed *Great Treks*, you'll love Jeff Salvage's other adventure *One Dress, One Woman, One World*. Experience the world through the eyes of a bride by joining Jennifer and Jeff Salvage on their journey. *One Dress, One Woman, One World* chronicles 100,000 miles of travel with the loving couple and Jennifer's unbelievably versatile wedding dress on one trip of a lifetime after another. Covering over 85 locations across 6 continents Jennifer's escapades are unprecedented. Read her firsthand account while looking through her husband's lens and witness the fun, hardship and splendor colorfully displayed through these inspirational photographs.

It's the perfect gift for a bride to be, photographer, travel enthusiast or anyone with a hunger for adventure, beauty or an appreciation of the arts.

Purchase the book or view samples of the unbelievable photos at *www.onedressonewoman.com* or *www.amazon.com*.

SUPERCHARGE Your Walking Workout by Learning to Race Walk

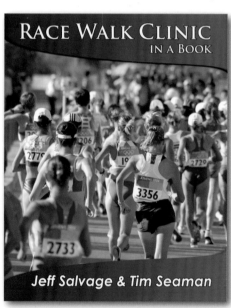

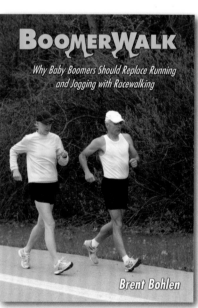

If you have a big trek coming up, why not prepare by getting more from your walking workout and learn to race walk? Visit *www.racewalk.com*, the #1 source for race walking information on the internet and learn from Jeff Salvage, Tim Seaman or Brent Bohlen how to become more efficient with your walking stride.

Don't forget to visit www.greattreks.com often for more trekking information.